Global Labour in the Fourth Industrial Revolution

Studies in Critical Social Sciences

VOLUME 242

The titles published in this series are listed at *brill.com/scss*

Global Labour in the Fourth Industrial Revolution

How COVID-19 Accelerated Humanity's Degradation

By

Adrián Sotelo Valencia

Foreword by

Andrés Piqueras

Translated by

David Stiles Sparks

TUTA SUB AEGIDE PALLAS · 1683 ·

BRILL

LEIDEN | BOSTON

Cover illustration: "The digital factory", 2022. Courtesy of Marietta V. Solanes.

Library of Congress Cataloging-in-Publication Data

Names: Sotelo Valencia, Adrián, author. | Piqueras Infante, Andrés, writer of foreword. | Stiles Sparks, David, translator.
Title: Global labour in the fourth industrial revolution : how COVID-19 accelerated humanity's degradation / by Adrián Sotelo Valencia ; foreword by Andrés Piqueras ; translated by David Stiles Sparks.
Description: Leiden ; Boston : Brill, [2023] | Series: Studies in critical social sciences, 1573-4234 ; Vol. 242 | Includes bibliographical references and index. | Summary: "In this latest work by the prolific Mexican theorist Adrián Sotelo Valencia, the COVID-19 pandemic is shown to have merely exacerbated the profound world capitalist crisis rooted in the 1970s structural exhaustion of the third industrial revolution. Sotelo explains how the current 4.0 revolution whose articulating axis is the development and expansion of artificial intelligence, Big Data, algorithms, 3D printing, the Internet of Things, and digital platforms constitutes a global strategy of capital and the state aimed at detaining the global capitalist crisis. The Digital Revolution heralds a new international division of labour with severe repercussions for labour, especially in dependent countries like Mexico. The foreword by Andrés Piqueras of the Universidad Jaume I de Castellón underlines the urgency to heed this insightful analysis"– Provided by publisher.
Identifiers: LCCN 2023002040 (print) | LCCN 2023002041 (ebook) | ISBN 9789004532700 (hardback) | ISBN 9789004532717 (ebook)
Subjects: LCSH: Labor–History–21st century. | Economic history–21st century. | COVID-19 Pandemic, 2020–Influence. | COVID-19 Pandemic, 2020–Economic aspects. | Globalization–History–21st century.
Classification: LCC HD4855 .S6713 2023 (print) | LCC HD4855 (ebook) | DDC 331.01–dc23/eng/20230126
LC record available at https://lccn.loc.gov/2023002040
LC ebook record available at https://lccn.loc.gov/2023002041

Typeface for the Latin, Greek, and Cyrillic scripts: "Brill". See and download: brill.com/brill-typeface.

ISSN 1573-4234
ISBN 978-90-04-53270-0 (hardback)
ISBN 978-90-04-53271-7 (e-book)

To Mary, my rock and companion
To John Saxe-Fernández, mentor and guide

Contents

Tables, Graphs, Diagrams and Figures

Tables

Graphs

Diagrams

Figures

Foreword

There are two main ways for social science to confront what happens above, below, and through that which the ideological apparatuses of our socioeconomic system define as "reality." One of them—the most common, comfortable, and easy—consists of ignoring everything that does not fall within the parameters included in that construction, or else to grant them the status of "anomaly," "aberration," or another string of adjectives linked to irrationality or "what should not be." Unfortunately, this is where we find the majority, "orthodox" social science, which, in addition, due to the neoliberal offensive to eradicate critical-alternative thinking from the Universities and to discipline scientific activity, is trapped in the vortex of the curricularization of everything it does. That is to say, the knowledge it is supposed to have is subject to the most immediate commodification possible. To this end, the new elites who manage knowledge must also ensure that the production of knowledge is enclosed in a privatized and highly elitist circuit, removed from society, which is part of the process of dispossession of collective wealth and very specifically, in this case, of scientific knowledge. Submitting to this procedure obtains the privilege of entering into the standards of "curricularly profitable science," alien to the commitment with the common and the service to society. It also benefits from recurrence to—and permanence in—the dominant scientific circles that nurture and cite each other.

From these political-academic dynamics and impositions, most of the "scientific" books and articles come out with no other purpose than to increase the CVs of those who design them, or at least to try to avoid the marginalization of their authors, i.e., that their persons remain "without academic value"—often expresses as the necessity for academics to "publish or perish." They are, therefore, texts that tend to reproduce the dominant conventions, the majority currents of orthodox science, and which, on the other hand, are usually forgotten as soon as they are written, since they contribute hardly anything to the understanding of what is going on, when they do not contribute decisively to hindering the understanding of social processes. Curiously, however, in this last case we find ourselves before a partial exception, since with the hegemonic irruption of neoliberal-postmodernism, the more confusion academic elaborations manage to introduce, the greater the resonance they tend to reach in certain spheres of the academic market and its corresponding social diffusion. Of course, in order to do so, one must be among the stardom of Confucianism (books such as *Empire, A Thousand Plateaus, Changing the*

World Without Taking Power, among many others, could well be at the apex of this said classification).

What is normal, however, is that in both cases forcing teachers to achieve and maintain a permanent "productivity" translated into publications as a standard of evaluation of their work has the result that it has: to generate, as in the rest of the market, superfluous and redundant merchandise with rapid obsolescence. All of which is compatible with the accelerated and very worrying absence of epistemological foundations, methodological procedures worthy of the name, and theoretical rigor in academic and scientific research and analysis in general, at least as far as the social sciences are concerned.

We must bear in mind that as far as these sciences are concerned, our social system lives for the expanded reproduction of the capital that is its "blood" by consuming the energies of the parts that constitute it—that is to say, of us. It has so many more possibilities of achieving this the more unconscious we are of it (every order of domination would disintegrate if those who suffer it were aware of its foundations and conditions as my teacher Ibáñez used to say). That is why the institutional devices of management, control, and social administration have the purpose (through their intermediary specialists: the social scientists) of extracting information from society converted into "people" and returning it in the form of entropy (difficulty in understanding the order that maintains the state of things; hindering the union for joint intervention and for the formation of collective subjects; hindering common reflection). They want us to be isolated and "individuals"—as if we were only a version of ourselves (the one that the social order models for each one)—so that our "subjectivity" is as similar as possible to the one that the owners of the order want. So that this subjectivity, orphan of "archeological" analysis, becomes as it manifests itself an object of study that "confirms" what they want it to be—that is to say, a reinforcement and "proof" of that order.

That is why postmodern science promotes the leap from materialism to idealism—the abandonment of the concern for knowing how things are in order to become ardently interested in interpreting them—in "subjectivizing" reality. "The fall into interpretation and language and the denial of the capitalist structure by postmodernism have in common the rejection of the capacity to know and transform the existence that revolves around the central and cohesive genetic-structural role of commodity production," says the tireless knowledge activist and social fighter Gil de San Vicente.

Contrary to all this, there is a way of knowing and facing the world that seeks to go to the root of things. Yes, obviously, we are talking about "radical science" (actually meta science), the only one that is capable of knowing in depth what is happening and therefore being able to prevent to some extent what may happen, and thus also harbor the possibility of contributing to transform what is known from the point of view of society itself.

In order to gauge the significance of this way of doing science, there is nothing like resorting to Marx's insistence that the greater or lesser reason of ideas—it is worth saying here the theory—is not settled in the world of ideas themselves but in the world of social practice, as he states for example in the second thesis on Feuerbach ("The question whether objective truth can be attributed to human thinking is not a question of theory but is a practical question. Man must prove the truth—i.e., the reality and power, the this-sidedness of his thinking in practice. The dispute over the reality or non-reality of thinking that is isolated from practice is a purely scholastic question."). Such positioning has its translation in that there is no better validation in the social sciences than their capacity to solve human problems and improve people's lives. Far from the preaching of the dominant ideology converted into "objectivity" regarding the need for "neutrality" of scientific approaches, the scientific-political praxis proposed by Engels and Marx appeals to the unavoidable commitment of knowledge to what is known and to those who are known. When we speak of Social Sciences, this inevitably implies praxis with a political purpose.

The objective of the dialectical-materialist—and with it of critical-alternative science—is none other than to collaborate in the conversion of individuals into subjects and for them to (re)situate themselves in the social field—to draw the spaces of power in which we move so that we can collectively analyze as subjects of knowledge (now everyone becomes a 'researcher') our subjections, elevating the social system itself to a privileged object of study. That is to say, contrary to what the dominant science does, it is about injecting negentropy to the subjects and entropy to power by undermining the basis on which it is sustained (the privatization and exclusivity of knowledge, the separation of the subordinates).

Here we are before a book of this second category. And as such, it is Marxist (let us not forget that since the 19th century Marxism has constituted the most profound, far-reaching, and potentially transformative alternative-critical praxis that exists up to the present). We Marxists have long known what are the root causes that make capitalism a system permanently condemned to crisis and to ever greater crises. And we know this because we have the basic, root knowledge of the chronic illness from which capitalism suffers, an ailment from which it cannot escape and which aggravates its state tendentially, even if it manages in a passing way to fight it, counteract it, or postpone at times its most deleterious effects. This disease expresses itself in crises that sometimes turn into recessions and even depressions and have a wide range of external manifestations: underconsumption or overproduction; financial, due to macroeconomic imbalances, excess, or shortage of money; or shocks caused by competition itself. Such manifestations of crises often serve orthodox economic science to elaborate causal explanations that are superficial if not directly erroneous. In reality the systemic crises of capitalism start from a common denominator which Marx discovered for us and which this science refuses to understand: the fall of value as surplus value. Which is implied in the intrinsic tendency to the over-accumulation of capital. This is the "chronic disease" of the capitalist mode of production.

And it is such because capitalist development entails a tendency towards greater utilization of (and innovation in) capital-intensive technologies, which entails a lower utilization of labor power per unit of capital put into production. In other words, capitalism presents a tendency to reduce living labor (human beings) in the direct production of commodities. A circumstance that implicitly carries the recurrent process of over-accumulation of invested capital per unit of value (and therefore of surplus value) that it is capable of generating.

Value reflects an abstract time that tends to average out—the time socially necessary to obtain a given commodity (object or service) according to the technological development reached at each historical moment. Throughout the course of capitalism, this technological advance has followed the arrow from manufacturing to robotization, passing through the processes of mechanization and automation: Manufacturing is Mechanization is Automation is Robotization-artificial intelligence. What does this mean? That as the relative weight of fixed capital (machinery or technology in general) increases over variable capital (human beings) in the organic composition of capital, productivity may increase but not so much value nor surplus value. That is a lower value is generated in proportion to productivity since the time socially necessary to produce commodities decreases. It also means that the abstract human labor proper to the capitalist wage relation is losing relevance in the generation of value. "Living labor" (human beings) is being relegated as an agent of production, while "dead labor" (machines) takes center stage.

In short the over-accumulation of capital occurs when productive capital—that which is capable of reproducing itself indefinitely in the cycle money-commodities (means of production and labor power), production, new commodities new(greater) money (M-C-P-C'-M')—is not capable of growing in a new cycle to the extent corresponding to the level previously acquired and, therefore, cannot complete its cycle of valorization, generating a capital that compensates for the capital invested (it cannot even conserve the same value it already had before beginning the new cycle of valorization). With this the material conditions of production and reproduction of the social existence of capital—that is, of society itself—are also decomposed.

This disease has its symptoms today in the different processes of morbid displacement that shake capitalism. Indeed, when the process gets stuck in the primary circuit of accumulation (the industrial circuit, where surplus value is produced according to a dynamic of expanded reproduction and where the cycles of valuation are a function of the production and circulation of commodities), three types of displacements tend to be prioritized or accentuated: one spatial within the primary circuit of accumulation, another spatiotemporal towards the secondary and tertiary circuit of accumulation, and a third absolute, renouncing accumulation, i.e. outside production: speculative finance enters here (these displacements accompany the technical-organizational displacement—towards new lines of production, use of new technologies, etc.—and displacement between branches or even sectors of activity, which are permanently present in the dynamics of capitalist accumulation and competition).

The spatial displacement is towards places where the technical composition of capital is lower and therefore the danger of over-accumulation is not imminent. Towards "peripheral" territories within each State and towards the peripheries of the System, wherever there are more possibilities of making investments profitable in a movement towards locations with better conditions for the profitability of the investment (proximity of raw materials, exactions or fiscal advantages, a labor force with less social bargaining power and cheaper, etc.).

The temporary displacement of surplus capital consists of capital flows away from the field of immediate production and consumption (primary circuit of the economy) to invest in productive infrastructure to be made profitable in a more or less distant future (secondary circuit of the economy: facilities, new energy generation capacity, new routes for the transfer of goods and labor force, etc.) or in social spending that favors research and development and, in general, the qualification of the labor force in the future (tertiary circuit of the economy; secondary circuit of the economy: facilities, capacity for the generation of new energy, new routes for the transfer of goods and labor force, etc.) or in social spending that favors research and development and, in general, the qualification of the labor force in the future (tertiary circuit of the economy; the immediacy and short-termism of the "interest" of the different capitalists, however, never allowed them to finish betting openly on this temporary displacement of profit, so they had to receive the "push" of the class struggle that made it possible for the State—as "collective capitalist"—to assume these tasks with very different enthusiasm in some social formations than in others).

However, at present this temporal displacement is being integrated into a type of spatiotemporal displacement in which investment is directed to areas of the secondary circuit that do not represent a source of productive investment in the future but a speculative one such as the land, housing, and mortgage markets, for example.

Financial displacement for its part implies a kind of transmutation of the means of accumulation of capital by which the process of valorization through the production of exchange values and the consequent expanded reproduction of capital (M-C-M') is subordinated to the monetary way of realization of profit (M-M'), unleashing the most fictitious and unreal movement of capitalist accumulation: the mirage that money "produces" money by itself without the mediation of labor. Finance capital speculates upwards with the realization of supposed future profits (mortgaging the present at the expense of the future). Financialization also underpins and reinforces the other displacements.

Globalization and its dynamics of corporate relocation as well as the neo-liberal political-economic offensive were, thus, neither natural nor casual processes but the forced result to compensate for a time for the fall of the rate of profit in the central economies of the capitalist system. In the first case, as I said, by investing capital in the peripheral economies or in branches of activity where the process of over-accumulation had not yet taken place and where more living labor can still be incorporated for the extraction of surplus value (thus, re-starting an extensive accumulation of capital); also, by expanding at the same time the market, the speed of rotation of capital, and the shortening of the life of products. In the second case, through the neo-liberal onslaught by imposing higher rates of exploitation of the labor force and less redistribution of the profit achieved to the population as a whole; also, by seeking new spaces of valorization where previously common goods and life-preserving human activities were inscribed (that is, the whole of the social wealth that remained outside the market, which also implies on an internal scale a new wave of dispossession and extensive accumulation of capital). All this is also implied by the intensification of the use of nature as a cheap source of energy and resources.

The combination of all these processes has provided a temporary margin to capitalism, which has "bought some time" in Streeck's allusion, but, in the end, one after the other, they show their exhaustion to continue compensating the tendential fall of the rate of profit. Over-accumulation arrives faster than desired in the peripheral economies, some of which are converted by means of the massive investment of external capital into "emerging" ones; the speed and extent at which the market reproduces itself cannot counteract the magnitude at which value falls; the increase in exploitation tending to increase surplus value reaches a moment in which it does not compensate for the fall in value; at the same time the impoverishment of society is contradictory with the capitalist realization (or sale of what is produced). As for the commodification of life-sustaining activities and of social wealth in general, for the most part it aims at appropriating more of the value already generated ("value harvesting") rather than creating new value through abstract labor. For their part, the ecological limits inherent in all these dynamics become unnoticeable, although it is important to bear in mind from the outset that it is the "internal" limit of capital that presses the system to its "external" or ecological limit and not the other way around.

Throughout its history, capitalism has suffered two Long Duration Crises. The 1870s inaugurated the first of them. The same one that would lead several recoveries in between to the purely European imperialist phase and to growing tensions between the main powers that would lead to two world wars; the same one that made possible the greatest disconnection with the capitalist world known until today (the Soviet Revolution) and provoked the greatest stock market crash and led to a worldwide shock: the Great Depression of the 1930s.

In the 1970s, the Second Long Capitalist Crisis occurred from which the world elites have been trying to escape without success. They have tried everything: neo-liberal and neo-Keynesian measures, globalization, massive credit, "quantitative flexibility," financial speculation with its corresponding stock market bubbles ... But the result has been a trail of crises of which we had the penultimate outbreak in 2007–2008. When they were convincing us that we would get out of it, we were hit by a pandemic that once again destroyed the economic and social indicators of most of the world (with the almost sole exception of China).

This time the crisis of value has not manifested itself financially nor through the Banks. On the contrary, both types of institutions seemed to be called to save us through the creation and distribution of money, but today we see that they only make things worse because the disease is the same, only the symptoms change. That seems to be enough, however, for mainstream science to cling to these elements—the most epiphenomenal of the processes—to give each time a version of what is happening (of course, as many as different medical professionals would give if each one tried to explain a disease from a different symptom such as fever, joint pain, skin rash, prostration, or dark circles under the eyes, for example). That is why as I said before we Marxists, unlike official economics in particular, have been able and can not only foresee the crises and their course but also explain them (one thing cannot go without the other, of course), since going to the root of things—being radical—allows us to transcend the surface phenomena to dive into the deep understanding of what is happening. Thus, for example, we know that the over-accumulation of capital entails among other important destructive dynamics: 1) a structural tendency towards the elimination of employment or desalarization; 2) a growing devalorization of the labor force; and 3) the generalized "brutalization" of labor relations.

Adrián Sotelo gives a full explanation of all this in this book, but he also does so by delving into the intricacies of the 4th Industrial Revolution through which we have begun to pass, so that he is able to explain, contrary to the official propaganda on the hopeful beneficial effects of that revolution for humanity, how it comes to abound in all the processes of social and environmental destruction of a capitalism that in its degenerative phase increasingly encourages the development of destructive forces instead of productive ones.

This is how Sotelo formulates his main thesis in this regard:

> The current industrial revolution—also called digital or 4.0—is the product of the crisis and exhaustion of the structural and technological devices of the previous revolution—also called scientific-technical—which began in the course of the seventies of the last century, supported by the development of automation, computing, and the Internet.

Thus, the digital revolution arises from that crisis and poses a new global restructuring of the capitalist system based on devices identified as Big Data, Internet of Things, artificial intelligence, algorithms, and 3D technology, among others. "This is a real revolution of working time and the collective worker that translates into a widening of the production of surplus value and the accumulation of capital through increased exploitation by articulating different categories, activities, and functions that run in the digitized value chains, in productive and service activities, as well as in those related to distribution and consumption [...] Digital platforms such as telecommuting and home office as well as the components of the fourth industrial revolution are projected as a whole to restructure and recycle capitalism in a new structural dimension that allows it to overcome the crisis and contradictions of the stage prior to the coronavirus, where the great industrial and technological revolutions took place and could not resolve them," concludes Sotelo.

This means that the author attends with ease to the dynamics of the ongoing material transformation of labor processes, with the implications that the set of technologies of the 4th Industrial Revolution has for the subsumption of social subjectivity and for the disciplining and (super)exploitation of labor. Because Sotelo—as it could not be otherwise in a Marxist analysis—is based on the inquiry of the validity of the law of value (as opposed to so much current negation of it) to articulate the dimensions that constitute it in the present industrial "revolution." On the one hand, he points to its technical devices that displace human labor (such as Big Data or Artificial Intelligence), but on the other, he does not lose sight of either the digital factories where business engineering takes place—which require a highly qualified labor force—or the vast and hard processes of material production that aim at the procurement of raw materials (such as lithium, mainly) essential to sustain this new form of capitalism apparently "dematerialized" and alien to value.

This digital-computerized-automated model, which our author theorizes as a substitute for the Toyota Production System (TPS), has a multidimensional impact on the world of work: on its organization, on the precariousness of labor, and on the deterioration of wages and labor costs in general—a precise and necessary way of analytically concretizing by the author what we have been saying so far. For this very reason, Adrian Sotelo successfully combines the analysis of the role of this "platform capitalism" with the breakdown of a process that has constituted one of his most constant concerns and most valuable contributions: that of the super-exploitation of the labor force (which is implied in the set of circumstances described and which I only noted before in parentheses). A concept that Sotelo has long been analyzing in its different dimensions and in its disparate predominance depending on whether it is applied in the central or in the peripheral social formations of the capitalist world system.

Let us pause here for a moment, because if a good part of the labor force is permanently unemployed, underemployed, or "self-employed"—if there is no expectation that it will be needed in more and more productive processes—then, for the capitalists, there is no longer any need for education, medical care, social safety net, stable jobs, or higher wages (this is also part of super-exploitation, as Sotelo will explain in these pages). Unlike the industrial capitalist—who had to begin to "take care" of the reproduction of his labor force when the reserve army of labor ran out and organized itself for struggle—a capitalist who is increasingly dedicated to financial speculation and who has in android robotization a future bet on the substitution of physical and intellectual labor sees no need to worry about the working population or society in general. He or she remains confident in the illusion of being able to live outside human labor and society itself. That is why today capital, driven by the decadence of its rate of profit, has also begun to suck the social wealth, to bleed the body from which any economy draws its life: society itself. This is what some of us have called a process of autophagocytosis, which as can be easily understood is suicidal.

For now in the face of the current systemic chaos generated with economic debacle included and in the face of their undeniable ineptitude to safeguard not even the health of their populations in the face of the current pandemic, the elites of global capital have announced at the World Economic Forum in January 2021 the "Great Reset" of capitalism—a turn of the screw to the loss of democracy, to the population control, to the precariousness of the labor markets, to the generalized impoverishment, to the environmental deterioration. The same elites announce it as the convergence of economic, monetary, technological, medical, genomic, environmental, military, and governmental systems. In economic and monetary policy terms, the Great Reset implies an enormous concentration of wealth, on the one hand, and the probable issuance of a universal basic income, on the other, to "maintain" unemployed populations. It could include a move to a digital currency with centralization of bank accounts and Banks, immediate real-time taxation, increased negative interest rates, and centralized surveillance and control of spending and debt. The Great Reset also means the issuance of medical passports soon to be digitized, including medical history, genetic makeup, and registries of former diseases had. Covid-19 is providing ideal training for populations to accept such things. The Great Reset also accentuates war as a device of accumulation and an instrument of economic, geostrategic, and international relations, especially against Russia and China.

This book also prepares us to understand the whole framework of domination in progress, to prevent the "new capitalism" that is coming which has already begun to settle among us, spurred on by the latest pandemic. In line with this, our esteemed and dear author is also capable of linking the broad analytical contents on the current capitalist crisis with the end of the "long expansion" of the United States and the decline of its hegemony, which leads to an increase in its warmongering and destructive dynamics.

Perhaps in the face of Sotelo's expository forcefulness on what a degenerating capitalism supposes, he offers us readers some proposals to get out of all this—to fight it in the immediate—even though the proposition of the construction of socialism crosses all his book and evidences it more and more necessary in the face of capitalist barbarism, as Luxemburg already anticipated.

There remains also the latent discussion for the future as to whether or not the system is capable of surpassing itself at least in certain territories of the planet, towards an automated mode of production with android machines that no longer requires "living labor"—whether it will have the energy to do so and how far human agency of the new struggles around the class relation could be bypassed on that path.

Marx paradoxically with himself already indicated that only when a mode of production has exhausted all its potentialities is it ready to be replaced by another. What underlies this book by Adrián Sotelo—to my understanding with which I feel akin because it is also a part of my own theoretical proposal—is that we have probably reached that moment, but without this translating itself into probable prospects of transformation in favor of the large majorities, at least for now.

In these circumstances as I have pointed out elsewhere, the phase of decomposition of the system need not be short, especially as long as there remain niches of surplus value and cheap energy to palliate the accelerated decline in value. Its demise will not occur as we are already seeing as an instantaneous collapse or sudden collapse—its marked trajectory of decline may even have small (and increasingly) transient upturns. But what does seem beyond doubt is that without human intervention to overcome it outside the law of value (or to prevent that sort of "passive revolution" of its elites towards a hypothetical automated mode of production) and without a revolutionary leap towards the achievement of forms or ways of life capable of achieving social cohesion and socio-natural equilibrium, the agony of the capitalist mode of production will entail ever greater doses of suffering, hardship, and death for humanity.

I believe that this is what our author wants to warn us about when he includes in the title of this work such forceful words as "Humanity diminished."

I ask the reader to be enlightened and strengthened through the knowledge of the world in which they live by this book by Adrián Sotelo that is in their hands. In this way they will have—and we will also have—more possibilities of transforming it.

Andrés Piqueras
Professor of Sociology and Social Anthropology
Universitat Jaume I of Castellón

Introduction

> Nature builds no machines, no locomotives, railways, electric telegraphs, self-acting mules, etc. These are products of human industry; natural material transformed into organs of the human will over nature, or of human participation in nature. They are organs of the human brain, created by the human hand; the power of knowledge, objectified. The development of fixed capital indicates to what degree general social knowledge has become a direct force of production, and to what degree, hence, the conditions of the process of social life itself have come under the control of the general intellect and been transformed in accordance with it; to what degree the powers of social production have been produced, not only in the form of knowledge, but also as immediate organs of social practice, of the real-life process.
>
> KARL MARX, *Grundrisse*, Vol.II

World capitalism is experiencing a powerful, anti-human, and profound crisis that affects practically all nations of the world. Its most conspicuous expression consists in trying to solve this crisis through the implementation of what specialists and authors have called the "fourth industrial revolution," which would be based on the first revolution and other devices and applications such as Big Data, 3D technologies, the Internet of Things, algorithms, Machine Learning, which are pompously publicized by the hegemonic media linked to international capital business corporations.

Before the outbreak of the medical-health crisis caused by Covid-19 in the world, the thesis of the "end of work"—supported by specialists and institutions of international prestige, including prestigious Nobel Prize winners in some discipline of the social sciences (especially economics)—had gained strength. One of the positive aspects, if it can be called that, of the current health crisis that confined a good part of humanity to their homes—although another part had no choice but to continue working in the streets exposed to contagion and even death—was having revealed the social and labor reality of capitalism in the sense that the only "factor of production" (as neoclassicals like to call it)—creator of value, wealth, and surplus value—is precisely

 | DOI:10.1163/9789004532717_002

the labor force, albeit in conjunction with the means of production. In this sense this will be a central thesis in the post-pandemic period: *without labor and without value the capitalist mode of production simply does not function and plunges into a profound crisis that it is unable to overcome.*

On the other hand—just as in the past in the sphere of morphological but not essential changes of capitalism—its various crises demanded profound restructuring and mutations of its productive, technological, labor, business-organizational apparatuses, and even in its political regimes in order to overcome them today in the midst of the structural and health crisis caused by the coronavirus; the business system and its hegemonic corporations are demanding a global restructuring that will allow them to restore their diminished growth rates and, above all, to increase profitability and the production of surplus value without upsetting the juridical, institutional, macroeconomic, and socio-political bases of the capitalist mode of production.

This is the framework of enunciation of the title of this book: it expresses one of the fundamental contradictions of the current global capitalist system to the extent that it tends to displace the worker and the living labor force from the production process through the application of the devices of the fourth digital-industrial revolution. To that same extent, it affects the whole of humanity by reducing its radius of action and importance—together with the workers—in the solution of the great problems and issues related to the preservation of its own existence, which is at the same time that of nature.

In this context, our central thesis is that in the same way that the English industrial revolution unleashed in the mid-18th century was produced to consolidate the interests of the bourgeoisie and rising capital in the face of the dying feudal world, the current restructuring driven by the revolution 4.0 substantially preserves the capitalist mode of production and adjusts it to the interests of big capital and its powerful transnational corporations in order to constitute a new paradigmatic configuration capable of guaranteeing, at least temporarily, a recovery of the average rate of economic growth while overcoming, at the same time, the previous so-called flexible Toyota Production System (TPS) of intensified production.

Part 1 of this book unfolds and analyzes this central thesis in the analysis of the capitalist social crisis as a human hecatomb in an epoch of decadence of that system. We consider in Chapter 1 the health effects of the outbreak of the infectious disease caused by the coronavirus and in Chapter 2 its projection in the increase of the precariousness of the world of work and the extension of super-exploitation to the advanced capitalist countries.

Part 2 deals specifically with the expansion, crisis, and deterioration of capitalism. Chapter 3 discusses the end of the expansion of the growth of the

U.S. economy and the problems of hegemony-supremacy that it is experiencing at the international level in the face of the arrival of new powers in the context of a multilateral and polycentric world.

Part 3 focuses on the subject of the digital or platform revolution itself. Chapter 4 shows a close correlation between disaster capitalism and the enormous benefit received from it by the ruling rich and super-rich classes derived from tragic events such as epidemics, wars, and/or devastating environmental disasters such as earthquakes. We focus specifically on the world of labor and analyze its reality in the hellish work environment of Mexican maquiladoras heavily exposed to the ravages of the coronavirus.

In Chapter 5 we critically analyze what has been called "platform capitalism" and the advent of the digital factory as a result of the 4.0 revolution. Finally, Chapter 6 endeavors to carry out an analysis of the relationship between this industrial revolution and the labor-value theory in order to demonstrate that its devices are directly or indirectly linked to the production of value and surplus value, contrary to the "end of work" thesis that denies these relationships. Unfortunately, the world had to experience the greatest crisis of humanity—above all else emphasized by the number of people involved (7.7 billion according to the latest available UN report for 2019)—and become aware of its historical, existential, and ontological moment in which it debates its own existence.

Capitalism—which is the declining world system at the service of the minority ruling social classes—is historically incapable of resolving the global crisis of humanity. Only the construction of a new social, human, and socialist formation built by the workers in alliance with the popular classes will be capable of stopping and overcoming the global hecatomb of humanity into which capitalism as a whole has engulfed it.

PART 1

Capitalism and the Human Hecatomb

CHAPTER 1

The Coronavirus Pandemic Demolishes the "End of Work" Fallacy

1 Introduction

In this chapter we consider that among other ideological effects the coronavirus health crisis—which paralyzed most of the world economy for a long time—highlighted the fallacy that integrates the multiple theses of the "end of labor" and its centrality in the environment of capitalist relations of production to supposedly give way to a "new" post-industrial or post-capitalist society that would no longer have anything or very little to do with human labor power in terms of the law of value and the critique of political economy.

We critically review some theses in this regard and conclude that although there have been *morphological changes* in the labor/capital relationship—but not in its essence—there are no solid theoretical-methodological arguments to postulate that this relationship has been displaced and overcome.

1.1 *Debates and the Re-articulation of the World of Work*

In the course of the eighties and nineties of the last century, a boom of ideas, hypotheses, theses, and theories was unleashed that proclaimed a supposed "end of work" as a central category of the capitalist system by virtue of the advent of a "post-industrial" stage that transferred the axis of the production of wealth and social welfare to technological development and science with no connection, or little connection, with the labor force. In this way on the surface of society the ideological impression was created, always delusional—which will be strengthened by the fictitious capital that feeds its ideologist with the theories of the end of work, given that it erases the trace of surplus value at the same time that it generates profit—that finally! capital managed to become "independent" of the labor force and at the same time to "solve" the problem of the production of wealth and surplus value *without* the intervention of the latter. It was thought then that a magic formula had been found to produce surplus value and wealth *without the participation of* the human labor force—with *machines*, technology,[1] science, and, finally, fictitious capital and

1 Marx's (2010: 623) premise of the appropriation of living labor by capital is generally overlooked in the sense that is is "... the analysis and application of mechanical and chemical

 DOI:10.1163/9789004532717_003

its concomitant fictitious profits (Carcanholo, 2013). In this way we would have finally arrived at the candid world of Pangloss*.

When fictitious capital emerges as the hegemonic device of capital in the world from the mid-seventies and in the course of the eighties of the last century, as Carcanholo (2013: vol. 2: 137) says:

> The truth is that since the 1980s capital and its ideologists—including economists—claimed to have found in practice a magic formula to guarantee the generation of economic wealth without the need to use human labor. Some even went so far as to think that capital would end up no longer needing the labor force to produce economic surplus to guarantee its profitability. Labor, therefore, would have lost its centrality; technology, information, and the mastery of knowledge were elevated to the category of magical entities capable of everything and the object of adoration. Finally, capital would no longer need to dirty its hands in production to realize itself as a being capable of by itself generating profits, high profits. Nature, too, would be secondary.

It should be clarified as Antunes (2018: 257) says that "… financial capital is not a separate and opposite alternative to the productive world but controls it to a large extent, and only a fraction of it—fictitious capital—is dislocated from production." This clarification is important because sometimes it is thought that this type of fictitious capital operates separately from the other cycles of capital (productive, commodities, and money) without understanding that what really happens when it becomes hegemonic is that it overdetermines the other cycles, imprinting them with its trajectories and logics. But this does not cease to generate illusions as Piqueras (2018: 59) opines: "… the maximum ('illusory') dream of the capitalist class is realized in appearance: that capital is self-reproducing beyond human labor, beyond material wealth, and beyond the energetic bases that make the latter possible."

One of the truths—and benefits at least for critical and transcendental thought—of the confinement, forced or not depending on the countries and regions, in their dwellings of more than half of the human population of the planet (calculated by the UN for the year 2019 in 7,700 million human beings) due to the effects of the expansion and attack of the medical health

laws, arising directly out of science, which enables the machine to perform the same labour as that previously performed by the worker." In this sense we glimpse the components of the fourth industrial revolution such as artificial intelligence and Big Data, albeit in an infinitely (potentially) more complex sense than that existing at the time of the German thinker.

pandemic is the incontestable and evident empirical demonstration—by the way, denied by the bourgeois and conservative thought during the epoch of neoliberal imperialist capitalism since the eighties of the last century—that at world level *capitalism as a mode of production, life, and work cannot function or sustain itself for a second without the labor force of the worker as the essential engine of the production of wealth, value, surplus value, and corporate profit.* That as Marx scientifically demonstrated, the worker and his labor can exist *without* capital, but capital cannot exist *without* them. Hence, in the midst of the pandemic, capital and the capitalists—in general widely supported by their respective governments—are constantly pressing for the opening of all the so-called "essential"[2] activities such as mining, automobile, steel, and others for which they have invented true business myths such as that of "herd immunity"—as in Sweden, where it was supposedly applied and has been a failure and which basically pontifies that the economic openings of capitalism can "coexist" with the pandemic without endangering the health and life of the population and of the workers.

This confirms the thesis of the *centrality of labor* and its *subject*—the *worker*—in spite of the intense expansion of the chimerical "cognitive capitalism"—computerized, digital, or platform capitalism[3]—currently in

2 In capitalism the essential or non-essential character of a product, activity, or employment is defined according to the profitability of capital and the weight, size, and monopolistic extension of private investments. Not by its social and human utility, which in another historical context would be fundamentally determined and defined by the capacity to satisfy social needs (*use value*) such as health, food, housing, or education. In the midst of the pandemic, factories and productive processes not essential for the bulk of the working population—articulated in the hegemonic chains of production of value and surplus value such as the automotive, electronics, production of parts and components for the industrial-military complex of the United States from Mexican territory—are operating at 100%. Marini states that "... necessary consumer goods are those that enter into the composition of workers' consumption and determine, therefore, the value of their labor force" (1979: 52).

3 See, for example, Srnicek (2016: 27–29) where he debates the issue of the meaning of concepts such as "cognitive economy," "immaterial," "information," and "knowledge," taking a stand for the thesis that argues that "data" (the "information") constitute the "raw material" of advanced capitalism of the 21st century without drawing the ultimate consequences of this approach in the sense that these "data" or information *without* the assistance of the cognitive labor force (of the engineer, the technician, or the skilled worker) constitute not only a theoretical but an empirical emptiness by not contemplating its intimate connection with the productive processes and the concrete materiality of constant capital, for example, with the chips that contain the "immaterial" data and information or with the production of batteries for computers and smart phones and other devices that would be practically nonexistent without the mining activity, for example, of lithium, which is extracted by nothing less than the labor force of the miner-worker.

vogue and which many assumed had replaced the law of value/labor and labor power itself in the terms in which Marx formulated it (see Rubin 1972).

Far from being confirmed, the theses of the "end of work" (see Antunes 2001) raised by Marxist and non-Marxist authors have been completely disproved by the reality of a capitalism that in the best case, its average growth rate will be negative in the post-pandemic period from 2020 onwards and will give way to a much more aggressive, deep, and permanent structural crisis of the capitalist mode of production that would be approaching this mode to its imminent degradation and/or extinction, depending on the class struggle and subjective factors such as proletarian organization, the rise of class and human consciousness of workers, and, in general, of the proletariat and other social strata oppressed and exploited by the regime of capital in general.[4]

The current global capitalist crisis has demonstrated without so much science or wisdom that the system *cannot* exist *without the* exploitation of the labor force (physical and psychic) *nor without* the assistance of its *subject*: the worker. Furthermore, it disables all the hypothetical accumulation of theses and ideas (articulated with the "theories of the end of labor") that Tyrians and Trojans have been wielding to "demonstrate" that the system "can" function *without labor* power and *without the* production of value and surplus value, according to the illustrious organic intellectuals of the system for the benefit of capital and its bearers: entrepreneurs of all kinds. And the main argument they put forward is the increasing substitution of the living labor force by machines with greater emphasis on the current and incremental phase of the 4.0 revolution: "Intelligent machines cannot extinguish living labor. On the contrary, their introduction is done through the intellectual work of the worker who, by interacting with the computerized machine, also ends up transferring part of his new intellectual attributes to the new machine that results from this process" (Antunes and Sotelo 2003: 113).

This substitution of living labor for dead labor is proclaimed by the main postmodern theories of the "end of labor": Keynesian, functionalist, and neoclassical theories, as well as some Marxist approaches and currents that have yielded theoretical-epistemological and methodological ground to the influence of conservative theories that basically believe that capitalism is capable of infinite self-reproduction *without* labor. As István Mészáros (1995: 66) expresses when referring to the imperative necessity of capital to submit the worker to its alienated dominion: "Fantasies about the coming of totally

4 For a vision that denies without foundation the revolutionary character of the proletariat, see Postone 2003.

automated and worker-free capitalist production process are generated as an imaginary elimination of this problem."

The profound crisis that shook world capitalism between the 1960s and 1970s had an intense impact on thought and ideology in the following decades. We could say that, henceforth, the theses that at the level of thought were raised as a reflection of this capitalist structural crisis were synthesized in the formulas of the "end of work" and the "end of ideologies." Regarding the former, for example, Rifkin's work entitled *The End of Work* (1995), originally published in English; in relation to the latter, the book *The End of Ideologies* (1960) by the American sociologist Daniel Bell, published in English and later in Spanish in 2015. Subsequently, this same author published another book in English (1973) then translated and published in Spanish (1989) where he reinforces the thesis of the end of work and ideologies with a clear message of eviction of Marxism—in particular of Marx's theory of value that constitutes the essential support of Marxist political economy.

Other authors such as Dominique Méda (1995) and Claus Offe (1985 and 1992) point in the same direction. In 1993 another book appeared that argues bluntly—misinterpreting Marx's theory—(Postone, 2003: 325, author's italics) "... that [Marx's] presentation's argumentative thrust implies quite clearly that overcoming capitalism would *not* entail the self-realization of the proletariat. The logic of Marx's presentation does not support the notion that the proletariat is the revolutionary Subject." The author bases this assertion on the fact that as capitalist industrial production develops. " ... [proletarian labor] becomes increasingly superfluous" from the perspective of social wealth without demonstrating it, but contradictorily, he asserts that this does not occur in relation to the production of value (360). This duality was early noticed by Marx mainly in the *Grundrisse*, without deriving from there as Postone does the dismissal of the proletariat as a revolutionary and transforming subject. On the contrary both in this work as in the later ones as in *Capital*, Marx will do nothing but reaffirm with conviction this revolutionary character of the proletariat as the *fundamental force* of the global transformation towards a system and mode of production of life and work that is non-capitalist.

Thus, the doors were opened wide for the construction and reflection of the ideological aspect of what would later be called "single thinking," which assumed one of its greatest expressions and influences in Fukuyama's *The End of History* (1992) when capitalism seemed to be on a trajectory of stabilization and lasting growth during the Clinton administration in the United States (see Chapter 3 below).

In the eighties and nineties of the last century, this ideology of the single thought—true panegyrist of capital—was reinforced, which will mark an important "abyssal line" as Santos (2018) calls it as a hegemonic expression of Western thought that will have important ramifications in practically all social and human sciences. In such a way that the ideological roots would have been laid for the full validity of neoliberal ideology and its political power by considering that all human[5] and social development is only possible if it is based on the "free" development of "market forces" without extra-economic interventions of social and political forces such as the State, political parties, popular and social organizations, and institutions because they supposedly spoil the "free functioning of markets." The Ecuadorian sociologist Agustín Cueva (1993:247) calls this form of neoliberal thinking of the new right that emerged with force in the course of the eighties of the last century under the protection of the electoral triumphs of the conservatives Ronald Reagan in the United States and Margaret Thatcher in England as "… a *neo-Darwinism* applied to the field of the economy, with the market as the 'natural selector' of the best endowed entrepreneurial 'species'." Supposedly, the "market" ensures *per se* the progress of society by its own mechanical dynamics without intervention of extra-economic forces and institutions that spoil its "free" functioning. The fact that savage capitalism in its current neoliberal phase is in decline and increasingly with regressive rates of economic growth proves the falsity of statements such as the following: "… free markets and stable political systems are a necessary precondition for economic growth" (Fukuyama, 1992). If there has been anything in the last three decades of neoliberalism, it is precisely regression, depression, systemic crises, fiscal deficits, increased unemployment and job insecurity, inequality, poverty, and misery—phenomena that neoliberals of all stripes simply prefer to ignore in their theoretical lucubrations.

From the perspective of the antagonistic labor-capital relation, these works—together with others written by prominent thinkers such as André Gorz (1980, 1982, 1997, 1998, 2003, January 7, 2008), Reich (1992), Castel (1998) and Jürgen Habermas (1984) *inter alia*—contributed directly or indirectly to consolidate the idea-force that Labor (in the ontological sense of Lukács (1978)) had been theoretically and ideologically "devalued" as the main productive force of contemporary capitalist society. Its place in the productive sphere would be taken by science and technology as well as by machinery in its most ultramodern and sophisticated version—that is robotics, telematics, the Internet of Things, and artificial intelligence (AI), which as Klein says (*The Intercept*, May 8, 2020):

5 The term "human" understood here in the sense used by Mészáros (1970: 13, author's italics): "… in Marx's view man is neither 'human' nor 'natural' alone but both: i.e., '*humanly* natural' and '*naturally* human' at the same time."

> It's a future that claims to be run on "artificial intelligence" but is actually held together by tens of millions of anonymous workers tucked away in warehouses, data centers, content moderation mills, electronic sweatshops, lithium mines, industrial farms, meat-processing plants, and prisons, where they are left unprotected from disease and hyperexploitation. It's a future in which our every move, our every word, our every relationship is trackable, traceable, and data-mineable by unprecedented collaborations between government and tech giants.

On the level of circulation, it is argued that these forces are based on the market *in abstract*—fetishized—and on the financial system, supposedly without the intervention of the State as proclaimed by the neoliberal *think tanks* of all conservative currents.

It, thus, entered a fetishistic universe of ideological alienation (Mészáros, 1970 and Kohan, 2013), aimed at presenting capitalism as a system in "perfect and perpetual equilibrium" without abrupt fluctuations and where the dependence of capital on labor and in general on the world of labor would have been finally "solved" (?) while ensuring the general "welfare" of the population thanks to the "great benefits" of modern technology and science.

The reality will be very different from that portrayed by those conservative currents to the extent that from the perspective of labor sociology the binomial super-exploitation-precariousness[6] of labor (Sotelo, 2016a and 2020) was imposed as the epicenter of the relations of production and labor practically all over the world, including the main countries of advanced central capitalism that have been precipitated by the paths of structural capitalist crisis and chronic depression to the point of being immersed in a complex and variegated process of structural quasi-stagnation that recalls the best theses raised by Marxist authors of the stature of the Americans Paul Sweezy and Harry Magdoff (2009)[7] in the United States; or by neo-Keynesians such as the

---

6 The super-exploitation of labor is a category derived from the labor-value theory and expresses the specificity of the social and production relations operating in specifically dependent and underdeveloped economic-social formations. It was Marini who provided a specific theory on the nature of such societies based on the tools of Marxist political economy, in particular of *Capital*, which contains a general theory on the development, crisis, and decadence of capitalism. The thesis of the extension of the super-exploitation of labor was raised by the Brazilian author among other works in his *Preface* (1993) and in 1996. Other authors who have detected this issue of the extension of the super-exploitation of labor to advanced capitalism are Martins (2011, 2017 and 2020); Alves (2018) and Antunes (2018). I deepened the problem from the perspective of Marxist dependency theory in Sotelo (2020).

7 Lenin (1963:75) is one of the pioneers of the concept of "stagnation," which he defines in relation to capitalist monopoly that "... inevitably engenders a tendency of stagnation

Austrian Josef Steindl (1976),[8] among many others who projected and amazingly approached the contemporary era of a decaying capitalism that Piqueras (2018: 9, author's italics) characterizes as the "*terminal phase* of capitalism" that not only initiated a long, structural, and systemic cycle of fall of its economic growth variables, particularly since the 2008–2009 crisis[9]—which let it be said in passing contrasts with the period of greatest expansion experienced by capitalism as a global system after the Great Patriotic War (GPW) (officially called "World War II")[10]—but in addition, declines in labor productivity, GDP, product per capita, and profitability of capital in the productive sphere were recorded in full benefit of the speculative fictitious capital that is currently dominant within the cycles of production and reproduction of global social capital. This behavior seems to be secular insofar as it draws a tendency more and more coincident and pronounced with the empirical reality of capitalism, towards structural stagnation and the increase of recessive and depressive processes.

2 Conclusion

The doomsayers of the "end of history" and of labor have been totally wrong in supposing that capitalism and the universalization of "liberal democracy" in the (Western) world had reached the civilizational peak, setting up capitalism and the Western bourgeois society in decadence hit by the world pandemic

---

and decay ... But the tendency to stagnation and decay, which is characteristic of monopoly, continues to operate, and in some branches of industry, in some countries, for certain periods of time, it gains the upper hand." It is useful to clarify that in note 322: 879–880, the Progress Publishing of Moscow points out that originally this book by Lenin was entitled: *Imperialism, the Highest Stage of Capitalism* (1963) in Petrograd in a publishing house of the time called Parus. De Bernis (1988:19, note 2) confirms this information. For his part, Theotônio Dos Santos (1971) analyzes the antecedents of the crisis in the United States. It is possible to compare the conception and meaning of the concept of "stagnation" with that offered, for example, by Celso Furtado (1966) and which of course is not shared by authors of dependency theory such as Dos Santos (2002) and Marini (1985).

8 Sweezy and Magdoff (2009: 11) consider this book by Steindl originally published in English in 1952 to be "... the most complete and penetrating study ever made on the problem of stagnation" (i.e. of capitalism!).

9 See: Robinson (2008). For an analysis of capitalist crises from the perspective of Kondratiev cycles see: Mandel (1976 and 1995).

10 To the extent that it was the former Soviet Union that truly defeated the Nazis and contributed millions of dead in the world war, it is actually referred to as the Great Patriotic War (GPP).

with the United States ("American First" *dixit* Trump) as its epicenter and which has thrown millions of workers into unemployment as the "ideal model" (*dixit* Weber or Fukuyama); primarily women and young people in the course of the first half of 2020—after the registration of the first case of Covid-19[11] on January 21 of that year—with all the foreseeable and unpredictable consequences that await us in terms of labor, environmental, health, education, housing, and, in general, in human life.

The civilizational and planetary crisis of capitalism, which creates and recreates what Sassen (2014) calls "predatory formations,"[12] is indicating that there no longer exists in the *global-geographical time-space, place-space-accommodation* for humanity. For this reason, and all the above, it is necessary a radical, root, transformative, post-pandemic, anti-capitalist, and socialist change capable of ensuring the construction of a new social, moral, ethical, cultural, civilizational, human, and planetary world where everyone fits, without restrictions and distinctions of any kind. Without xenophobia, racism, or social classes. This would be, indeed, an authentic *new post-capitalist normality*.

---

11 The first case of Covid-19 was reported in Mexico on February 27, 2020, and one day later two more cases were confirmed: one in a Mexican and one in an Italian citizen.

12 These "predatory formations" are all the expulsions of people, communities, migrations, and immigrations, which consist of "... the mix of elements that generates each of the particular expulsions ... as a kind of predatory formation. That is to say, these expulsions are not simply the result of an individual's, a firm's. or a government's decision or action". (Sassen: 2014: 77), but rather the "... systemic logic at work in each of those preparatory formations" (78). See Felix's (2019) treatment and application of Sassen's theory to the case of Brazil in the chapter on "Expulsões" (pp. 185–228).

CHAPTER 2

Labor Precariousness and Extension of the Super-Exploitation of Labor

1 Introduction

International organizations such as the ILO, the World Bank, and ECLAC (CEPAL) recognize the high degree of precariousness existing in labor relations in most of the world's countries. However, this concept is considered *in itself* as if it were autonomous and detached from the conditions of exploitation and the capitalist organization of labor. Here we place it as a constituent of wage labor, regardless of the fact that it brings better conditions of income and benefits to some categories of the world of work. We understand, then, the precariousness of work that is occurring practically throughout the system as a process of *actualization of* the *condition of precariousness* experienced by most of the world's workers, aggravated even by the medical-health emergency of the coronavirus. In addition, insofar as it deteriorates living conditions and the consumption fund, we consider this process of precarization as the vehicle to impose and generalize the Super-exploitation of labor in the advanced capitalist countries.

1.1 *Globalization of the Law of Value and the Super-Exploitation of Labor*

The treatment of the processes of precarization and super-exploitation of the labor force in dependent countries cannot follow the analytical trajectories of the countries of advanced capitalism where the great industrial revolutions that accompanied their development unfolded. It is necessary to understand that this process was born in countries such as England, France, or Germany in confrontation with the feudal mode of production that was dominant in the world at least until the unfolding of the industrial revolution in the 18th century. From here the cycle of money capital turned to the sphere of production for the manufacture of commodities and the obtaining of value and surplus value as a result of the process of exploitation of wage labor by capital. This is what Marx studied in his fundamental works, both in the *Grundrisse* and in *Capital*.

Things are different in the economies and countries that were born on the periphery of the expansion of advanced world capitalism—first as colonies,

 | DOI:10.1163/9789004532717_004

then as dependent entities, and later, once the nation-states were consolidated, underdeveloped as a product of that historical-structural subjection and subordination.

In this sense, Marini (July-September 1977: 79) states that in a first historical phase "[i]n the dependent countries, the sphere of production is closely articulated with the flow of circulation of money capital and commodity capital (in the form of means of production), originating in the advanced capitalist countries" at that time, mainly England. But in a second stage, which corresponds to Latin American industrialization (1930–1945, 1945–1982), "… in any hypothesis, this flow once internalized constitutes a determining factor in the configuration of the economic cycle of the dependent country" (*idem.*), which affects both the spheres of production and those of circulation, exchange, and consumption. In this way, a dependent *cycle of its own* is constituted, which necessarily reproduces itself according to international variables and the predominance of the mode of production of the hegemonic centers of the advanced capitalist countries (for further details see Marini, 1979).

The above corresponds to the methodological approach he makes in his seminal work, *Dialectic of Dependency* (1973 and 2022), regarding the dependent specificity of capitalism in the underdeveloped countries of the periphery of world capitalism:

> A second problem concerns the method used in the essay, which is made explicit in the indication of the need to start from circulation towards production in order to then undertake the study of the circulation that this engenders. This, which has raised some objections, *corresponds rigorously to the path followed by Marx*. Suffice it to recall how in *Capital*, the first sections of Book I are devoted to problems proper to the sphere of circulation and only from the third section onwards does the study of production begin; likewise, once the examination of general questions has been completed, the particular questions of the capitalist mode of production are analyzed in the same way in the following two books. Beyond the simple formal ordering of the exposition, this has to do with the very essence of the dialectical method, which makes the theoretical examination of a problem coincide with its historical development; this is how this methodological orientation not only corresponds to the general formula of capital but also accounts for the transformation of simple mercantile production into capitalist mercantile production.
>
> MARINI, 1973: 83–84

And the form that the *cycle itself* of the dependent economy ends up assuming within and in the process of industrialization is the following:

> Starting, then, from the mode of circulation that characterized the export economy, the dependent industrial economy reproduces in a specific form the accumulation of capital based on the super-exploitation of the worker. Consequently, it also reproduces the mode of circulation that corresponds to that type of accumulation, although in a modified form: it is no longer the dissociation between the production and circulation of goods in function of the world market that operates but the separation between the upper and lower spheres of circulation in the very interior of the economy—a separation that, not being counteracted by the factors that act in the classic capitalist economy, acquires a much more radical character.
>
> MARINI, 1973: 63

In another text that Marini considers complementary to his work after analyzing the phases of the capital cycle of the dependent economy in theoretical terms: the two phases of the circulation of capital (C-M-C)...(P)...(M-C') mediated by productive capital (P) in terms of the origin of the money-capital (investment) that triggers the process of accumulation, the author concludes that:

> ... with respect to the analysis of the formation of money capital and its effect in the circulation phase c1 of the capital cycle in the dependent economy, what must be pointed out is the importance that the state and foreign capital have there. Consequently, from now on and independently of the problems of realization that we will consider later, we can affirm that the economic cycle of the dependent economy—the different phases of expansion and recession through which it passes—is directly articulated with the exterior, and is susceptible to a large extent to be influenced by the state.
>
> MARINI (1979: 43)

As the economy was privatized—yielding ever larger slices to private capital (national and foreign) mainly through privatizations—the State gradually relinquished its role as a direct factor of capital accumulation and proportionally transferred this role to private capital, particularly foreign capital, which came to hold in private ownership productive capital assets in the dependent countries. The other aspect of the capital cycle pointed out by Marini is the radical and structural character assumed by the importation of fixed capital from abroad,[1] such as machinery, technologies, and tools, which leads the author to declare that "[w]hat characterizes the dependent economy is the acute form that it acquires this characteristic and the fact that it responds to the very structure of its historical process of capital accumulation" (1979: 45), even in the phase of industrialization where dependence in some areas is reduced but not annulled as was the main approach of ECLAC.

As dependent capitalism developed in that first process of consolidation of its economic cycle—*overdetermined* by the world economy—a new phenomenon of generalization of the law of value was generated, which corresponds to the decade of the eighties of the last century, coinciding with the so-called "globalization,"[2] which is indeed so but in the following sense:

---

1 Bambirra (1978: 28–29) describes the process of structural dependence that forges its own capital cycle: "... it is not possible to analyze the process of reproduction of the dependent capitalist system detached from the world capitalist system simply because the dependent reproduction of the system passes through the exterior, that is to say, at first sectors I (production goods) and II (manufactured consumer goods) are abroad, then, with the development of the industrialization process, sector II develops within several of the Latin American economies but sector I does not; for the system to reproduce itself it has to import machinery. From the 1950s onwards, sector I begins to be installed in Latin America (in some cases before) but it continues to depend, for its own operation and expansion, on foreign machinery. This machinery, from this period on, does not arrive as merchandise-machinery but as capital-machinery, that is, in the form of direct foreign investments. This is the specificity of the dependent reproduction of the system: the accumulation of capital passes through the exterior through the importation of machinery; then, when this begins to be produced internally -only in some countries and with many limitations since the leading sectors, such as electronics, nuclear energy, etc., are monopolies of the most developed countries-, it is controlled directly by foreign groups, and although it already begins to supply the needs of machines of sector II -which by the way also happens to be controlled in great part by foreign capital- it continues to depend on the machinery-capital of sector I of the developed capitalist countries".

2 The origin of the concept of "globalization" is attributed to Harvard University professor Theodore Levitt (May 1983) in an article published in the *Harvard Business Review* entitled: "The Globalization of Markets." For more on the concept of "globalization," see: Mittelman, 2000 and Guillén, 2005: 26–29. In relation to the concept "neoliberalism," Bellamy (March 11, 2019) points out that its origin is found in Ludwig von Mises' book *The Nation, the State and the Economy* published in 1919 in English. An antecedent of neoliberalism and an authentic radiography prior to the Washington Consensus (1989) is the *Study* published in 1992, known as *El Ladrillo* (1992) because of the weight it had due to the number of pages; it was first distributed among the high military commanders of the Pinochet dictatorship that deposed the legitimate and constitutional government of the *Unidad Popular* ("Popular Unity") in September 1973. In their conclusions, the authors of frankly conservative and anti-communist profile boast about the "virtues" of the dictatorship and the implementation of a "market economy," concluding that: "[t]he model of a social market economy proposed to replace the existing one had logical coherence and offered a possibility to get out of

> The universalization of the law of value that we are witnessing raises a fundamental question: the increasingly accentuated impossibility of effecting transfers of value between individual and social (i.e., national) capitals through monopoly prices; will it tend in the long run to eliminate the super-exploitation of labor as a compensatory factor used by capitals that in the process of transfer must give up part of the value they have created? … The answer must take into consideration that the reduction of opportunities to provoke transfers of value through the use of mechanisms that violate the law of value such as monopoly prices will only accentuate the need to *maximize those transfers that derive naturally from the very manner in which the law operates or, rather, that are associated with its functioning.* These transfers are those that make for the diversity of the organic composition of capitals within or between branches and can only be counteracted if the capitals that are harmed in this game *artificially alter their organic composition by reducing the variable capital without the corresponding reduction of the mass of labor which they exploit.* This is only possible by increasing the intensity and duration of labor without equivalent compensation or, frankly, by reducing wages, i.e., by super-exploitation of labor power.
>
> It must be borne in mind that the tendency towards increase super-exploitation does not apply only to the capitals that transfer value in the process of transfer but also to those that appropriate it since it is evident that this allows them to take possession of quantities of value greater than those they could normally incorporate. In other words, the universalization of the law of value by tending to permit only those transfers, which in this context can be considered *legitimate*, does not aim at the suppression of the super-exploitation of labor but rather at its aggravation.
>
> MARINI, *Preface*, 1993: 11–12

With this approach—which coincides with the thesis of Piqueras (2018a: 105) regarding how the globalization of capital implies the globalization of the general laws of the accumulation of capital and value as well as of the labor-capital contradiction—Marini distinguishes two historical-structural situations that arise before and after the generalization of the law of value, which some call "globalization": (a) in the first period, transfers of value operate from

underdevelopment. Once the model was adopted and faced with the inevitable difficulties that arise in any social and economic organization, there is no doubt that the merit of having maintained the course without losing the true and final objective corresponds entirely to the then President of the Republic" (referring to the dictator Pinochet).

a predominantly monopoly situation, while (b) in the second such transfers from some capitals to others—and from labor power to these capitals—are generated mostly as a function of competition and changes in the organic composition of capital characterized by the reduction of investment in variable capital (labor power), including not only wages but also labor costs, with the mass of labor used and exploited by capital remaining constant. For this to happen, the intensity of labor and the working day must be increased and wages reduced in order to increase the rate of profit which is the fundamental and ultimate end—and law—of capitalism (Roberts, 2016). Thus, even against those who believe that with the greater the development of the organic composition of capital via elevation of the productivity of labor and constant capital, the super-exploitation of labor tends to reduce, if not to cease, Marini demonstrates the opposite: that in spite of all the advances that this composition of capital registers including its technical part, the super-exploitation of labor—as a mechanism of expropriation of value[3] and surplus value—does not diminish but increases, showing this phenomenon in the inverse proportion that is expressed in the reduction of variable capital in wages including labor costs, without reducing the *mass* of labor that is the object of exploitation by capital.

An additional observation to Marini's approach consists in the fact that super-exploitation not only benefits the (dependent) capitalists who cede value and are compensated for it through these transfers but also the capitalists of the advanced countries who appropriate it, thus benefiting themselves twice over: through the appropriation of part of the value coming from the dependent country and by resorting to this procedure against the labor force of the same central country whose workers are also subject to super-exploitation through the expropriation of a part of their consumption fund and, therefore, of their wages (Sotelo, 2020).

In both cases the super-exploitation of labor by capital is applied in general to the collective worker and not only the individual and creates the institutional-material-political basis for its extension in varying degrees and intensities to advanced capitalism.[4] This process depends, of course, on the

3 The super-exploitation of labor understood as a "... *mode of production* founded exclusively on the *greater exploitation* of the worker *and not on the development of his* productive capacity" (Marini, 1973: 40, our italics). It also implies the expropriation of part of the workers' consumption fund as a specificity of super-exploitation, not understanding it as a simple "violation of the law of value."

4 To the extent that the category of the super-exploitation of labor *increasingly* assumes a strategic position in the global capitalist system—as well as precariousness and labor flexibility implemented in most of the countries of the world as one of its main vehicles—we consider

class struggle—on the degree of organization of the proletariat and the working class of those countries—as well as on their capacity to put up effective resistance against capital through strikes, mobilizations, wage increases, and all kinds of actions and resistance. In many countries such as the United States, the attack on unions—particularly the independent and progressive ones and the concomitant fall in the rate of unionization—constitutes a requisite for the imposition of the super-exploitation of labor and the fall in wages. To this conversation contributes Robinson (2014: 173) who points out in the United States, the deindustrialization, the flexibilization of labor, and the increase of competition among workers themselves for a job in the context of an increase in unemployment and underemployment, as is happening today in that country and in others of advanced capitalism immersed in crisis and recession.

Another aspect of the super-exploitation of labor on which we have insisted (Sotelo, 2016a and 2020) is, first, the tendency and, then, its structural extension to advanced capitalism (Marini, 1996). Such a phenomenon began from the eighties of the last century with the structural crisis of capitalism that came from the previous decade (1974–1975) and was subsequently extended with the restructuring and crisis of Fordism-Taylorism[5] of mass production of

proposing that by virtue of the above approaches the different disciplines that affect the contemporary critical sociology of labor (economics, political science, anthropology) should integrate into their theoretical-methodological and analytical apparatuses this category as an important contribution and conceptual, analytical instrument of Latin American critical thought for the understanding of the dynamics of the world of work, as well as an important contribution and conceptual and analytical instrument of Latin American critical thought for understanding the dynamics of the world of work as a whole, inserted in the turbulent and contradictory scenario of the crisis and the permanent mutations to which the world of work is exposed in a process of degradation and restructuring. This does not imply discarding any category or concept coming from the social sciences that is at the same time a faithful reflection of the socio-labor reality but to articulate them and use them in function of the hypotheses and premises contained in the theory of the super-exploitation of labor as an analytical basis of dependency and its dynamics inserted in the turbulent and contradictory world economy.

5 In a book written in 1952, Weil (2014) speaks of the "turnstile of subordination" to describe the subjection of the manual labor force or execution of the worker to capital, depriving him of his intellectual-cognitive skills. Enriching her analysis, the author adds that Frederick Winslow Taylor "set up his laboratory to be able to say to the workers: it is wrong that you have done that work in one hour, it should be done in half an hour. His aim was to take away from the workers the possibility of determining for themselves the procedures and the rhythm of their work and to put in the hands of the management the choice of the movements to execute in the course of production ... his primary concern was to find the means to force the workers to give the factory the maximum of their working capacity. For him, the laboratory was a means of research but first and foremost a means of coercion" (Weil, 2014: 231).

automobiles and goods of various nature, with the consequent destructuring of the welfare state that spread after the Great Patriotic War (GPW), fundamentally in advanced capitalism. Instead of the crisis came the slowdown of capitalism with an average growth rate of 3% and with a strong predominance of fictitious capital in which "... the real economy becomes an appendix of the speculative bubbles sustained by the financial industry" (Gorz, January 7, 2008).

With restructuring came industrial reengineering and labor flexibility, and with the welfare crisis came the emergence of the imperialist corporate state and neoliberal [allegedly] free market capitalism. The ideologists of the various conservative and right-wing currents called all this "globalization," a euphemism that hides the profound structural and civilizational crisis of capitalism as well as its contradictions and socio-economic inequalities.

Articulated, these processes from the perspective of the world of work and the law of value intensified the precarization of the labor force and its subject—the worker (Sotelo, 2016 and *La izquierda Diario,* June 30, 2020)—to transform them into a flexible and polyvalent entity easily adaptable to the needs of accumulation and valorization of capital and with a high replacement rate (job rotation, unemployment, underemployment) according to the dynamics and behavior of the industrial reserve army at the local, regional, and international level.

At the same time, global and advanced capitalism generated the macroeconomic, institutional, and financial conditions so that in order to raise the rates of profit and profitability of capital (see Tables 2 and 3), the form of production of surplus value through the *expropriation of* a portion of the value of labor power to capitalize it in the accumulation of capital could operate with greater efficiency.

We argue, therefore, that in the period prior to the world crisis of the mid-seventies of the twentieth century, this form of exploitation and production of surplus value was exclusive to the dependent and underdeveloped capitalist economies—as formulated at the time by the Marxist theory of dependency and, in particular, its main exponent, Marini (1973)—being only accidental or conjunctural in the advanced ones. Here, as up to now, relative surplus value prevailed hegemonically, which was articulated with absolute surplus value and the intensification of the labor force (Sotelo, 2020).

The globalization of capital, the hegemonic advance of fictitious capital, and the contraction of the rates of growth and profit deployed even more the super-exploitation of labor in the systems of production and in the remunerations of workers and their working conditions in the advanced countries without upsetting the hegemony of relative surplus value—which is the structural sustenance of advanced capitalism—that gravitates around fictitious capital, monopolies, and the *dismeasure of labour power*.[6]

Since the first decade of 2000, several realities and contradictions that had been hidden in the ideological and disciplinary mantle of neoliberalism and "globalization" have emerged, which in order to be sustained must necessarily be understood as the form in which "… the law of value … manifests itself in our days … beyond national borders" (Marini, *Preface*, 1993: 11 and 1996: 49–68), unfolding in: a) the growing difficulties of capital to produce value and surplus value—configuring what we have called the *dismeasure of labour power* that affects its *expanded reproduction*—and b) a new social division of labor that erects the *worker* as a labor force that is exploited by capital in the *main producing force* of *extraordinary profits* (Marini, 1996: 65 and April-June 1979).

The first contradiction caused the concentration of capital in the financial sphere and its conversion into fictitious capital (Chesnais, November 1993: 21–53; Carcanholo and Nakatani, 2015: 89–124) due to the fall on historical average of the growth rate of the world economy (see Graph 1); while the second—in the face of the increasing homogenization of constant capital on a global scale whose *source code* and industrial and intellectual property remain in the hands of the great scientific-technological centers of the imperialist countries (see Dos Santos, 1987), particularly fixed capital under the form of private property of the large transnational corporations—extended the intercapitalist competition for the reduction of labor costs and wages under the influence of the increase in the rate of exploitation of labor to raise the average rate of profit. For both strategies, scientific-technological development has been of enormous importance as has the deployment of the new organization of labor based on the Toyota Production System (TPS) of Japanese origin and on the flexible automation of productive processes (Coriat, 1992, Gounet, 1999 and De Oliveira, 2004).

In the second decade of the 21st century, the precariousness of labor became generalized, characterized by a) the loss of economic, social, labor,

6 By the dismeasure of labour power, we mean the process that—by virtue of the development of the productive and technological-scientific forces of capitalism—reduces the socially necessary labor time—which determines the value of labor power and, in general, that of commodities—at the same time that immediate labor ceases to be a sufficient factor to measure the value of commodities (social wealth) and, therefore, to increase surplus value and in the long run the rate of profit, which reaffirms its tendency to fall, stimulating simultaneously the development of fictitious capital (Marx, 2010; Sotelo, 2010 and Alves, 2018). This, according to Marx (2010: 615), is synthesized in the process by which "[t]he increase of the productive force of labour and the greatest possible negation of necessary labour is the necessary tendency of capital, as we have seen."

and institutional rights of workers articulated with a high turnover rate (which in many cases implies layoffs, mobility, and redistribution of tasks and labor flexibility under the cover of deregulated temporary contracts) and b) the *extension of* the super-exploitation of labor to the economic-productive system of the countries of advanced capitalism, although with its specific, historical-structural modalities and limits, which we indicate below.

To elucidate this issue of the *extension* of the super-exploitation of labor in the developed world, in summary, we distinguish the *operative super-exploitation of labor* from what we call the *constituent super-exploitation of labor.* While the former operates in advanced capitalism, the latter occurs in dependent and underdeveloped capitalism. From the point of view of labor-value theory and political economy, this difference consists basically in the fact that the first (*operative super-exploitation of labor*) is subordinated to the relative surplus value that is hegemonic in the economic and productive system as well as in the accumulation and reproduction of capital of the imperialist center, while the second (*constitutive super-exploitation of labor*) *overdetermines*—and to some extent hinders—relative surplus value, which is subordinated to the socio-labor and political hegemony of the regime of dependent super-exploitation of labor *under* the custody and participation of the State through institutions, laws, codes, and regulations. This way of seeing things resolves the issue of those who claim that *extending* the super-exploitation of labor category to advanced capitalism "dissolves" the specificity of dependency and only accepts such extension for times of crisis in a conjunctural manner. On the contrary, by arguing for the constituent and operative character of the category of dependency while maintaining its structural character that becomes more acute in periods of crisis, our thesis preserves the specificity of dependency and world capitalism without breaking their relations of domination and conflict within the imperialism-dependency scheme to the benefit of the former.

Hence, the value of Marini's approach (1973: 100, author's italics) regarding the central task of the Marxist theory of dependency relative to the dependent economy, certainly little understood by his critics: "The task is therefore to *determine the character assumed in the dependent economy, the production of relative surplus value, and the increase in the productivity of labor.*"

This thesis has given rise to controversies and confusions—most of the time due to its being misunderstood by scholars—that have led to a dead end.[7] The

---

7 Regarding what Mészáros (1970: 11–12) says in relation to the critics of Marx's *Economic and Philosophical Manuscripts*, the same can be said in reference to the critics of Marini's *The Dialectics of Dependency*: "The narrow 'literal' reading of isolated passages (not to speak of the ideologically motivated misreadings of similarly isolated aphorisms and passages) can

constitutive super-exploitation of labor does not contradict capitalist development in its dependent and underdeveloped modality in the same way that the *operative super-exploitation of labor* adapts and unfolds under its specific modalities in the productive systems and in the social organization of labor in the advanced capitalist countries: the United States, England or Japan.

From the foregoing it does not follow—as has been incorrectly and even maliciously interpreted—that scientific-technological development in dependent countries "does not contribute" to raising labor productivity. On the contrary, the productivity-technology dialectic *does* in fact occur, and it is deployed both by private enterprises and by the State in their development and industrialization processes but in a subordinate, dependent manner under the predominance of the super-exploitation of labor regime.

This relationship between the super-exploitation of labor and productivity with scientific-technological development (relative surplus value) can be seen in two texts by Marini himself. In the first (1973: 71–72) he writes:

> ... by influencing a productive structure based on the greater exploitation of the workers, technical progress made it possible for the capitalist to intensify the rate of work of the worker, to raise their productivity, and, simultaneously, to sustain the tendency to remunerate them in a lower proportion to their real value.

In another essay he argues along the same lines:

> ... once an economic process is set in motion on the basis of super-exploitation, a monstrous mechanism is set in motion, whose perversity—far from being mitigated—is accentuated when the dependent economy resorts to the increase of productivity through technological development.
>
> MARINI, 1978: 63–64

This substantial difference between advanced and dependent capitalism consists in the fact that in the former the regime of production of relative surplus

---

only produce theories [... that] are based on the method of transforming isolated quotations into sensationalist slogans." This counter-critique fits like a glove to authors like Cardoso, Faletto, or Singer who tried to disarticulate Marini's thought and, in general, that of the Marxist theory of Dependency without success.

value is hegemonic both in terms of its economic-structural configuration and its political regime and determines the social and production relations of the productive systems and work processes, while in the dependent economies, this regime is subordinated to the old forms of capitalist production, to absolute surplus value, and to the super-exploitation of labor that historically preceded relative surplus value.[8] Here too, needless to say, the State and its public policies play a central role, especially as regards labor, wage, and social welfare legislation for the working population.

The important thing is to determine whether the super-exploitation of labor is implanted and develops under the guidance of the economic cycle and relative surplus value with the structural limits and blockages that these impose on it in advanced capitalism—*operative super-exploitation of labor*—or whether it constitutes the *hegemon of* the cycle of capital, of the relations of exploitation, of surplus value, and of the organization of labor in the dependent countries—*constitutive super-exploitation of labor.*

1.2 *The Extension of the Super-Exploitation of Labor Does Not Cancel the Dependency: It Only Redefines It*

It is necessary to clarify, briefly, that the extension of the super-exploitation of labor to central capitalism in no way annuls the (category of) dependency or takes away its specificity because it continues to orbit around the axis of the super-exploitation of labor. Nor does the imperialist economy lose its own since the axis of its processes of production, accumulation, reproduction, and exploitation of labor continues to orbit hegemonically around relative surplus value (science and technology applied to the production of commodities), around which the super-exploitation of labor is configured in a subordinate but structural manner under the protection of state and private institutions that guarantee its existence and reproduction. Finally, neither do we agree with those who accept the extension and operation of the super-exploitation of labor in advanced capitalism only in times of crisis and that when it is supposedly overcome, it loses its validity. We reaffirm: this operation is structural

8 In fact, this is a *locus* from which to understand, *ab initio*, the historical-structural genesis of Latin American underdevelopment as a by-product of the development of world imperialist capitalism (Frank, 1969: 207–208) and the constitution of structural dependency—although we clarify that in order to understand and encompass the phenomenon in its totality, it is necessary to introduce, *ex post*, the socio-political analysis (State, consciousness and class struggle, popular and revolutionary movements, etcetera) which, at the same time, overdetermine both relative surplus value and the super-exploitation of labor. I address this issue in Sotelo, 2019, Part 2, chapter 4. See also: Biondi and Felix (2018).

and can only be understood in terms of the relations of dependence with the world capitalist economy, not in an isolated or disconnected manner.

This is consistent with the definition of dependency as the:

> … relationship of subordination between formally independent nations, in whose framework the relations of production of the subordinate nations are modified or recreated to ensure the extended reproduction of dependence.
>
> MARINI, 1973: 18[9]

The implications of this definition of dependency does not result in its negation by the fact of the extension of the super-exploitation of labor to central capitalism. On the contrary, they redefine its relations of production and labor in function of the structural subordination that assures its extended reproduction. Of course, the class struggle between labor and capital can modify in any direction—favorable or unfavorable—the correlation of forces between relative surplus value and the super-exploitation of labor in the countries of advanced capitalism.

The reproduction of the social formations and politically independent nations of Latin America and the Caribbean is subordinated through multiple economic, social, and political mechanisms by the hegemonic nations of advanced capitalism—specifically by the United States as an imperialist power since at least the post-GPW period.

---

9 In an atypical way within the school of regulation, Professor De Bernis (1988: 172) offers a definition of dependency very close to the Latin American tradition: "… it can … be defined as the situation of a nation that does not contain within itself its own principle of regulation or—what is equivalent—is not constituted as a productive system; this makes it appear that dependency is nothing but the passive of domination [and] allows us to understand the nature of the process of underdevelopment and gives development the objective of creating the conditions of an autonomous (national or regional) productive system." It is interesting to note that unlike the Marxist theory of dependency, the category of dependency in this school is subordinated to the category of "regulation," whose introducer in the social sciences, alongside Michel Aglietta (2015), was precisely Professor De Bernis. For a study and exposition of the Regulation School, see Boyer, 2002, who in his book *Regulation Theory* (p. 41) defines regulation as "… a set of procedures and individual and collective behaviour patterns which must simultaneously reproduce social relations through the conjunction of institutional forms which are historically determined and supported by the current accumulation regime. Furthermore, a mode of régulation ensures the compatibility of a set of decentralised decisions, without requiring agents to internalise the principles governing the overall dynamic of the system."

Since the eighties of the previous century, the dialectic between *constitutive super-exploitation of labor* and *operative super-exploitation of labor* overdetermines the process of labor precariousness as a contemporary form of super-exploitation of labor, which at the same time permeates and subordinates the social relations of production, labor organization, and exploitation throughout the world (see Perondi, 2020). It pushes wages downward through inter-capitalist and inter-labor competition—which Marx calls *subjective competition* while that between workers and capitalists is *objective*[10] *competition* (Mészáros, 1970: 140–146); it stimulates flexibility and labor deregulation of the labor force; it increases unemployment and underemployment, as well as labor informality; it manages to obtain growing masses of value and surplus value for the accumulation and reproduction of capital even while reducing nominal and real wages and *expropriates a part of the value of the labor force of the working class and of its consumption-fund as a mechanism that compensates capital for the fall of its profit rates and, in general, of the profitability of capital.*

The problem is that these phenomena worsened and spread around in connection with the expansion of the capitalist crisis and the pandemic of the coronavirus that aggravated it (Sotelo, April 6, 2020) along with its dire consequences for workers and the popular and oppressed classes of human societies that since long ago have experienced an exponential decline and deterioration of their living, working, human, cultural, and environmental conditions. Capital, governments, and businessmen are only interested in their own salvation at the cost of the lives of millions of human beings.

2 Conclusion

The secular crisis of capitalism—particularly aggravated after the world crisis of 2008–2009 and derived from sharp falls in the rates of economic growth and productivity—affected the production of surplus value and capital profit, provoking a strong and intense precarization of labor and the extension of the super-exploitation of labor in the countries of advanced capitalism themselves.

10 "… because private property isolates everyone in his own crude solitariness, and because, nevertheless, everyone has the same interest as his neighbour, one landowner stands antagonistically confronted by another, one capitalist by another, one worker by another. In this discord of identical interests resulting precisely from this identity is consummated the immorality of mankind's condition hitherto; and this consummation is competition" (Engels, 2010: n.p.).

These mutations in the global system did not annul the relations of dependency and underdevelopment with capitalist imperialism: they only redefined them in function of the global restructuring of big capital which maintains them as a *sine qua non* condition of its own reproduction.

PART 2

Expansion, Crisis, and the Deterioration of Capitalism

CHAPTER 3

The Crisis of World Capitalism

1 Introduction

In this chapter we argue that the current crisis—not only of capitalism but also of its mode of production, life, and work—is the deepest that has occurred in recent decades. It is expressed in the diminished average rates of economic growth that it has produced in recent years, independently of the periods of crisis in which it experiences revival and relative economic growth in an environment in which the latter periods are increasingly being reduced. In this context we note the crisis of hegemony-supremacy experienced by U.S. imperialism in light of the rise of new powers that are emerging as its rivals, particularly Russia and China. This only exacerbates the depth of the crisis and places it on the backs of the majority of humanity: the workers who are displaced into unemployment, misery, low wages, and labor and social precariousness.

For many years the United States was considered the locomotive of the development of Western capitalism after the GPW. Indeed, it seemed that its trajectory marked "a manifest destiny" that promised to make it "forever" the world's leading power. Although there was a period particularly during the 1990s in which the country experienced a certain sustained—albeit moderate—growth from the 2000s, to date and in the context of it becoming the epicenter of the global coronavirus pandemic, it never reached the levels of development it achieved during the so-called "golden years" of post-war capitalism.

Thus, the United States as the commander of Western imperialism is experiencing one of its greatest historical crises and in the context of the crisis of world capitalism, has reached the limit of its expansion, which places it in the conflictive, multipolar world as a power that will have to settle both its decline and loss of hegemony.

1.1 *Coronavirus-Accelerated System Decline*

In every economic crisis, capital and its system of socio-labor metabolism seize the opportunity to restructure its economies, businesses, and work processes in order to impose—generally without social consensus as a rule—new relations of exploitation and labor organization on workers of all categories and productive systems. Starting with massive layoffs—as happened, for example, (not without strong protests) with the closure of Nissan in Barcelona, which

 | DOI:10.1163/9789004532717_005

simply announced to the unions and the Spanish government the closure of its plants in Barcelona, jeopardizing 25,000 jobs. As well as the French Renault in the northern city of Maubeuge, where thousands of people demonstrated against the decision of the automobile manufacturer (a subsidiary of Renault Maubeuge Construction Automobile) to cut 15,000 jobs in the world, of which 4,600 correspond to that country. Or the declaration of bankruptcy of LATAM Airlines, the largest air transport group in Latin America, which announced that the company and its subsidiaries in Chile, Peru, Colombia, Ecuador, and the United States had filed for Chapter 11 of the US bankruptcy law, becoming one of the many victims of the capitalist crisis and the health emergency that paralyzed flights. The same situation occurred with Colombia's Avianca Holdings and Australia's Virgin Australia Holdings when they filed for "protection" while they restructured their debts and adjusted their workforces.

All this contrasts with the period before the coronavirus. Thus, it is known that world capitalism experienced a long expansionary cycle after the GPW.

As Theotonio dos Santos (1971: 93) states:

> ... during the entire post-war period, capitalism faced a relatively favorable situation with a sustained expansion of world trade and national income. During this period, the uneven character of capitalist development provoked important changes in the correlation of forces within it. In particular, the growth of Japan and Germany and in the background that of continental Europe far exceeded the growth of the United States (and England).

Baran and Sweezy (1966: 246) also corroborate this expansion on the basis of the increase in population consumption and military expenditures of the *military industrial complex* that led the United States to become the hegemon of the area of Western capitalism: "... never since the height of the railroad epoch [the second half of the 19th century to the first years of the 20th century] has the American economy been subject in peacetime to such powerful stimuli."

Marini (1995: 17) synthesizes this historical process:

> ... the system that was implemented in 1944–45 put an end to a long period of disorganization of the world economic and political system that began with the war of 1914, went through the great depression of 1929, and reached its peak in the Second World War. The post-war order was marked by a series of elements, including the division of the world into two camps: capitalist and socialist. In the former, the hegemony of

> the United States was unquestionable, while the latter, in rapid expansion, had the Soviet Union as its epicenter.

Dos Santos (2002: 81) points out that in that period "… restructuring was based on the implementation of the scientific and technical revolution and on the worldwide expansion and diffusion of mass production technologies, particularly in the durable goods sector" with strong influence of the centers and capitals of advanced countries.

In general, the post-war expansion extended until the *crisis* of the mid-1970s (1974–1975), which represented a real *stage of transition* towards what would later be known as "neoliberalism" and "globalization" put in place and generalized from the following two decades onwards (a point of agreement between both Marini, 1995: 17, and Robinson, 2008: 22–26): for the former, it marks the transition to a "new world economy," while for the latter, "[t]he global capitalist crisis that began in the 1970s is generally identified as the turning point for globalization and … marks the transition to a new transnational stage in the system."[1] Or as O'Connor writes, capitalist crises "… are the cauldron in which capital qualitatively restructures itself for economic, social, and political renewal and further accumulation" (Robinson, 2014: 154).

At this stage capitalism shows fluctuating behavior with a marked tendency to decline—despite the relative recovery from the 2007–2008 crisis observed between 2010–2019—as shown in Graph 1 below, which summarizes the process by decades:

Since the end of the nineties of the previous century between 1997–2006, the world economy grew 3.4%; during the capitalist crisis of 2009, the global economic product was negative (-2.1%) according to ECLAC (September 2010: 18), while it experienced a weak recovery by averaging 2.8% between 2011–2019, with only 2.5% grown in the last year (ECLAC, April 3, 2020). Based on this grown rate in the long period between 1997–2019, the average growth rate was

1 Some authors such as Martins (2020: 172 et seq.) and Dos Santos (2002: 125 and 2004) argue that a new Kondratiev cycle of expansive tonality (A) began in the United States in 1994, which extended to the world economy during the following 25 years and would presumably end in 2019. Discussing the long cycles with Mandel and the Kondratievs, Jorge Beinstein in an interesting article (February 2009) warns that, *indeed*, theoretically, a long recovery of this type would have been recorded, but what actually happened, empirically, was that capitalism prolonged its long depressive cycle beyond the recovery point marked in the mid-nineties of the last century based on the performance of the "new economy" so touted by Keynesian thinking and the democrats. Based on the data presented in this book (see Table 1), we are inclined to agree with Beinstein's thesis, particularly aggravated by the intensification of the capitalist crisis of the coronavirus.

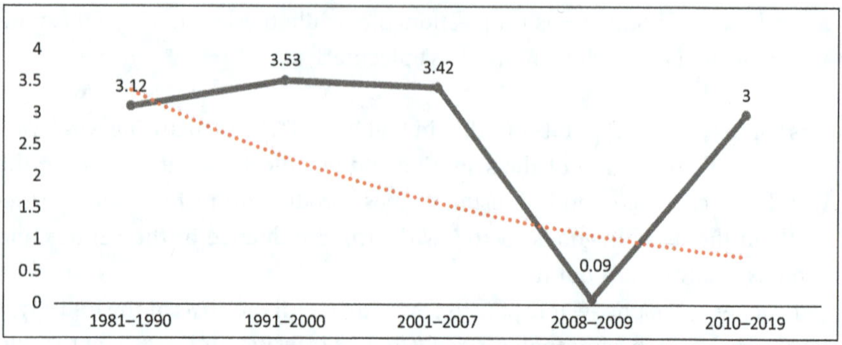

GRAPH 1 World GDP growth, 1981–2019 (%)
SOURCE: ELABORATION BY THE AUTHOR BASED ON DATA FROM WORLD BANK, N/D. DATA FOR 2019 CORRESPONDS TO IMF (2020)

a meager 2%—lower than the 3% that some analysts (Harvey, 2010: 109)[2] consider as the minimum necessary for capitalism to survive and reproduce itself and at the same time generate an environment conducive to growth in which to invest the capital surpluses created by the labor force. A thesis that Piqueras (2014: 142) also sustains regarding the reduction of investment spaces for which "[t]here seems to be no capitalist solution for such a challenge, beyond provoking false exits through new inflations of fictitious capital."

In a shorter time span, the World Bank (June 2020, Table 1.1: 4) shows that global capitalism has not scaled that proportion. On the contrary in 2017 it grew only 3.3%; in 2018, 3%; and in 2019, 2.4%, averaging 2.9% in that period.

The year 2019, prior to the coronavirus pandemic, took place in the context of a crisis of world capitalism in which most of the countries and societies of the planet were involved. Beyond the structural and heterogeneous behavior of the regions (Asia, Africa, Latin America and the Caribbean, United States, Europe, Oceania)—which was the "intermediate" form adopted by the globalization process according to Dos Santos (2002: 43), of course unequal and contradictory—the *median* of world compound growth was below 3%, including the share in the percentage of the most dynamic economies such as China and India (for its origins, cf. Amin, 1999). Thus, according to ECLAC (2019, Table 1: 21) and with projections for 2020, the "developed economies" fell from 1.7% in 2019 to 1.5% in 2020. The United States (which many still weight as the first capitalist power of the orb) goes from 2.3% in the first year to 1.9% in the

2 "No matter what kind of innovation or change occurs, the long-term survival of capitalism depends on the ability to achieve 3% compound growth" (Harvey, 2010: 109, translation ours).

second; Japan declines from 0.9% to 0.5%, respectively; the United Kingdom, from 1.3% to 1%; the Euro Zone grows minimally from 1.1% to 1.2%; the "emerging and developing economies" evolve from 3.9% to 4.3% between 2019 and 2020; "emerging" Asia rises from 5.9% to 6%; China declines from 6.1% in the first year to 5.8% in the second; India increases its development rate from 6% in the first year to 6.7% in the second; "emerging economies" in Europe increase from 1.8% to 2.4; the Middle East and Central Asia from 0.9% to 2.9% and Sub-Saharan Africa increases its rate from 3% to 3.4%, respectively.

For their part, the 28 countries of the European Union went from 2.3% in the first quarter of 2018 to 1.7% in the third quarter of 2019 (according to EUROSTAT, n.d.).

In its balance, ECLAC (2019: 21) highlights that:

> The slowdown is widespread in 2019 and affects developed and emerging economies. For the former, a growth of 1.7% is expected this year (2019) instead of the 2.3% observed in 2018. For emerging economies, meanwhile, growth of 3.9% is expected in 2019, compared to the 4.5% observed in 2018 ... For 2020, developed economies are expected to continue to slow down (to 1.5% growth), while emerging economies would recover their dynamism to a lesser extent (with a rise of 4.3%). With these percentages, the world's growth rate would reach levels in 2020 similar to those of 2019 ... The slowdown in developed economies in 2020 reaches the United States that, despite being in the longest expansion phase in its history,[3] would grow by less than 2% next year as the effect of the tax reform that gave impetus to the economy in 2018 and part of 2019 dissipates further.

Two issues stand out from the above quote: On the one hand, that regardless of the outbreak of the coronavirus pandemic officially recognized in December 2019 in China, the world capitalist economy was already slowing down and on the other, that the country most affected by Covid-19—the United States—was leading along the same path of global slowdown of economies, a phenomenon that would be expressed a few months later in an exponential manner throughout 2020.

The tragedy of today's pandemic capitalism is that it collapses like a house of cards, plunging the world into a pit of crisis and unemployment never seen

3 Based on a graph published by Duffin (*Statista*, February 3, 2020), we calculate an average annual growth between 2009 and 2019 (120 months) of 1.84% in that "expansionary" U.S. period. See Graph 2.

in its modern history. For example, the OECD (June 2020) estimates a drop in world GDP in 2020 of -6% in a less severe scenario of the infection, with an estimate of -7.6% in the event of a worsening of the disease; for the United Kingdom it would be -11.5% and -14%, respectively; Spain, -11.1% and -14.4%; the United States plummets -7.3% and -8.5%; China, -2.6% and -3.7%; Mexico, -7.5% and -8.6%; Colombia, -6.1% and -7.9%; Chile, -5.6% and -7.1%; Brazil, -7.4% and -9.1%; and Argentina, -8.3% and -10.1%.

In this context of structural crisis and serious mutations—epidemics, syndemics, and pandemics; structural racism and xenophobia; human and ecological devastation; imperialist wars and wars of extermination; neocolonialism; annexation of sovereign territories—all projections concerning the growth performance of the world capitalist economy are negative for the year 2020[4] as shown in the following table:

With the exception of China (2.0%)[5] and Turkey (0.5%), the other countries and regions show negative growth rates in 2020. Despite the optimism of international organizations such as the World Bank and the IMF, the crisis will extend into 2021 even though their predictions project generalized recoveries, affecting world trade which, according to WTO estimates (April 8, 2020),

4 In the vicinity of this contraction, unemployment could reach 25% of GDP; behaviors unimaginable even for the most lucid minds of neoliberal technocrats a few months ago. See: *Sputnik* (June 8, 2020). This situation is exacerbated when compared to the 2008–2009 financial crisis in which the United States lost 5% of its jobs and took about 119 months to recover pre-crisis levels. In Europe on the other hand, this loss was 3%, according to the German newspaper *Der Spiegel* (quoted in: *Sputnik*, July 25, 2020). The National Bureau of Economic Research officially recognized that this country entered recession in February 2020, marking the end of a long "... expansion that began in June 2009" and that showed an average annual growth rate of 2.3% until 2019. By 2020 it estimates a decline of -6.1% for the U.S. and -5.2 for the world economy. See: *Sputnik*, June 9, 2020. Recent data from the U.S. Department of Commerce (July 30, 2020) reveals a 32.9% drop in real GDP during the second quarter of 2020. During this same quarter, the strongest *ECONOMY* in the European Union, Germany, experienced a negative slump of 10.1%, according to the Statistiches Bundesamt (Destatis), July 30, 2020. While the World Bank (June 2020: Table 1.1: 4) projected world economic growth of -7.7% in 2020, Spain officially entered recession as its GDP plummeted -18.5%, according to the National Statistics Institute (INE, July 31, 2020), in the second quarter of 2020 and the unemployment rate reached 15.33% with around 3 million 368 thousand unemployed during the same period.

5 The National Bureau of Statistics of China (National Bureau of Statistics, January 18, 2021) reported that the Chinese economy grew, on average, 2.3% in 2020, making it one of the few, if not the only one, to grow in the midst of the global capitalist recession and the exponential growth of the Covid-19 pandemic. While the United States, in the same year, had a contraction of -3.5%, according to the U.S. Department of Commerce, and Mexico -8.5% according to INEGI (January 29, 2021).

TABLE 1 Real gross domestic product as % of previous year with projections 2021–2022

	2018	2019	2020e	2021f	2022f
World	*3.0*	*2.3*	*-4.3*	*4.0*	*3.8*
Advanced economies	2.2	*1.6*	*-5.4*	*3.3*	*3.5*
United States	3.0	2.2	-3.6	3.5	3.3
Euro area	1.9	1.3	-7.4	3.6	4.0
Japan	0.6	0.3	-5.3	2.5	2.3
Emerging market/developing economies	*4.3*	*3.6*	-2.6	*5.0*	*4.2*
EMDEs excluding China	3.2	2.3	-5.0	3.4	3.6
Commodity-exporting EMDES	2.0	1.6	-4.8	3.0	3.2
Other EMDES	5.7	4.8	-1.3	6.1	4.8
Other EMDEs excluding China	4.8	3.2	-5.3	3.9	4.1
East Asia and Pacific	6.3	5.8	0.9	7.4	5.2
China	6.6	6.1	2.0	7.9	5.2
Indonesia	5.2	5.0	-2.2	4.4	4.8
Thailand	4.1	2.4	-6.5	4.0	4.7
Europe and Central Asia	3.4	2.3	-2.9	3.3	3.9
Russian Federation	2.5	1.3	-4.0	2.6	3.0
Turkey	3.0	0.9	0.5	4.5	5.0
Poland	5.4	4.5	-3.4	3.5	4.3
Latin America and the Caribbean	1.9	1.0	-6.9	3.7	2.8
Brazil	1.8	1.4	-4.5	3.0	2.5
Mexico	2.2	0-.1	-9.0	3.7	2.6
Argentina	-2.6	-2.1	-10.6	4.9	1.9
Middle East and North Africa	0.5	0.1	-5.0	2.1	3.1
Saudi Arabia	2.4	0.3	-5.4	2.0	2.2
Iran, Islamic Rep.[3]	-6.0	-6.8	-3.7	1.5	1.7
Egypt, Arab Rep.[2]	5.3	5.6	3.6	2.7	5.8
South Asia	6.5	4.4	-6.7	3.3	3.8
India[3]	6.1	4.2	-9.6	5.4	5.2
Pakistan[2]	5.5	1.9	-1.5	0.5	2.0
Bangladesh[2]	7.9	8.2	2.0	1.6	3.4
Sub-Saharan Africa	2.6	2.4	-3.7	2.7	3.3

TABLE 1 Real gross domestic product as % of previous year (*cont.*)

	2018	2019	2020e	2021f	2022f
Nigeria	1.9	2.2	-4.1	1.1	1.8
South Africa	0.8	0.2	-7.8	3.3	1.7
Angola	-2.0	-0.9	-4.0	0.9	3.5

1. Headline aggregate growth rates are calculated using GDP weights at 2010 prices and market exchange rates.
2. GDP growth rates are on a fiscal year basis. Aggregates that include these countries are calculated using data compiled on a calendar year basis. Pakistan's growth rates are based on GDP at factor cost. The column labeled 2019 refers to FY2018/19.
3. Columns indicate fiscal year. For example, 2018 refers to FY2018/19.
4. World growth rates are calculated using purchasing power parity (PPP) weights, which attribute a greater share of global GDP to emerging market and developing economies (EMDEs) than market exchange rates.
5. World trade volume of goods and nonfactor services.
6. "Oil price" is the simple average of Brent, Dubai, and West Texas Intermediate prices. The non-energy index is the weighted average of 39 commodity prices (7 metals, 5 fertilizers, 27 agricultural commodities). For additional details, please see https://www.worldbank.org/commodities.

Note: e = estimate; f = forecast. World Bank forecasts are frequently updated based on new information. Consequently, projections presented here may differ from those contained in other World Bank documents, even if basic assessments of countries' prospects do not differ at any given date. Country classifications and lists of EMDEs are presented in table 1.2 include: Brazil, the Russian Federation, India, China, and South Africa. Due to lack of reliable data of adequate quality, the World Bank is currently not publishing economic output, income, or growth data for Turkmenistan and Bolivarian Republic of Venezuela. Turkmenistan and Bolivarian Republic of Venezuela are excluded from cross-country macroeconomic aggregates.

SOURCE: WORLD BANK, JANUARY 2021

will experience a fall of between -13% and -32% in 2020 due to the negative economic-financial and socio-labor effects of the coronavirus.

Therefore, most of the serious studies and analyses conclude and certify that in the best of cases, a country that manages to grow at least 2% average annual growth—as would be the case of China—would already be at the "top" of such behavior in the "best" global expectation, compared to negative falls in most of the capitalist countries of the Western world such as the United States and Eastern world such as Japan, those that make up the European Union, and, of course, those of Latin America and the Caribbean, as well as most of Africa and Asia.

The World Bank (June 2020, Table 1.1.1: 17) estimates that global GDP will experience its worst performance and the largest drop since the GPW, plummeting -5.2% and *per capita* output -6.2%, with Latin America and the Caribbean being the most affected region with severe drops of -7.2% and -8.1%, respectively, accompanied by unprecedented increases in structural unemployment, underemployment, and precarious employment; poverty; and informality (in this regard see: World Bank, 2020).

This crisis and its contradictions operate as a function of the sharp fall in the rate of profit (Tables 2 and 3) and the problems of the contraction of international trade.

In relation to the behavior of the rate of profit, we observe how, during the long post-war period until 2017, it declines just over 18%, the opposite occurring during 1982–1997, when it increases 23.6% along with the increase in the rate of surplus value of 37%, and then falls, in 1997–2017, -9.9% and -6.8% respectively as shown in the following table 2:

We add that along with the economic crisis "… the pandemic slump has driven global corporate profits down by around 25% in the first half of 2020—a bigger fall than in the Great Recession. " (Roberts, September 20, 2020).

1.2 *The End of the "Long Expansion" in the United States: The Locomotive Slows Down*

In the wake of the 2008–2009 capitalist-financial crisis that shook the world—particularly affecting the working classes and other categories that live off the sale of their labor power—the corporate media and the system's organic intellectuals began to speak of a "post-crisis American miracle," expressed in an "expansion" that accumulated 128 months of "sustained" growth in the United States (*The Economist*, June 24, 2019).

As can be seen in Graph 2 in the last period of expansion that occurred between June 2009 and February 2020 (before and during the outbreak of the pandemic), the U.S. economy grew by 2.3% for 128 consecutive months.

It is presumed that something similar to what was announced in the 1990s as the "new economy" (Kelly, 1997 and Mandel, December 26, 1996)—based on the third techno-industrial revolution based on automation and computers—occurred when the average GDP growth rate was 3.6%. But, despite the length of the last expansion (128 months), the GDP growth rate's annual average was only 2.3% (Graph 2), lower than the average annual GDP growth rate in the US from 1982–1990, which was 4.3%, and that of 1991–2001, which was 3.6%. It even remains below the average of the two Bill Clinton administrations, precisely where the enigmatic "miracle" of the "new economy" occurred and in which the average growth rate reached 3.1% (See Graph 3) but without

TABLE 2 G-20: Rate of profit, organic composition of capital, and rate of surplus value, 1950–2017 (%)

Period	Profit rate	Organic composition of capital	Capital gains tax
1950–2017	-18.7	12.6	-8.4
1950–1966	11.3	4.0	15.7
1966–1982	-34.5	-5.6	-38.1
1982–1997	23.6	11.0	37.2
1997–2017	-9.9	3.4	-6.8

SOURCE: ROBERTS, SEPTEMBER 20, 2020

surpassing the highest growth achieved between 1940–1950 during the second post-war period which was 4.5% (Valenzuela, 2017: Table 1: 14).

As a corollary of the above, it can be concluded that the shorter the expansionary cycle of the U.S. economy, the higher its economic growth rate and vice versa as shown in Figure 2, comparing the GDP of the period November 1970-November 1973 with that of June 2009-February 2020. In the former in 36 months, the average growth rate was 5.1%, while in the latter in 128 months, it dropped to 2.3%.

This behavior—which implied the recovery of the rate of profit and economic growth in the United States particularly in its manufacturing industry during the 1990s and in Bill Clinton's two terms in office—is the combined product "… wage repression and painful, very large-scale processes of rationalization and technical change in manufacturing …" (Brenner, 2006: 260). This author also indicates that between 1990–1996 the wage increase was only 0.2% (2006: 254), a meager amount that does not even compensate somewhat for the increases in consumer goods of the basic U.S. market basket that—however weak they may be—affect both the value of the labor force in a negative sense and the consumption fund of the working family, especially if we consider items such as housing, health, food, and transportation (we address this issue in Sotelo, 2020: 198 *et al.*). For the researchers of the Economic Policy Institute, Lawrence Mischel and Josh Bivens (May 13, 2021), this situation of wage deterioration is due among other causes to the open gap between the average remunerations received by workers (*typical workers*) and the increases in productivity, responsible for a reduction of about 10 dollars per hour and per

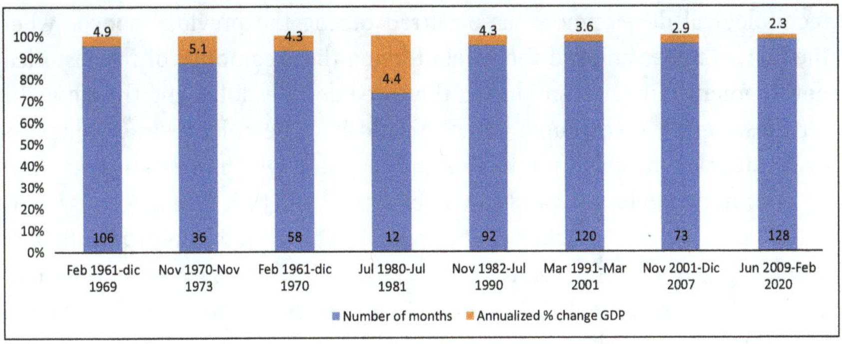

GRAPH 2 United States: economic expansions, selected periods between February 1961 and February 2020 (in quantity and % of GDP)
SOURCE: ECONOMIC COMMISSION FOR LATIN AMERICA AND THE CARIBBEAN (ECLAC), BASED ON DATA FROM THE NATIONAL BUREAU OF ECONOMIC RESEARCH (NBER) AND THE BUREAU OF ECONOMIC ANALYSIS OF THE U.S. DEPARTMENT OF COMMERCE, CIT. IN: ECLAC, AUGUST 2020, GRAPH 1: 2

worker during the last four decades, which translates to a loss of approximately 43% in the whole economy between 1979 and 2017.

Unlike the period of the "new economy"—the subsequent and last "exceptional period" (2009–2019) prior to the outbreak of the coronavirus pandemic—the US growth has as its cause and results in good measure from the tax reforms implemented by Donald Trump in December 2017, coupled with his protectionist policies that resulted in absolute benefits for capital and the ruling classes of that country of around 2 trillion dollars by way of tax cuts at the cost of the reduction of important social services for the working classes such as Medicare. Therefore, it is not a question of "exceptional" growth and expansion derived from increases in the productivity of labor and

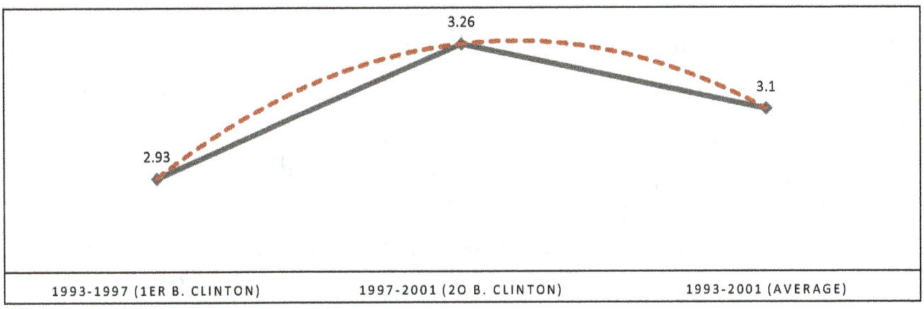

GRAPH 3 United States. Average growth rates in %. during the Bill Clinton regime (1993–2001)
SOURCE: CALCULATIONS BASED ON DATA FROM THE WORLD BANK, N.D.

technological development, as occurred during the previous epochs when the United States enjoyed the label of being the locomotive of the historical development of capitalism during the three decades following the GPW. But for these reforms, economic growth would have been lower in a context of stagnant wage rates and productive employment, which in recent years have deteriorated (Sotelo, 2020 and Lawrence Mishel and Josh Bivens, May 13, 2021). Although 2018 saw a slight improvement in the overall rate of profitability, according to Roberts (November 4, 2019) "[i]n 2018, on my measure, US overall profitability rose very slightly over 2017 (probably due to Trump's corporate tax cuts). But profitability in 2018 was still 5–7% below the 2014 peak." So, it is a far cry from the recovery that would have occurred if the 2014 peak had been reached and surpassed. Incidentally, Roberts in the same cited source indicates a similar trajectory of the EU economies.

In short, the rate of profit worsened since it had been experiencing strong historical setbacks since the second post-war period as shown in Table 3 below:

This is what leads the author to affirm that "... [o]ver the whole post-war period up to 2019, there was a secular fall in the US rate of profit on the HC measure of 31% and on the CC measure 31%!,"[6] fundamentally due to the increase in the organic composition of capital and the fall of the rate of surplus value since 1946 by about 10% (Roberts, September 13, 2020). An interesting conclusion of the author in this same article, which operates as a corollary of the historical process of capitalism, is the one that states that during the neoliberal period:

> ... from 1982 to 1997, the rate of surplus value increased 16%, more than the organic composition of capital (11%), so the rate of profit increased 9%. Since 1997, the U.S. rate of profit has fallen about 6% because the organic composition of capital has increased by almost 17%, outpacing the increase in the rate of profit (3%).

The author concludes for 2020 that "[a]ssuming a 7% fall in US real GDP, I calculate that we can expect a 25% fall in the rate of profit " (Roberts, September 13, 2020).

Finally, the current phase of neoliberal imperialism since the financial and trade crisis of 2008–2009 is linked to the strong trade disputes between China and the United States, expressed in the mutual imposition of strong

6 HC corresponds to historical costs, while CC corresponds to current costs, differentiated by inflation variations according to the author.

TABLE 3 United States: Rate of profit, organic capital of composition, and capital gains rate. 1950–2017 (%)

Period	Rate of profit		Organic composition of capital	Capital gains rate
	HC	CC*		
1946–2019	-31%	-31%	60%	-10%
1965–1982	-20%	-35%	—	—
1982–1997	9%	29%	11%	16%
1997–2017	-6%	—	17%	3%

SOURCE: ROBERTS, SEPTEMBER 13, 2020
*HC = Historical Costs; CC = Current Costs as calculated by the author

"sanctions" and taxes on the exports of both countries as indicated above. It also manifests itself in the technological area with the Trump administration's attack against the Chinese company Huawei that leads the way particularly in fifth generation technologies (5G) and, in general, with the protectionist policy implemented by Trump in an attempt to counteract the enormous difficulties that the US economy is currently experiencing. Its origin is in the 1990s, expressed in the fact that the recovery caused the economic conversion into a "service economy" to the detriment of the industrial sector and to the benefit of the interests of financial capital (Beinstein, 2001: 183–184) in such a way that the US GDP represented 32% of the world product in 1965 and by 1995 had fallen to 25% (Beinstein, 2001: 184). Still, in 2019 it stood at 24.8%, while China had a share of 16.3% in the latter year according to the IMF (January 12, 2020).

Many authors (Brenner, 2006, Shaikh, 2006, Roberts, 2016) agree that the objective of the system (to increase the rate of profit and the general profitability of capital) is achieved at the cost of increasing the exploitation of the labor force and the repression of wages, regardless of the behavior of unemployment and employment rates because capitalists adjust them to their business cycles and their profitability needs. Although this stimulated sustained economic growth as the year 2000 approached, signs of a slowdown in world and U.S. growth were already evident and the World Bank (February 2001) announced that "there will be a 'soft landing' for the U.S. economy, rather than a full-blown recession."

Together with the concentration of income to the benefit of the ruling classes, the increase in social inequality, and the fall in workers' real wages, it can be seen that as the GDP increases, a deficit in the trade balance is produced and the public debt grows, which was covered by loans mainly from Western Europe and Japan in the course of the nineties (Beinstein, 2001: 194–195). From the year 2000 onwards, the "American miracle"—caused by the "new economy"—has flatly vanished and exhibited on a large scale and volume its socio-economic and political contradictions.

In the second part of the 1990s—at the height of the "new economy" that promised to overcome the capitalist crisis and at the same time generate a new long wave of economic growth based on the boom in computer and telematic technologies that helped to characterize capitalism as "cognitive"[7]—Castel (1998), particularly in the United States, argued that in the face of the crisis of what he calls the "wage society" the social welfare state was the only device left within the rational logic of that crisis to maintain the cohesion of what the author calls the "Social Question."[8]

Thus, during the decade of the seventies:

> There was indeed a powerful synergy between economic growth with its corollary, quasi-full employment, and the development of labor rights and social protection. The wage society seemed to follow an upward trajectory that in the same movement ensured collective enrichment and promoted a better sharing of opportunities and guarantees.
>
> CASTEL, 1998: 493

It is necessary to relativize this author's assertions when he generalizes workers' rights, collective enrichment, and the "better sharing of opportunities and guarantees" that he assures us occurred by virtue of this "synergy" between full

---

7 For the "knowledge" or digital economy, see Srnicek, 2016. The myth of growth based on technologies and knowledge *without labor force* led many authors to make statements such as the following: " In the 21st century, a shift to an economy dominated by the production and consumption of intangibles, such as the trade in know-how and ideas, could spur the above-average growth rates of a long boom" (Miller, 1999). As we have seen, this premise has not only been fulfilled in the 21st century, but global capitalism is far from guaranteeing its minimum reproduction without resorting to the constant economic, commercial, and financial crises that have introduced it into a pit of structural quasi-stagnation. See also OECD (1999).

8 "... fundamental aporia in which a society experiences the enigma of its cohesion and tries to avoid the risk of its fracture. It is a challenge that questions the capacity of a society or a nation to guarantee its existence as a whole articulated by relations of interdependence" (Castel, 1998, 30).

employment and economic growth; this did occur, indeed, but in a *restricted way* among the high professional categories of the labor aristocracy and in some qualified segments of the labor force, not in the collective mass worker typical of Fordism-Taylorism in advanced capitalism (Coriat, 1985) of the era of the social welfare state.

Castel indicates that this upward trajectory of the wage society (the central social issue of the time)—and we add of the social welfare State—in his words "was interrupted" and with it "… the very idea of progress lost its cohesion" (Castel, 1998: 493), whose place was occupied by precariousness and labor and wage flexibility in the contour of a minimal entrepreneurial capitalist State.

Despite the relative guarantees provided by such a social state in the history of capitalism, the uncertainties and aporias of the system for the working class have always been a constant that is exacerbated in times of crisis and even more so with neoliberalism, understood in the sense defined above by Cueva (1993: 247 and Dardot and Laval, July 24, 2019).

Thus, Castel (1998: 446) writes in relation to the labor market in France in the thirties: "… it was dominated by a mobility full of uncertainties under the threat of resignation against which labor legislation did not protect. Hiring by task, by the hour, or by the day was the most frequent. In most cases, there is neither a written contract nor a preliminary stipulation of the duration of the contract."

The paradox of our times is that this uncertainty and the permanent risk of job loss have become the epicenter of the social and labor relations that characterize the world of work practically everywhere, not to describe this situation as the French author does as the great (new) social question of the 21st century to which significant titles of publications such as Beck's "risk" (1992) or Stiglitz's "malaise" (2002) allude.

1.2.1 The Hegemonic Crisis of U.S. Imperialism

On the international level, the indirect military conflict between Russia and the United States stands out, where the latter does not accept the status of the existence of a multipolar and polycentric world (see: Sotelo, April 23, 2020) that flatly and historically discarded all hegemonic unilateralism in international relations as occurred after the fall of the Berlin Wall and the USSR. This is a matter which, of course, goes against all imperialist supremacism in international relations, especially of the American and other—let us say minor—imperialisms, such as the German, French, Italian, or British. The still dominant imperialism (of Trump and Biden)—although more and more sustained in repression and war as ways of increasing the accumulation of capital in its favor—has replanted the supremacist doctrine of "American exceptionalism," together with the accompanying slogan "America first" in Latin America through the resurrection of the deadly and outdated Monroe Doctrine, promoted by the hawks of the Pentagon with the help of their Latin American pawns in the counterinsurgent "Lima Group" and organized and directed by Washington and by such fellow organizations as the neocolonialist OAS directed by the sadly "famous" Almagro.

The truth is that the crisis goes far beyond these dimensions to encompass social, cultural, environmental, civilizational, spiritual, and human dimensions that affect all categories of the world of work: from the most unskilled sectors, to the billions of informal workers (2.06 billion, according to the ILO, April 29, 2020, Table A3: 15), and the unemployed, including the most qualified workers with high levels of education, training, and technological skills located at the highest levels of the production and consumption systems interspersed with cutting-edge technologies, digitalization, and artificial intelligence.

In another context and latitude—particularly with regard to the problem of the hegemony or supremacy of US imperialism at the international level[9]—in 2019, the Syrian Arab army, supported by Russia, practically liquidated the terrorist hosts that remained in some strongholds of the country thanks only to the support of Washington that at the same time is using its Zionist vassal to maintain their harassment and presence in Syrian oil zones. Otherwise, the Syrian government would have decreed a ceasefire, total peace, and begun the reconstruction of the country overwhelmed by 10 years of war against the terrorist hosts since its beginning on March 15, 2011.

The "sanctions" imposed by U.S. imperialism—in this context of economic contraction and falling profit rates against progressive sovereign nations—have been unsuccessful in countries such as North Korea, Iran, Cuba, and Venezuela,[10] among others, despite being directed against the people in order

9 Relative decline warned by the British historian Paul Kennedy (1987: 515) through his concept of "imperial overstretch," as England had in its time before and the United States today, which possesses and distributes around 800 military bases all over the planet (9 of which are installed in Colombia), not precisely with peace and development objectives.

10 Within the framework of the strategic and solidarity agreements between the Islamic Republic of Iran and Venezuela and in open defiance of US imperialism, the former sent 1.53 million barrels of gasoline and refining components to Venezuela in 5 vessels between May 24 and June 1, 2020. The vessels were escorted by the Bolivarian Army Navy and Aviation after the US threatened to use force to prevent the arrival of the Iranian vessels to Venezuelan coasts. The arrival of the vessels in Venezuelan territorial waters of the Iranian ships *Fortune*, which arrived on May 25, 2020; the *Forest*, on May 26, 2020; the *Petunia*, on May 27, 2020; the *Faxon*, on May 28, 2020; and the *Clavel*, on June 1, 2020 (see: https://twitter.com/armadafanb/status/1266065998878310406) marks for the first time a challenge to

to deteriorate and undermine the legitimacy of the governments of those countries and make possible by these means a *coup d'état* or military intervention to favor U.S. interests and, later, appropriate the natural resources of those sovereign nations.

The trade war provoked by US belligerence and Donald Trump's protectionist policy against China within the framework of the technological-digital conflict between both powers for its control, which somehow continues under the Biden administration, has affected the two powerful economies and accelerated a presumed agreement between both contenders—although, as practice shows and as has happened many times, the US government cannot be trusted. It imposes its interests through threats and blackmail as it did with Honduras, Guatemala, El Salvador, and Mexico by imposing its xenophobic and racist immigration policy on them, turning them *into* what is called a "safe third country."[11] In the same way, the United States imposed on Mexico the "United States-Mexico-Canada" Free Trade Agreement (USMCA)—also known as T-MEC—that replaced NAFTA[12] and was authorized by the Mexican Congress and the U.S. House of Representatives, conditioned to the implementation of a neoliberal labor reform[13] that the Mexican government executed in haste

the arrogance and supremacy of US imperialism. Together with having become the epicenter of the global Covid-19 pandemic and losing ground in world arms markets, for example, through India's purchase from Russia of the Russian S-400 Triumf air defense systems for a total value of 5 billion dollars, for which it threatened to impose "sanctions on that country," it is precipitating its crisis of hegemony in an increasingly multipolar and polycentric world in the presence of the arrival of new economic powers of truly nuclear proportions such as China and Russia. See: *Sputnik*, May 26, 2020. For a geopolitical analysis of the significance of Venezuela-Iran relations, see: Teruggi (May 26, 2020).

11 As Smith (November 6, 2019) accurately asserts, "[o]n the front of migration, Trump has managed to use the tremendous asymmetry of power between the United States and Mexico to convince or compel the new centre-left populist president of that country, Andrés Manuel López Obrador, to carry out the policing of Central American migrants in Mexico on behalf of the US border regime." To say that the Mexican president is "center-left" is an exaggeration of the terms since he himself has not described himself as such, much less his political practices as a ruler, which are inclined, rather, to the deployment of a neoliberal developmentalism or, better, a developmentalist neoliberalism with populist overtones in some aspects very similar to the practices of Echeverrism in the seventies of the previous century.

12 The Decree Promulgating the "Protocol Replacing the North American Free Trade Agreement with the Agreement between the United Mexican States, the United States of America, and Canada" was published in the Official Gazette of the Federation (DOF, June 29, 2020) and became effective as of July 1, 2020.

13 In a document issued by 27 U.S. Congressmen (Congress of the United States, July 23, 2020) and addressed to Eugene Scalia, U.S. Secretary of Labor, and Robert Lighthizer, U.S.

and without consulting the workers as well as the acceptance of U.S. policies on "labor aggregates"[14] and "rules of origin" that fundamentally favor its large transnational companies in that country and in other countries belonging to "North America" (see Sotelo, March 20, 2020).

In military matters, tension increased between Russia and the United States and its armed wing NATO when the latter country formally withdrew from the Intermediate-Range Nuclear Forces Treaty (INF) in August 2019, which somehow intensified the arms race and increased international tension in terms of (probable) military and nuclear confrontation between great powers where China is no exception.

The political and geostrategic chess involved Latin America and the Caribbean in the whirlwinds of the crisis and the restructuring of global labor and capital as well as in the social and class struggles occurring with force throughout the region. Said struggles are not only against neoliberalism but also against capitalism and imperialism that is expressed in its ruling classes and in the backwards and pro-imperialist right wing that accept and promote dependence and underdevelopment embedded in patterns of capital accumulation socially exclusive and privatizing, extractivist, and primary-exporting, rooted in the interests of national and foreign private capital.[15]

Trade Representative—in frank interference in Mexican affairs that violates national sovereignty—they point out that, according to them, Mexico "does not comply, nor does it have the capacity to comply," with its commitments in labor matters acquired with the signing of the T-MEC last December 10, 2019 between the representatives of the three countries, due both to the fact that no progress is being made in the "democratization of unions" and the fact that the 180 million dollars that the US Congress authorized are not being used for the implementation of reforms to the labor justice system.

14 The United States monitors Mexico through its "labor attachés" from its embassy in Mexico. These are enigmatic figures imposed by the United States to supervise from its embassy the Mexican labor legislation based on the ratification of the Treaty between Mexico, the United States, and Canada (called T-MEC for its acronym in Spanish or USMCA for its acronym in English). In this regard, see: Sotelo, December 17, 2019. Within this logic and the mandate of the USMCA, the first phase of the labor reform (released by the STyPS on May 1, 2019) began in eight states of the country (Campeche, Chiapas, Durango, State of Mexico, San Luis Potosí, Tabasco, and Zacatecas, and in Hidalgo in 2021), which highlights the replacement of the Conciliation and Arbitration Boards (In Spanish: Juntas de Conciliación y Arbitraje or JCyA) and the entry into operation of the Federal Center for Labor Conciliation and Registration (In Spanish: Centro Federal de Conciliación y Registro Laboral or CFCRL) to move labor justice to a "… new system with the operation of specialized labor courts dependent on the Judicial Branch," very similar to that of the United States, see: *La Jornada*, November 18, 2020.

15 Bellamy (March 11, 2019) correctly clarifies that neoliberalism and capitalism are not two separate realities that could be "overcome" one without the other, "… because an alternative to neoliberalism that keeps the capitalist system unscathed is impossible."

In Latin America in the context of a slowdown in the region of its economic growth rate—which went from an annual average of 1% in 2018 to 0.1% in 2019 with projection to grow a meager 1.3% in 2020 according to ECLAC (2019, Table VIII,1: 113)[16]—the changes and imbalances in the correlation of forces between the so-called progressive governments, which are not necessarily left-wing, and the openly neoliberal, conservative, and right-wing and ultra-right-wing governments aligned with the United States stand out, which in the context of the systematic attacks by Washington and its allies against the government and the people of Venezuela[17] are expressed in the electoral triumph of the *Frente de Todos* [*Everyone's Front*] campaign that launched the candidacy of Alberto Fernández and Cristina Fernández in Argentina (president and vice president, respectively) with 48.24% of the votes, against the 40.28% obtained by the business candidate of the right Mauricio Macri of the *Coalición Juntos por el Cambio* [*Coalition Together for Change*].

With the decisive support of the US government and the Organization of American States (OAS), the police-military and civilian coup d'état (November 10, 2019) was perpetrated against the constitutional and legitimate government of President Evo Morales in Bolivia (see Sotelo, November 30, 2019), resulting in deaths and injuries of civilians and the departure to Mexico of the Bolivian president and other members of his cabinet, exiled and politically persecuted first to Mexico and later to Argentina. Subsequently after 9 months of dictatorship, el Movimiento al Socialismo (MAS) (In English: Movement to Socialism) regained power through parliamentary elections, defeating the dictatorship and the fascist right-wing parties in collusion with Washington.

Let it be said in passing, the above demonstrates that there are no infallible progressive or conservative cycles with mechanical temporalities and

---

16 It is worth noting that once the Covid-19 pandemic broke out ECLAC (April 21, 2020, Table 6: 16) corrected its projections to estimate a GDP of -5.3% for Latin America and the Caribbean in 2020. See Table 1 where it can be seen that Latin America and the Caribbean as a whole decreased -6.9%.

17 In his book, Bolton (2020: 225–259)—one of the hawks of the US ultra-right and former National Security Advisor—describes the "causes" from his imperialist, ideological perspective of the failure of Trump's imperialist policy to destroy the Bolivarian government of Venezuela and its constitutional president Nicolás Maduro Moros. The hawk shamelessly narrates that his boss Trump, with frank colonialist and annexationist phraseology, told him that he needed a military solution for Venezuela—to invade it with gringo troops or not—because Venezuela "… is part of the United States" ("Trump insisted he wanted military options for Venezuela and then keep it because *it's really part of the United States*" (Bolton, 2020: 206). Likewise, he states (2020: 206) that Trump commented to the Secretary of Homeland Security that "… it would be *'cool'* to *invade* Venezuela". Italics and bold ours.

predetermined durability (see Petras and Morley 1999: 124–147 and Sotelo, October 4, 2015); but that, on the contrary, such processes in one sense or another depend on class struggles and on the insurgency and mobilization of the working and popular masses, as well as at certain junctures on the peculiar characteristics of the political-electoral processes. What is a constant in the Latin American political and media scenario in the recent *coups d'état* that have taken place under various modalities (soft *coups*, parliamentary, judicial, Guaidó or Añez style self-appointments, etc.) is the determined permanence and intervention of US imperialism to fracture and dissolve any hint of liberation struggle of the people that is aimed at conquering power and moving towards new forms of economy, society, and culture completely adverse to capitalism in decadence.

Another element in favor of this thesis is the insurrectional processes that occurred before the outbreak of the coronavirus pandemic in Ecuador, Chile, Bolivia, Haiti, and to a lesser extent in Colombia. In these countries, conservative-neoliberal governments unconditional to Washington's interventionist policies have been imposed. But the movements in struggle have not only put in check market and privatizing neoliberalism—exemplified in Chile—but have also exposed the historical limits of capitalism itself as a way of life, production, and labor at the global, regional, and local levels.

2 Conclusion

The capitalist system in its current imperialist and monopolistic phase—which some characterize as neoliberal—is in a process of decline not only because of its inability to meet the needs and demands of the population, but also fundamentally because it is facing serious problems in the production of new value and surplus value to ensure high rates of profitability and economic growth. This has led the main power of the Western world (the United States) to experience a sharp decline in its economic and to a certain extent military power with great powers emerging as competitive protagonists in a multipolar and polycentric world.

Much of the literature and prestigious publications report on the growing difficulties experienced by the United States both internally and in the space of global geopolitics. But most of the time, this situation is covered up by promising that there will soon be a recovery that will result in US's rehabilitation as the first world power ("unilateralism," "America First" *dixit* Trump), ignoring the obvious reality that the world exists in an environment of strong contradictory and competitive processes in the face of the arrival of great powers, in particular of China as an entity that in recent years has positioned itself as a strong protagonist, of the first order, in the international economy that seriously disputes world hegemony.

PART 3

The Sociology of Digitalization: The World of Dehumanized Labor in the Vicissitudes of the Global Hecatomb of Post-pandemic Capitalism

CHAPTER 4

The Pandemic Accelerates and Deepens the Crisis of Capitalism and Enriches the Multibillionaires

1 Introduction

In this chapter we consider that the coronavirus health crisis arose in the immediate vicinity of the capitalist crisis, accelerating the processes of precariousness, job destruction, social impoverishment, and falling incomes of the working classes. We also show that so-called neoliberalism, whose policies effectively exacerbated the coronavirus health crisis, in no way represents a "solution to the crisis" since at its base it is only a political device used by big capital and the State to manage said crisis at the expense of the living, working, and health conditions of the world's working populations.

In this context we see how a highly internationalized industry dependent on large transnational corporations, such as the maquiladora export industry that operates mainly on the border between Mexico and the United States, subordinates the working and health conditions of the workers employed to the needs and strategic interests of large transnational corporations, as well as to the geopolitical prerogatives of the U.S. government. The social result is *COVIDcide* due to the complacency of the Mexican federal and state governments in subordinating health policy to the interests of these companies and to the political-economic definition of the productive and service sectors and industries that should remain open and operating during the coronavirus health emergency.

1.1 *The World of Work in the Post-pandemic Period*

What will the world be like post-pandemic? A brave and innocent question. But highly problematic and difficult to answer, even for specialists in the field.

The March 2020 outbreak of the coronavirus pandemic—whose ubiquity drastically changed visions, expectations, feelings, and the course of the contemporary history of capitalism—became a global pandemic according to the World Health Organization (WHO), which officially recognized it on March 11, 2020, and spread to most of the countries of the world: first in China, then in Europe, and later in the United States, which ended up becoming the world epicenter of the pandemic.

 DOI:10.1163/9789004532717_006

Regardless of the causes that provoked it—where there is always a human action responsible or co-responsible, and among which include, with much strength and consistency, the deliberate action of the US government that was formally held accountable by nations, specialists and academics from various parts of the world (see for example *Hispantv*, March 18, 2020)—the health crisis was considered one of the worst in human history that spread to advanced countries and to dependent and underdeveloped countries (an interesting analysis for debate in Ramonet, April 25, 2020).

This pandemic or syndemic[1] is a *consequence* of destructive capitalism and not the other way around, as deceptively spread by the mainstream Western media following the ideological guidelines, geopolitics, and the "fifth generation war"[2] that the United States is pushing against nations that oppose or hinder its imperialist interests.

Analyzing the causes of the health crisis, Roberts (December 2, 2020) indicates that:

> The pandemic slump also has a different 'proximate' cause. In a sense, this unprecedented global slump, affecting 97% of the world's nations, kicked off because of an 'exogenous event'—the spread of a deadly virus. But, as has been argued by ecologists and in this blog, the rapacious drive for profits by capitalist companies in fossil fuel exploration, timber logging, mining and urban expansion without regard for nature, created the conditions for the emergence of a succession of pathogens deadly to the human body to which it lacked immunity. In that sense, the slump was not 'exogenous'.

ECLAC (April 3, 2020: 2) recognizes the antecedence of the world capitalist crisis to the pandemic:

---

1 The concept of "syndemia" was coined by medical anthropologist Merrill Singer in the 1990s (see BBC News, October 9, 2020). It consists of the interaction between the disease itself and the structural and socio-environmental conditions affecting the most unprotected human beings subject to high social inequality sponsored by the capitalist system. Therefore, the treatments applied (healthy distance, use of masks, vaccines, etc.) to try to overcome the disease, by attacking only its effects, but not the causes that originate it, are condemned to be insufficient and unable to prevent its spread.

2 See Colmenarez, 2014. A presentation of the book by its author in an interview with Telesur (March 24, 2015). The concept of "fifth generation" is equated with "hybrid warfare" and is attributed to an article written by Mattis and Hoffman (2005).

> The economic performance of the world economy was already weak before the COVID-19 pandemic. In the period 2011–2019, the average global growth rate was 2.8%, significantly lower than the 3.4% of the 1997–2006 period. In 2019, the world economy recorded its worst performance since 2009 with a growth rate of only 2.5%. Even before the pandemic, global GDP growth forecasts for 2020 had been revised downward.

Similarly, in relation to the behavior of the rate of profit in the United States, Roberts (September 13, 2020, my italics), supports this thesis when he states that:

> The mass of profits fell 3% in 2019. Indeed, the period from 2014 to 2019 is now the longest period of contraction in US profitability since 1946. *That suggests the US economy was already heading into a slump in 2020 before the COVID pandemic hit.* (italics mine).

This is the global context in which from the beginning the pandemic emerged in the Chinese city of Wuhan, capital of the province of Hubei in the center of the country. As it was controlled in the Asian giant to the point of practically stopping it, COVID-19 uncontrollably spread to Europe and later to the United States, which became its epicenter. Along with this context, we have leaders like Trump, described as a denier of the pandemic, along with other presidents such as Bolsonaro of Brazil, Sebastián Piñera of Chile, the Prime Minister of the United Kingdom, Boris Johnson; or those who half-heartedly "accepted" it, such as the president of Mexico who was accused of promoting a "neoliberal denialist model." Irresponsibly and without knowledge of the cause, on several occasions AMLO reiterated and insisted that his country was "immune" to the disease because it was a "Chinese virus" and therefore a "Chinese pandemic" (See *The New York Times*, May 29, 2020) with[3] no international ramifications, which later led to the US exit from the WHO under the "argument" that this

3 At the time of writing this text (May 22, 2021), the United States has 33 million 862,888 COVID-19 cases, of which 5,860,013 are actively infected and 603,446 dead in the midst of the most severe crisis of the US capitalist economy—with millions of unemployed so far, a fall in its GDP of -3.6%, and an unprecedented social crisis exacerbated by the brutal and racist murder of George Floyd on May 25, 2020, an unarmed African-American man at the hands of a police officer, Derek Chauvin, in Minneapolis, Minnesota, and to whom he anguishedly warned and pleaded "I can't breathe" that went viral on social media around the world. The vicious crime triggered a wave of mobilizations and protests—which the racist president disqualified and labeled as "infiltrated" by his "enemies"—in at least 30 US cities that forced the Trump administration to deploy the National Guard and impose a "curfew"—in the best tradition of Latin American military dictatorships—in 25 major cities to supposedly "control the violence." With his sexist and threatening language, President Trump labeled the

body was controlled by China, and which the UN confirmed on July 7, 2020 (*Sputnik*, July 7, 2020). Another denialist, the extreme right-wing Brazilian president Jair Bolsonaro—supposedly "infected" by Covid-19[4]—called the pandemic "uma simples gripesinha" (a harmless "little flu") and always refused to keep a healthy distance and use mouth covers, putting in grave danger hundreds of thousands of people who irresponsibly attended his rallies and public meetings.

What is certain is that the disease was installed in the whirlwind of the capitalist crisis, such a crisis that preconstituted and overdetermined the macroeconomic, social, environmental, spiritual, psychic, sanitary, human, and labor *status quo* of the world [deteriorated and precarious!] with its serious and deep historical deficiencies and social inequalities. These inequalities include: an abysmal division of social classes, of human "races," of genders, and of structural and systemic racisms that historically prevail in the United States; intense migratory movements and social[5] mobility; very pronounced tendencies towards economic deceleration and recession; an increase in unemployment rates and falls in employment; intense processes of deregulation, flexibilization, and precarization of the labor world (pre)constructed

anti-fascist and left-wing movement called *Antifa*—those who protested the death-murder of George Floyd—"thugs," "extreme left-wing criminals," and "terrorists." On his Twitter account, he boasted about inciting his police forces to violence: "When the looting begins, the violence begins. Thank you." This repressive and bloody episode is part of the long United States history of class struggles and anti-racist mobilizations, including the Watts Riots in 1965 for the arbitrary arrest of an African-American motorcyclist, Marquette Frye, for drunk driving; the hundreds of protests in the Long Hot Summer in 1967 against unemployment and police brutality in cities like Newark and Detroit, in 1965; the Easter Week protest in 1968 for the assassination of Martin Luther King at the hands of a sniper; the Los Angeles protest in 1992, when a jury composed of white jurors acquitted police officers who assaulted a cab driver, Rodney King; the Baltimore protests in 2015 for the killing of African-American Freddie Gray, among others that tarnish the American nation and make it the most violent in the world.

4 We put "infected" in quotation marks because when the news became known and went viral on social networks, suspicions arose that it was a ruse by the Brazilian president to promote the hydroxychloroquine (used against malaria) by appearing on TV with a smiling photo showing a box of the drug, despite the fact that serious scientific studies conducted in the United States, Great Britain, other countries such as China and Russia, and by the WHO had denounced that chloroquine and hydroxychloroquine, while completely harmless to combat and overcome COVID-19, are harmful and even deadly due to their side effects that can damage the heart. But all of this is amusing and scornful to those leaders in the "denialist" group.

5 Felix (2019) studies the relationship between spatial mobility, the super-exploitation of labor, and mercantile circulation of the labor force with emphasis on small rural production in mining activity in the Eastern Amazon of Brazil.

historically in the antagonistic labor-capital[6] relationship; contraction of international markets and trade; fall in labor costs and in real—and not only nominal—wages received by workers; and in many places, strong processes of repression and containment of workers', peasants', teachers', students' and popular movements in various regions of the world, particularly in Latin America in the most repressive and genocidal countries of the region: Colombia, El Salvador, Honduras, Guatemala, Ecuador, Bolivia (following the *coup d'état*), Peru, Chile, Paraguay, Haiti and Brazil, among others.

It is no coincidence that the *downturn* of the global capitalist system is greater than all previous downturns (see chapter 3)—including the Great Depression of the 1930—and that its center of gravitation has been constituted precisely in the United States itself, which is the axis of world *imperialism* and the coronavirus disease.

Today—by virtue of the intimate interconnection provided by the Internet, artificial intelligence, Big Data, computer and telematics technologies, Industry 4.0, the Big-Economy, telework, and the Home Office (see Figure 3)—the dissemination of facts and events occurring in the world are transmitted in real time through social networks and the media, just as crises and their disastrous effects are bifurcated through the "demonstration effect"[7] (imitation-assimilation) to all regions, countries, and localities of the planet affecting millions of human beings simultaneously.

Thus, social labor in whatever form it takes (precarious, polyvalent, flexible, informal, part-time, fragmented, contracted, zero-hour, home-based, material, immaterial, virtual, etc.)—contrary to what the ideologists of the "end of labor" and of fictitious capital maintain as we saw in Part 1 of this book—constitutes the axis of the capitalist production of commodities and of the surplus value appropriated by capital. But due to the crisis presented by the methods of production of this surplus value (traditionally produced by absolute and relative surplus value), the super-exploitation of labor is erected as the third

6 As Robinson says (2008: 22): "The new capital-labor relation that constitutes the essence of flexibility did not appear overnight; it has come about gradually through the ongoing rollback of earlier reciprocities and social wages involving great struggles and ongoing conflicts."

7 The "demonstration effect" is a concept from functionalist sociology that indicates the process by which "traditional," "rural," "illiterate," and "a-historical" (inappropriately labeled as such) societies such as those of Latin America "assume" and "incorporate" the values, languages, cultures, modernities, and institutions of supposedly "superior" industrial and modern societies into their social, economic, and political systems (having as their "ideal model" evidently the North American one). For this topic, see: Germani (1968), especially Part 2, Chapter 3. In the same vein, but from the approach of neoclassical economics, Rostow (1971). For an analysis and critique, Sotelo, 2005.

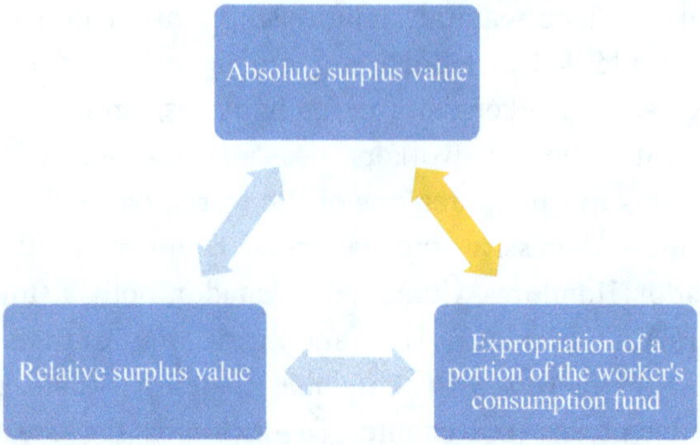

DIAGRAM 1 The super-exploitation of labor as a mechanism of production of surplus value
SOURCE: ELABORATION OF THE AUTHOR

mechanism of production of surplus value (*expropriation* of shares of the consumption fund and of the value of the labor force of the worker that is derived from the flows of capitalist accumulation; see Diagram 1 below), as we have seen, the decisive axis and objective of the production of extraordinary profits in the globalized capitalist system that characterizes the current neoliberal and imperialist phase of this system.[8]

Including in the United States, the result is that in order to make ends meet, the worker needs to work more than one job. As Reilly (*Time*: September 13, 2018) ironically exclaims in relation to the job of an elementary or high school teacher in the United States: "Work three jobs and donate blood plasma to pay bills!" It's as clear as day: the salary or wage is simply not enough to live on!

In disaster capitalism (Klein 2007), essentially predatory, crises and disasters like the Covid-19 pandemic, other historically significant diseases such as cholera or the "Spanish flu" that shook the world between January 1918 and December 1920 with a death toll that fluctuated between 40 and 50 million people, or other major disasters such as earthquakes and wars offer infinite opportunities for business and capital to deepen and extend the radius of action of labor precarity as a form that the super-exploitation of labor assumes in advanced capitalist countries and, thus, becomes an operative mechanism

8 In this regard, see the interesting theoretical-empirical study of the super-exploitation of labor in the Brazilian sugarcane industry by Biondi (2018), where the author demonstrates the *expropriation* of the sugarcane worker-peasant through the expropriation of a portion of the consumption fund and the value of the worker-peasant's labor force by the capital-landlord of agribusiness.

articulated to the relative surplus value producing regime that maintains hegemony in the system of relations and methods of labor exploitation (for an examination of the Covid-fictitious capital relation, see Roberts, January 25, 2021). As an example of the above, Roberts points out that when faced with the fall in their sales, companies such as General Motors, Chrysler, Ford, and Fiat changed their production of cars in the pandemic for the manufacture of fans, masks, and face shields (ECLAC, August 2020: 15). This is the clear proof that big businessmen are driven by the threads of competition and profitability, rather than by the production of goods and products that satisfy social and human needs in the context of non-profit horizons and social solidarity in the face of great human catastrophes, as would be ethically and existentially correct in socialist, humane, solidary, and rationally planned societies. But this is not the case. Despite the decline in employment and workers' incomes, Collins, Ocampo, and Paslaski (April 23, 2020) reveal in their study that the great beneficiary of the pandemic has been precisely big capital and its business figures.

The authors report that:

- Between January 1, 2020 and April 10, 2020, 34 of the nation's 170 wealthiest billionaires increased their wealth by tens of millions of dollars. Eight increased their net worth by more than $1 billion.
- As of April 15, U.S. tycoon Jeff Bezos' fortune had increased by approximately $25 billion since January 1, 2020. This is larger than the Gross Domestic Product of Honduras, $23.9 billion in 2018.
- Between March 18 and April 10, 2020, more than 22 million people lost their jobs as the unemployment rate rose to 15%. During the same three weeks, U.S. billionaire wealth increased by $282 billion: a gain of nearly 10%.
- Billionaire wealth in the U.S. rebounded rapidly after the 2008 financial crisis and between 2010 and 2020 increased 80.6%, more than five times the median increase in U.S. household wealth.
- Between 1990 and 2020, such wealth increased 1130%, an increase of more than 200 times the 5.37% growth of the average U.S. wealth.
- As a percentage of overall wealth, the fiscal (tax) obligations of U.S. billionaires declined 79% between 1980 and 2018.

In a report by OXFAM (July 2020: 2), the authors indicate that:

> COVID-19 does not affect everyone equally. An elite remains immune to the contagion of the economic crisis. Since the beginning of the confinements, there are 8 new billionaires in Latin America and the Caribbean—people with a wealth of more than US$ 1 billion. The wealthiest individuals have increased their fortune by US$ 48.2 billion since March 2020,

TABLE 4 8 Existing billionaires who increased their wealth with COVID-19 vaccine investments

Name	Role/description	Wealth 2021 (billions)	Wealth 2020 (billions)	Walth increase (billions)
Jiang Rensheng and family	Chair, Zhifei Biological products	$ 24.40	$ 7.60	$16.80
Cyrus Poonawalla	Founder, Serum Institute of India	$ 12.70	$ 8.20	$4.50
Tse Ping	Sinopharm	$ 8.90	$ 7.30	$1.60
Wu Guanjiang	Co-founder, Zhifei Biological products	$ 5.10	$ 1.80	$3.30
Thomas Struengmann and family	Portfolio includes Germany's BioNTech and Uruguay's Mega Pharma	$ 11.00	$ 9.60	$1.40
Andreas Struengmann and family	Portfolio includes Germany's BioNTech and Uruguay's Mega Pharma	$ 11.00	$ 9.60	$1.40
Pankaj Patel	Controls listed company Cadila Healthcare. The company now manufactures drugs to treat Covid-19 such as Remdesivir from Gilead. Its Covid-19 vaccine, ZyCoV-D, is undergoing clinical trials.	$ 5.00	$ 2.90	$2.10
Patrick Soon-Shiong	ImmunityBio—selected for the US federal government's "Operation Warp Speed" to help quickly develop a Covid-19 vaccine.	$ 7.50	$ 6.40	$1.10

SOURCE: BASED ON OXFAM, MAY 20, 2021, "COVID VACCINES CREATE 9 NEW BILLIONAIRES …"

> which is equivalent to one third of the total stimulus packages of all countries in the region.

The report also notes that large U.S. corporations are the biggest global beneficiaries, including Visa, Microsoft, Pfizer, Intel, Facebook, Oracle, AbbVie, Apple, Cisco Systems, Merck, Johnson & Johnson, Google, Verizon, Comcast, HomeDepot, AT&T, Protec&Gamble, UnitedHealth, Charter, Amazon, Chevron, Walmart and CVS Health, in order of decreasing importance in terms of the number of profits made during the pandemic in the year 2020 (OXFAM, July 2020: 5). This same agency published a report detailing that the COVID-19 vaccine "business" spawned 9 new billionaires, while 8 existing billionaires have seen their fortunes increase by an estimated $32 billion as seen in the chart 4:

OXFAM says that the list of new billionaire beneficiaries of the COVID-19 vaccine "business" is topped by the CEOs of Moderna and BioNTech, with wealth of about $4 billion each. The list also includes two Moderna company investors and its chairman. The report concludes:

> These billionaires are the human face of the huge profits many pharmaceutical corporations are making from the monopoly they hold on these vaccines. These vaccines were funded by public money and should be first and foremost a global public good, not a private profit opportunity. We need to urgently end these monopolies so that we can scale up vaccine production, drive down prices and vaccinate the world. Vaccine billionaires are being created as stocks in pharmaceutical firms rise rapidly in expectation of huge profits from the COVID-19 vaccines over which these firms have monopoly control. The alliance warned that these monopolies allow pharmaceutical corporations total control over the supply and price of vaccines, pushing up their profits while making it harder for poor countries, in particular, to secure the stocks they need.
>
> OXFAM, May 20, 2021

But this is more the exception for a few than the rule for many. As Roberts says (January 20, 2021):

> Sure, we hear all about the huge profits made by the likes of Amazon, Google, Netflix and the big banks during the 2020 pandemic slump, but the profits of the FAANGS are the exception to the rule. Total corporate profits (after government handouts are removed) have dropped by some 30%. And according to Bloomberg, in the US, almost 200 big corporations

> have joined the ranks of so-called 'zombie' firms since the onset of the pandemic. They now account for 20% of the top 3000 largest publicly-traded companies, with debts of $1.36 trillion. That means 527 of the 3000 companies didn't earn enough to meet their interest payments! So there remains a significant risk of a credit crunch and financial crash down the road, perhaps in 2021, when the Fed largesse is curtailed.

According to the Center for Multidisciplinary Analysis of the National Autonomous University of Mexico (CAM, July 15, 2020: 4–5), a large part of this situation of bonanza for a handful of large capitalists who rule the world is the result of the transfer and socialization of the losses caused to capital by the pandemic to the workers whose jobs and wages have been depleted by the crisis (see ILO, 2020). At the same time, it points out that the great monopolies of capital operating in the sphere of the circulation of goods and activities that are oriented to distribution and consumption through platforms facilitating the purchase and sale of goods and all those companies related to the ownership of data consumption (Apps) aimed at providing consumers the "home office" and "telework"—Amazon, Netflix, Zoom, Slack, among others. Transnational and monopolistic companies such as Inovio Pharmaceuticals in the health industry; MKM Partners, which developed an index to know the companies that benefit from Covid-19, are many others that profit from human misfortune and also enrich their owners and their families exponentially in the face of the deterioration and physical death of workers exposed not only to the onslaught of the pandemic but also to the high rates of poverty, job insecurity, and the super-exploitation of labor as in the case of the Mexican *maquiladoras* (see below). A veritable vaccine war against the SARS-Cov-2 virus has been unleashed by North American companies such as the pharmaceutical company Pfizer, associated with the German BioNTech and sponsored by the large Western monopolies and the hegemonic media campaigns against the proven effective vaccines of China, Cuba and Russia.

In the conditions of a virulent capitalism of disaster—which imposes itself with blood and fire in order to maintain its domination and profitability—the valorization of capital requires (*super*) exploitation and extensive volumes of unemployment and underemployment to survive, since these forces interact to drive wages downward, increase the rates of exploitation and competition among the same workers to get a job, even if it is precarious in terms of wages, labor, working conditions, social rights, and guarantees of permanence.

The billions of billions of dollars that the US imperial State manufactures with their little machines of "making money" (fictitious capital) correspond to the pre-existence of the surplus value produced by millions of workers all over the world and not only in the national space of that country: work that is formal or precarious, informal or agricultural, service or manufacturing; workers that are men and women, young, children or elderly located inside and outside each country whose labor, of course, goes mostly to the coffers of transnational monopolistic corporations for their accumulation and reproduction. That is why in the face of a pandemic such as COVID-19, for the businessmen it is a crime to stop the capitalist production of merchandise, value, and surplus value in the face of the need to defend the health and integrity of their workers who are relegated to second or third place in importance with respect to the mercantilist strategies and profitability of business.

Recalling Marx's premise that "money itself is worthless" (ignored by the theoreticians of the "end of labor" and of fictitious capital) or as Mészáros (1970: 192) says that "[g]old is a worthless metal without the need that transforms it into something greatly appreciated" and that this among other functions is the true expression of the value of labor power and, in general, of commodities (i.e. workers produce and are the source of all value), it is evident that the billionaire sums advanced by the US government in the first stage of the pandemic (equivalent to about 10% of its GDP) are necessarily compensated by the way of greater exploitation of the labor force accompanied by massive layoffs, wage restraint, and labor precariousness, in addition to other measures such as privatization of public services and health (see: *La Izquierda Diario*, June 24, 2020).

The COVID-19 pandemic highlighted the crisis and exhaustion of the universal globalized capitalist system, and not only of neoliberalism which is in itself a system to perpetuate and manage the crisis and not to solve it (Dardot and Laval, July 24, 2019), while showing the limitations to overcome it without attacking its own foundations rooted in property relations, exploitation, and private appropriation of wealth. With this insufficient arsenal of alternatives, the employers and the world right wing (the Bolsonaro, the Piñera, the Lenín Moreno, the Trump, the Macron, the Boris Johnson, characterized by their minimizing or denying attitude towards the coronavirus) as well as ultraneoliberal organizations such as the OECD and business organizations such as the Business Coordinating Council (Consejo Coordinador Empresarial) and the Confederation of Employers of the Mexican Republic (Confederación Patronal de la República Mexicana) that unleashed a whole campaign against the "healthy distance" and the preventive measures (such as quarantine) to avoid the possibility of infection, proclaiming that the best thing to do was not to curb economic activity (i.e. the exploitation of the labor force for the production and extraction of surplus value and profits) but to keep factories, services, and businesses open, without taking into account the dark exponential behavior of the coronavirus pandemic that threatens the health and life of the working and proletarian classes all over the world.

For workers and humanity, the seriousness of the health crisis in the main countries of advanced capitalism such as the United States, Italy, France, Spain, Portugal or Germany is the result of the dismantling of the welfare state that emerged after the GPW and the privatization of the social security and health systems to the extent that the World Health Organization (WHO) recognized that the United States became the epicenter of the pandemic. The pandemic forced the Trump administration to authorize the Paycheck Protection Program (PPP) which is a $669 billion business loan program derived from the U.S. federal government's Coronavirus Assistance, Relief, and Economic Security for Coronavirus Relief Act known as the CARES Act to help businesses continue to employ and pay workers.

Thus, in practice:

> The "stimulus" bills signed by Trump and passed by Democrats have already given away trillions to major corporations and tens of billions in tax cuts to the richest Americans. Even two-thirds of the original set of supposedly "small-business"-focused Paycheck Protection Program loans went to large corporations, such as Ritz Carlton, while gifting billions in fees to the banks that distributed the loans.
>
> BAKER, Sept. 03, 2020

In the midst of this human and social tragedy, President Trump insisted that it was necessary to "open the economy" and get back to work to overcome it no matter the toll of dead and sick that resulted (Sotelo, April 23, 2020).

In light of the tremendous numbers of deaths and infections resulting from COVID-19 in the United States, all of the resources wasted by Trump were completely unsuccessful in containing and overcoming it (see note 42).

It was public knowledge that the US government requested help from other countries such as South Korea and Germany to provide it with "test kits" against COVID-19, precisely because it lacked them as a security and prevention policy for its population—quite contrary to what happens with its geopolitical and military strategy, which is perfectly coherent and systematic when it comes to attacking and invading other countries and for which it invests billions and billions of dollars in its media-industrial-technological-financial-technological and military complex of fifth generation warfare.[9]

9 Under the pretext of "fighting drug trafficking," on April 1, 2020 Trump ordered to mobilize warships and warplanes near the Venezuelan coasts in the Caribbean Sea. This after the US regime accused without evidence the constitutional president of Venezuela, Nicolás Maduro Moros, and several members of his Cabinet of being "involved in a narco-terrorism plot" and

The lacerating effects on jobs and on the living and working conditions of the working populations of the planet were translated into thousands of layoffs in the most affected countries, which is where their employer classes deposited all the weight of the crisis due to the fall of their businesses and their rate of profit, which is the *engine* of their existence as Marx says (1973: 666) when he writes that this rate is: "… the most important law of modern political economy, and the most essential for understanding the most difficult relations."

Reuters (quoted in *Hispantv*, March 28, 2020) stated that about 23% of North Americans had been temporarily or permanently laid off due to the outbreak of the Covid-19 infection, as well as in other European countries such as in Italy where the working class responded to the ineffectiveness of the government measures to contain the disease (see: *La Izquierda Diario*, March 28, 2020). And the same happened in Latin America where workers experienced similar situations in conditions of widespread structural unemployment and informality, which in many countries like Mexico, Brazil, or Peru exceeds 60% of the working population.

The other critical scenario—together with a bulky and expansive unemployment, very extensive precarious work, labor informality and low-wage economies created in recent decades by neoliberalism—shows that according to ECLAC (April 3, 2020: 3) the economic impact of the pandemic could reduce China's growth to 3% in 2020; the United States, to -3.8%; Europe, to 2.3%; and the world average, to a percentage between -3% and -4%, configuring a scenario of deep recession and structural paralysis that will be difficult for contemporary capitalism to overcome and that will affect employment and wages on an unknown scale. Another publication highlights that a fall of -8% of GDP translates into a labor crisis that increases the open unemployment rate by 6.7% in Spain; while to a lesser extent in Germany, the 7% decrease in GDP causes an increase of 0.7% in the unemployment rate, with France and Italy in an intermediate situation (see: *El Captor*, April 15, 2020).

In this context we must point out an intense fall in the employment rate such that in the United States the number of unemployed people at the end of April 2020 was over 20 million, reaching an open unemployment rate of 14.7% of GDP, the highest obtained since the Great Depression of the thirties of the

---

offered 15 million dollars for their capture in the best Hollywood style of Old West movies. Basically, the purpose of this illegal and interfering action was to create a naval blockade against the Bolivarian country, information from *Hispantv*, April 4, 2020. For a contextual analysis see Fazio, April 5, 2020.

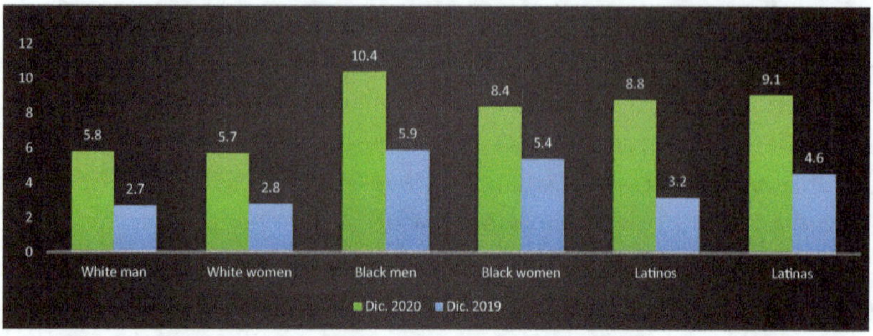

GRAPH 4 United States: Unemployment rates, December 2019-December 2020 (%)
SOURCE: "EPI ANALYSIS OF BUREAU OF LABOR STATISTICS (BLS) HOUSEHOLD DATA," TABLE A-2 AND TABLE A-3. *ECONOMIC POLICY INSTITUTE* (JANUARY 14, 2021)

previous century (Department of Labor, U.S. Bureau of Labor Statistics, July 2, 2020).[10]

The same source reports that in June 2020 job applications totaled 33 million, and couple with that, unemployment reached 18.9% for Hispanics, 16.7% for African Americans and 14.2% for what racist classifications call "whites."

In an annual comparison (December 2019-December 2020), the Economic Policy Institute (EPI) (January 14, 2021) establishes the unemployment rates by gender and racial difference in the following table:

Graph 4 shows that it is no coincidence that in a deeply classist, racist, and xenophobic capitalist society such as the U.S. it is precisely the sectors of African-American and Latino workers who are most affected by the crisis and unemployment. Coinciding with these figures, the Economic Policy Institute (July 24, 2020) estimates a historical unemployment of up to 30 million people

10 Although the Trump administration enacted The Coronavirus Aid, Relief, and Economic Security (CARES) Act by Congress on March 27, 2020—which makes it possible for unemployed workers to receive an additional weekly income of $600 (a total state outlay equivalent to covering some 5 million jobs nationwide) for an additional 13 weeks capped at July 31, 2020—it was not until August 8 when Trump by Executive Order authorized the extension of such unemployment aid but lowered the amount to $400 per week with a duration until December 27, 2020 (The Washington Post, August 8, 2020), which was insufficient to meet the most basic needs. However, neither the fall in the incomes of the majority of the population nor the daily and weekly increases in the demand for work by Americans were stopped. It is important to note that in accordance with Trump's anti-immigration and racist policies, undocumented workers—considered "essential" and who contribute $1.67 trillion to the national GDP and $425 billion to California's GDP—are excluded from federal subsidies granted by the government in the Covid-19 pandemic (UCLA, August 10, 2020.

receiving unemployment benefits. To get an idea of the size of this unemployment, one author asserts that: "It's as if all the jobs in all of the states beginning with the letter "M" simply disappeared in the last month. That's all the jobs in Maine, Maryland, Massachusetts, Michigan, Minnesota, Mississippi, Missouri, and Montana combined" (Gould, May 8, 2020).

In Mexico according to ECLAC-ILO (May 2020) although the percentage of wage earners with labor benefits improved from 62.3% in 2018 to 63.0% in 2019, in parallel, there was an increase in informality. Thus, the National Occupation and Employment Survey (NOES) (*Encuesta Nacional de Ocupación y Empleo*) indicates that in the last quarter of 2019 all modalities of informal employment totaled 31.3 million people, an increase of 2% over the same period of 2018 representing 56.2% of the employed population (INEGI, 2020, cit. in ECLAC-ILO, May 2020: 17). In the total informality, 50% is located in the activities of commerce, restaurants, and hotels in both Mexico and Latin America (ECLAC/ILO, May 2020: 21) and in which the participation of women (51.8%) is higher than that of men (46.8%) (ECLAC/ILO, May 2020: 27).

Things got so complicated in 2020 that while the Ministry of Labor and Social Welfare (*Secretaría del Trabajo y Previsión Social*) calculates that between January-April 2020, around 346,878 jobs were lost (*El Economista*, April 8, 2020). The Mexican Social Security Institute (*Instituto Mexicano del Seguro Social*) (IMSS, July 12, 2020) estimates a loss of 921,583 jobs between January and June 2020, of which 73% (some 672,755 jobs) were permanent with a monthly average of 83,311 jobs lost. The agency highlights that as of June 30, 2020, 19,499,859 jobs were registered in this agency; of those, 86.6% are permanent and 13.4% are temporary. In its *Quarterly Report January-March 2020*, the Bank of Mexico (May 26, 2020: 94) is more drastic in its projection, forecasting a loss of between 1,400,000 and 800,000 jobs in 2020 and between 200,000 and 400,000 jobs in 2021.[11]

For its part the National Council for the Evaluation of Social Development Policy (CONEVAL) (July 27, 2020: 2) summarizes in its diagnosis:

- The percentage of people in working poverty calculated from the Occupation and Employment Telephone Survey (OETS) in April and May of 2020 was 53.1% and 54.9%, respectively.
- With the OETS labor income decreased 6.2% from $1,516.93 in April to $1,422.24 in May.

11 It is reported that in Mexico more than 80% of the jobs recovered from the pandemic are low-wage jobs and about half of the new jobs created are temporary (*Animal Político*, January 11, 2021).

- Households surveyed through the OETS had follow up interviews in April and May. According to this information, the working conditions of 11.7% of people changed from not being in working poverty to being in working poverty, and 10.3% of people changed from being in working poverty to not being in working poverty.
- The follow-up indicates that among those who moved out of working poverty 27.4% were employed in the informal sector and 7.6% in the formal sector.
- The effects of the health contingency caused by COVID-19 occurred in unequal magnitudes in both the formal and informal sectors. Employment fell 13.7% in the formal sector and 27.2% in the informal sector between the first quarter (National Occupation and Employment Survey, NOES) and May (OETS) 2020.
- In percentage terms, the greatest loss of jobs is concentrated in the young and older adult groups. Between the first quarter (NOES) and May 2020, the 15 to 29 age group lost approximately 25.0% of jobs; in the 30 to 64 age group, 18.9%; and in the 65 and over group, 30.2%.
- Due to the uncertainty regarding the period necessary for the recovery of the labor market, a call is made to focus attention on the most vulnerable groups. These include households whose members depend on informal work or those who are employed in the sectors most affected by the health measures to contain the spread of COVID-19.

Although it lies in the socioeconomic and business effects of the pandemic, the cause of this job recession also lies in the fall in the growth rate of the national economy which ECLAC places for all of 2020 at -9.0% on average (see: ECLAC, April 21, 2020: 15); for comparison, the Bank of Mexico (May 26, 2020) conservatively estimated the rate at -8.8% in 2020, but the National Institute of Statistics and Geography (INEGI) (July 30, 2020) placed the rate of GDP at a barbaric -17.3%. In reality according to Table 1, the drop was -9.0%.

1.2 *COVID-Cide, Precariousness, and Death in Transnational* Maquilas *in Mexico*

The *Maquiladora* Export Industry (MEI)[12]—or rather, any activity that assembles cars, parts, and/or spare parts to produce a final product or merchandise

12 The *Maquiladora* Export Industry (MEI) is the industrial process for the transformation, manufacture, or repair of goods and components of foreign origin (mainly from the United States) that are imported for subsequent export (or in the case of Mexico to that same country) carried out by *maquiladora* companies, predominantly foreign, destined for export under the terms of the "*Decreto para el Fomento y Operación de la Industria*

that is later reexported to the country of origin—constitutes the essential link in the value chains of Mexico's dependent economy with few "backward" linkages with the national economy that is predominantly oriented toward the exterior (i.e., towards the United States). More than 85% of MEI companies are transnational and feed the transfer of value and surplus value to the North American economy. According to ProMéxico (November 8, 2017), 27% of Mexico's GDP comes from advanced manufacturing. This type of manufacturing—within 'industries 4.0' corresponding to the fourth industrial revolution[13]—consists of the application of technologies to make the production processes more efficient and optimize the quality of the product-goods in order to increase business competitiveness and, of course, surplus value and profit.

There are two types of technologies: a) process technology and, b) digital systems oriented to direct and control manufacturing production from computer devices such as scanner, touch screen, bar code reader, keyboard, stylus, mouse, webcam, etc.

In November 2018, there were around 6,000 *maquiladoras* throughout the country performing manufacturing and non-manufacturing type activities, with 90% of these factories located in the northern border according to the National Council of the *Maquiladora* and Manufacturing Export Industry (INDEX). The gross value of production exceeds 100 billion dollars—which translates to 70% of the country's total exports with more than three million "direct jobs" nationwide and more than seven million "indirect jobs," mostly of women whose salaries are at an estimated 30% below those of men (Meza, February 6, 2019). In March 2019, the number of establishments incorporated into the Manufacturing, *Maquiladora*, and Export Services Industry Program (IMMEX) was 6,215, 6,358 in February 2020, and 6,377 in March 2020. Of this total the largest proportion corresponds to the export-linked manufacturing sector (CEFP, May 29, 2020).

In terms of personnel, the MEI employs a total of 3,000,000 workers within 6 states bordering the United States—Baja California, Sonora, Chihuahua, Coahuila, Nuevo León and Tamaulipas. It absorbs 1,800,000 workers distributed in 3,700 companies—mainly transnationals producing electronics,

---

Maquiladora de Exportación y sus Reformas en México" ["the Decree for the Promotion and Operation of the *Maquiladora* Export Industry and its Reforms in Mexico"].

13 A video on the characteristics of industry 4.0 produced by the Government of Spain and the Ministry of Industry, Energy, and Tourism can be viewed on YouTube: https://www.youtube.com/watch?v=44W9IdwLLCs.

textiles, automobile and bus components, aerospace and war industries—expressing the strong dependence on the value chains of the U.S. economy.

In the context of the global pandemic of COVID-19, we have said that the pandemic itself was the pretext and serendipitous moment of opportunity that fit like a glove for big capital and the entrepreneurs that were economically 'harmed' by the closing of establishments because of the disease who were inserted in these platforms and other activities. Both the metropolitan bourgeoisie and the dependent bourgeoisie as exploiting dominant social classes—to justify the dismissal of millions of workers (in the United States alone there is talk of around 40 million unemployed claiming government aid during the first four months of the pandemic) to, thus, reduce their labor costs (i.e., wages and income of workers)—based their logic under the "argument" (Malthusian and Schumpeterian) of the potential closure or bankruptcy of their companies. However, many of them, such as the Mexican *maquiladoras* on the border with the United States, continued to operate as we saw above, even in the midst of the exponential expansion of the plague with thousands of sick and mortal victims who, of course, do not count in the system with its voracious metabolism of capital reproduction. Of the 6000 *maquiladora* companies in the country, it is estimated that 55% did not stop their activities during the pandemic, largely due to the pressures exerted by the US government. And the majority of those that did "stop" production—some companies formally declaring so—actually continued working without reporting it to the authorities, as the affected workers publicly denounced at the time (*Sin embargo*, October 8, 2020).

At the end of March 2020, the Mexican federal government declared a health emergency to prevent the spread of the virus, which included the closure of industries considered "non-essential" in areas of low spread until May 17 and in the rest of the country until June 1, 2020.

In view of the health emergency, the automotive industry temporarily halted production in Mexico and remained inactive from March 31 until May 18 when the "new normal" came into effect—when activities gradually resumed after the manufacturing of transportation equipment (where automotive production and exports are located) was considered an "essential activity."

This reclassification of the industries from non-essential to essential and the haste in opening them up was due to:

> ... pressure from large companies and the Pentagon ... On April 22, the National Association of U.S. Manufacturers, which represents 327 firms, sent a letter to President Andrés Manuel López Obrador to ask him to put Mexico's essential industries on par with the sectors catalogued as

> critical in the United States "in order to avoid interruptions in the supply and production chain in the industries," since their activities are considered vital to guarantee security, the economy, and public health in the face of the pandemic. He [AMLO] not only received this letter as pressure, but also the US Ambassador in Mexico and the US Undersecretary of Defense did their part. Thus, the federal government did not take long to give them the green light to resume activities legally.
>
> FRAGUA, June 12, 2020

After the federal authorities classified the automotive, mining, and construction industries as "essential" activities for all of Mexico on May 13, 2020 and the General Health Council declared the lightweight car, bus, truck, and aircraft manufacturing industry to be "essential" as of May 18, some automakers and industry suppliers began operations immediately as is the case of FCA, while other manufacturers such as GM, Ford, BMW, Honda, Nissan and Toyota restarted their production gradually.

Despite the workers' refusal to prematurely restart the opening of plants and the return to productive activities and the consequent labor exploitation, the federal government decreed on June 1, 2020 its resumption under the euphemism of the "new normal," when tens of thousands of workers lined up before dawn to return to the automotive factories along the northern border of Mexico and when many industries that had been catalogued as "essential" reopened their doors in the midst of the pandemic and a high rate of contagions; for example, in Ciudad Juarez, we have the registration of 20 dead Lear Corp employees when the federal government had already reported the death of more than 10,000 people from the coronavirus since the end of May, yet allowed the opening of automotive, aerospace, construction, and mining companies (Reuters, June 2, 2020).

Despite the provisions of the federal government, since the beginning of the pandemic between 50% and 80% of these production activities and companies remained in activity under precarious and unsanitary conditions according to workers' complaints, sources of contagion, spread of the virus, and worker deaths (Oprinari, May 31, 2020 and Reforma, July 7, 2020).

The deaths of 104 workers in Ciudad Juarez, Chihuahua, from *maquiladora* companies in that border town had already been reported as a result of Covid-19, of which 30 worked in one of the three plants of the US company Lear Corporation (*La izquierda diario*, May 25, 2020). There were also deaths from Covid-19 of workers from Regal with 10 victims; Mahle, Electrocomponentes de México, Electrolux, Hubbell, Commscope, Toro Company, Ethicon, Cordis, Syncreon, Flex, Keytronic, Optron, TPI, and Honeywell. In addition, three drivers

TABLE 5 Covid-19 contagions on the U.S.-Mexico border by State as of July 29, 2020

USA	California	Arizona	New Mexico	Texas
Active cases	487,855	168,361	20,136	421,817
Deaths	8, 908	3,470	632	6,831
Mexico	*Baja California*	*Sonora*	*Chihuahua*	*Coahuila*
Active cases	13,223	17,259	5,061	12,090
Deaths	2,572	1,879	872	595

SOURCE: *LA JORNADA* (JULY 31, 2020) AND *REFORMA* (JUNE 12, 2020)

of special trucks that transported the workers were killed by Covid-19, and for this reason they were nicknamed "death wagons." (*La jornada*, May 8, 2020).

Many workers confined to their homes by the pandemic only received 50% or 60% of their salary, which is equivalent to less than 3,000 pesos per month (around $150 USD or €141 EUR), completely insufficient to purchase the basic food basket. Others were forced to take "vacations" *without pay* and the less "lucky" ones, as one worker denounced, were simply fired by the transnational companies. This is a typical phenomenon of the super-exploitation of labor, consisting of *expropriating* part of the living and consumption fund of the working class in order to transfer it in favor of the accumulation of capital.[14]

News like the following is daily: "... there are 805 confirmed infections in Juarez, 348 in Chihuahua, 29 in Parral, 20 in Delicias, 13 in Cuauhtemoc, 9 in Meoqui and 6 in Bachiniva" (Barranco, May 21, 2020). News that, most of the time, was ignored by the authorities and the companies.

Despite the fact that the authorities of both the United States and Mexico decreed on March 21 a one-month closure of "non-essential" land transit along the border strip, which was extended four times (the last time being August 21,

14 This expropriation of part of the workers' consumption fund alludes to the specificity of super-exploitation, not understanding it as a simple "violation of the law of value". As Alves (January-March 2019: 46) rightly states: "Contrary to the fact that the super-exploitation of labor represents the 'violation' of the law of value, on the contrary, it expresses the affirmation of the very movement of the law of value in the conditions of the 'collapse' of the historical struggle of the class of wage-workers, the class struggle and the capacity of organized labor power to effectively assert its class interests (even with the affirmation of the anti-value as a public fund)". See this discussion in my book: Sotelo, 2019, Part 2, chapters 3 and 4.

2020), the number of infections in both countries continued to increase, reaching a total of 1,176,223 cases, of which 98,169 corresponded to four U.S. border states and 47,633 to four Mexican border states as can be seen in table 5.

The disorderly and unsecured openings caused legitimate strikes, work stoppages, and demonstrations to denounce the criminal actions of the *maquiladora* companies and businessmen who practice *COVID-cide:*

> In this difficult panorama, a wave of strikes and wildcat strikes, riot-like actions, and demonstrations broke out in April in dozens of *maquiladora* companies along the entire length and breadth of the border. As discussed here, some were at Creation Technologies, Clover Wireless, Honeywell, Pantronics and Skyworks (Mexicali), Tridonex, Autolive, VDO, Novalink (Matamoros), Legrand, and Hyundai (Tijuana). The slogan *¡Queremos vivir*! ["We want to live"] showed that the working class was demanding its most basic right: the right to life.
>
> OPRINARI, May 31, 2020

But the reality for thousands of workers is more rebellious than the official decrees and corporate statements regarding the high lethality rates of the disease, as the following report attests:

> Under the 'new reality' of the red traffic light[15] in effect since Friday, the essential *maquiladoras* maintain their activities with 100 percent of their workers; the aerospace and automotive industries—now newly essential —with 60 percent of their workforce; and the rest with 30 percent of their employees, in accordance with the decree of October 22. This level of authorized activity for the *maquiladora* industry contrasts with the restrictions established in the red traffic light announced by the State Government on May 30, when it announced the beginning of "the

15 To begin this return to social and economic activities on May 18, the Mexican government created a sanitary alert system based on traffic lights—using the colors green, yellow, orange, and red of a traffic light to easily categorize the different levels of COVID-19 infection by state and city and to establish zones of public health risk throughout the country. The idea was that the more a state or city advances in the traffic light (moving from red to green with fewer numbers of infections), the more non-essential activities and the reopening of non-essential spaces it would have. But as we have seen with the mobilization and protests of workers who were forced to work under unsafe health conditions while the pandemic was at its height and more significantly the death of numerous works, the actual use of this traffic light system was not always the case for various industries important to the interests of capital and the North American imperialist state.

> new normal" under the decree in effect since June 1. At that time—in 'the red'—the essential *maquiladoras* were authorized to maintain their activities with 100 percent of their employees; the aerospace and automotive manufacturing plants, with a labor capacity of 30 percent; and the rest, i.e., the non-essential ones, were asked to keep their operations suspended. Although the permissiveness of companies in this sector has progressed since the decree of August 10, when the capacity for aerospace and automotive companies was increased from 30 to 60 percent for the risk level marked in red. The non-essential ones remained closed and the essential ones operated at 100 percent. A review of these documents shows that *maquiladoras* are now allowed to operate almost under the restrictions authorized for the orange traffic light.
>
> GALLEGOS and MINJÁRES, October 26, 2020

Despite official and unofficial decrees of necessity or compulsion on the part of the employers, workers continued to work during the pandemic, and complaints multiplied as layoffs, cases of infection, and deaths were recorded in different companies and regions. The news was daily:

> Layoffs at Telemark, a subcontracting company of Qualfon Mexico; at TKM they continue to work and do not respect the healthy distance, denounce the employees. When an inspector arrives, they remove the personnel, and when the authorities leave, they order the work to restart. At Elektra it is reported that they change the location of the personnel so that they are not closed, they do not comply with sanitary and safety measures, and inside there are few fans; and they force them to work 12 hours for the "Hot Sale" (online sales) under threat of dismissal. And in subcontractors such as Staff E&I, S.A. de C.V. [16][Public Stock Corporations with Variable Capital], and Grupo Nach, layoffs are registered through electronic messages.
>
> information gathered from *La Izquierda Diario*, June 3, 2020

16 S.A. de C.V. = "sociedad anónima de capital variable," or in English, "Public Stock Corporations with Variable Capital." This is one of the most commonly used types of corporations in Mexico to form companies, where two or more owners become shareholders and contribute economic resources to a profit-making organization.

In companies such as Lear Corporation, a producer of harnesses and clothing for automobiles, the death of 6 workers was reported in the month of September 2020 (*La Izquierda Diario*, September 22, 2020).

This same source denounced that:

> After the government declared the *maquilas* essential at the request of Donald Trump, the conditions under which they have had to work have been deplorable. The thousands of workers' lives at risk because of the scandalous subordination to the policies of the U.S. government is unforgivable ... It is not possible for the [Mexican] government to paint itself as leftist, leaving so many families vulnerable. The million-dollar auto manufacturing, mining, construction, and transportation equipment companies (those included in the list of essential activities) have an obligation to provide free health protection equipment to all workers.

And even with the measures taken by the health authorities, 18 active outbreaks were reported in the state of Chihuahua: 3 in industrial plants and 1 in the CERESO "... where COVID-19 caused another 108 infections and 4 deaths" (*Sin embargo*, October 8, 2020). The same source reports as of its publication there were two active outbreaks in the *maquiladora* industry: one in the Xomox company and the other in Yazaki, which in total affect 59 infected persons.

In its balance sheet, the Ministry of Health of the State of Chihuahua concludes that "[u]pdated figures show that to date there have been 11 outbreaks of COVID-19 in industrial plants with a total of 115 people infected and 25 deaths recognized by the Ministry of Health" (*Sin embargo*, October 8, 2020).

2 Conclusion

The health emergency, which struck the world as a result of the coronavirus caused by Covid-19, aggravated a capitalist crisis that had already been developing since the previous period, at the same time as the exhaustion of the universal globalized capitalist system. Thus, it is not a "crisis of neoliberalism" in a vacuum, as is sometimes claimed, since neoliberalism itself is basically only a way to manage the crisis, but not to solve it. At the same time, the pandemic showed the limitations to overcome the crisis of the capitalist system without attacking its own foundations based on property relations, exploitation, and private appropriation of wealth, and highlighted that the system's only alternative is to increase unemployment, reduce workers' wages, and incomes, as well as to pressure national and local governments to keep in operation factories and services linked to the big multi-millionaire capitals, the beneficiaries of a capitalism of disaster that made of the health crisis a fabulous business.

In Mexico, the *maquila* industry, along with oil and tourism, has historically been one of the most important sectors of the Mexican economy, especially in terms of exports that mainly go to the United States. Its commercial, production, and export lines—controlled by North American transnational companies—imposed labor and sanitary regimes that led to deaths and contagions of coronavirus when workers were forced to go to the factories to avoid losing their jobs or keeping them with reductions in wages or benefits.

CHAPTER 5

Teleworking, Home Office, Digital Platforms and Super-Exploitation of Labor

1 Introduction

This chapter provides an analytical look at the different platforms used by capital and business administration such as telecommuting, remote work, and the home office to promote the use of cyberspace and, thus, extend the radius of action of the production of surplus value.

In contrast to the optimistic and uncritical visions, we seek to articulate these platforms with the process of exploitation and super-exploitation of labor that is generally made invisible under the "preciousness" of the forms superficially presented by technology and its media manifestations. One of these hidden realities is the conversion of the home into a workplace and domiciled space at the service of companies since, according to Alves (2021: 231), the "… pandemic of the new coronavirus accelerated the process of restructuring the 'work premises' [… while] capital 'invaded' the space of the home which it turned into a home-office."

1.1 *Platform Capitalism*

With the emergence of the Internet and information technologies, a series of qualifiers and characterizations of the new labor, productive, and business situation gained momentum, among which stands out that of "platform capitalism," which Srnicek (2016: 30) defines as the:

> … digital infrastructures that enable two or more groups to interact. They therefore position themselves as intermediaries that bring together different users: customers, advertisers, service providers, producers, suppliers, and even physical objects.

Using these digital platforms, the various tools and applications are manufactured and designed by the workers of large companies like Microsoft for the development of software and infrastructure or hardware (PCs, tablets, laptops,

 | DOI:10.1163/9789004532717_007

smartphones) for the later user by large companies[1] that are true monopolies or oligopolies of the electronic-computer-digital complex.

In agreement with Srnicek (2016: 32):

> Platforms, in sum, are a new type of firm; they are characterised by providing the infrastructure to intermediate between different user groups, by displaying monopoly tendencies driven by network effects, by employing cross-subsidisation to draw in different user groups, and by having a designed core architecture that governs the interaction possibilities.

Capitalism strives to overcome the limitations that hinder the *agglomeration* of masses of workers (*collective labor*) in the same space-time (*factory*). On the one hand, it is in its interest to concentrate the labor force both to extract from it the maximum value and surplus value; but on the other hand, it is necessary to disperse and confine the working class with the aim of preventing its organization according to its class and professional interests. And one of the means among many others used for both actions is *cyberspace*—virtual reality systematized in computer chips and expressed in computer networks that *tends* to affect more and more the *total working time*—constructed by means of information and communication technologies that manage to suppress both in the virtual environment and in real time the limitations of physical time and the spatial-temporal differences between the centers of production and the consumer markets. This is a veritable revolution of working time and of the collective worker that translates into a widening of the production of surplus value and the accumulation of capital through increased exploitation by articulating different categories, activities, and functions that run in the digitized value chains, in productive and service activities, as well as in those related to distribution and consumption.

The multiple forms and instruments that capital has to counteract its crisis of profitability and falling profit rate (see Tables 2 and 3) as well as to mold the organization of work to its interests and strategies lead to the imposition of work through procedures and devices interconnected to the network, among

1 As stated by Silvia Ribeiro (May 19, 2021), "As of the first quarter of 2021, the largest global companies in market capitalization (stock market value), are in order of volume Apple, Microsoft, Amazon, Alphabet (owner of Google), Facebook, Tencent, Tesla, Alibaba. All are technology-based companies. The first five are headquartered in the United States and are often referred to collectively as GAFAM (Google, Amazon, Facebook, Apple, Microsoft). Tencent and Alibaba are Chinese. Tesla is the company created by Elon Musk, currently the world's richest individual."

which stand out the "remote work" and the "home office" that had already been experimented and in some cases applied in the world of work (ILO, 2016).

In this context under the argument of experiencing difficulties derived from the pandemic, remote work is being imposed where there was none; or reforming and extending where it was already practiced, remote work (in the first instance apparently on a voluntary basis) or "telecommuting" which, although deployed by virtual means, is developed in real time through cyberspace, a virtual space for which computers and intelligent digital networks are used for educational, commercial, telemarketing, financial, and other activities.

Below, we discuss the plausibility of these platforms and tools being extended to the material industrial manufacturing process in order to valorize capital and create surplus value with a view to the production of profit.

1.1.1 Remote Work

Often, the distinction between the home office and remote work lies in the fact that in the former, the employee or worker can physically alternate between home and office and keep the legal fixed job with a fixed salary. Therefore, it is a hybrid organization of work related to the employer's interests, while in the latter, remote work prevails the physical and spatial mobility of (changing) locations in various activities such as sales, trade, Internet services, etc.

> On the other hand, the home office converts the home-family room, or part of it, into the *workplace itself*, while remote work, or telecommuting, is when the worker performs their functions from any place, which can be their home or other establishments such as offices or public spaces (gardens, parks, squares, etc.). Even inside or outside a country: for example, delivering a report to the company over long distances, grading students' academic records, or sending an activity report to an institution that requires it. A worker who becomes a kind of "digital nomad" as it is beginning to be called today.

Regarding the second form, an opinion of the Mexican Chamber of Deputies defines remote work as:

> ... the form of labor organization that consists of the performance of paid activities, without requiring the physical presence of the worker at a specific work site and using information and communication technologies as a support for contact between the worker and the employer.
>
> *La Silla Rota*, July 21, 2020

By virtue of the fact that telecommuting and the use of new information and commuting technologies (ICTs) imply changes in the organization of work and the productive process, the ILO (2016: 3) defines "remote work" as:

> a form of work organization with the following characteristics: a) the work is performed in a place other than the employer's main establishment or production plants, so that the worker does not maintain personal contact with other work colleagues, and b) new technologies make this separation possible by facilitating communication. Moreover, telework can be performed 'on-line' (with a direct computer connection) or 'off-line,' be organized individually or collectively, constitute all or part of the worker's tasks, and be performed by self-employed or salaried workers.

Without paying attention to the psychosocial and technical-labor[2] consequences, employers and work designers (ergonomists, psychologists, sociologists, industrial engineers) advertise the new forms of labor organization as the best of all possible worlds, making invisible the social relations of exploitation and domination between labor and capital that underlie them.

Varela (December 11, 2020) in an interview comments that the management that is being done of remote work (telecommuting),

> ... is dramatic ... When we most needed collective, team, creative work ... we are returning people to their homes, not transforming work into a cozy house, but our cozy house into work torture. The boundary between public and private life is disappearing, and the demand for work is greatly

---

2 According to Erika Villavicencio-Ayub, a specialist in occupational health from the Faculty of Psychology of the UNAM (*La izquierda Diario,* October 1, 2020, with information from Omar Morales), at least 75% of workers in Mexico suffer from stress, an issue that places Mexico among the first countries with the highest physical and emotional wear; before the pandemic, 25% of workers suffered from a mental disorder related to work activity. This "technostress" is related, the specialist points out, more to the excessive workload than to the skills in the handling of information and communication technologies, although we must clarify that under certain circumstances these also produce stress, such as the home office that stimulates exhausting workdays with increased work intensity that generate emotional imbalances causing what the psychologist calls "technostress," since it produces anxiety, headaches, mental and physical fatigue, and muscle aches. "To this we must add that the working conditions of workers in Mexico and in the world for decades are increasingly precarious, to the point that in most cases they do not have a contract, essential benefits such as social security, vacation, or Christmas bonus, not to mention that in most cases there is no right to unionization." For an approach to the world of work from the perspective of social psychology, see: Sergio Novoa (January-March 2019: 179–191).

> intensified. What happens with remote work is an intensification of the profit of companies because they diminish the immediate costs and invade the house of the people.

In contrast, David Moot (BBC News, October 4, 2020), British entrepreneur and founding partner of Oxford Capital, a British real estate investment firm, in this context exhibits 5 "models" of the telecommuting office:

1. Remote Office.
2. Hybrid Office: combines remote work with office work.
3. Remote Office Plus: a short time in the office and a longer time remotely.
4. Hub & Spoke (radial distribution): Expansive central office "with remote offices in other cities or countries to leverage local skills."
5. Quality Time: prioritizes the quality of production "without supervision";"itdoesn'tmatterifemployeesworkfrom9amto5pm;eachperson isdifferentandhastheircommitments."Theimportantthingistheresult, as the business marketing with a nose for the profit rate says.

But as sophisticated as it may seem, remote work "... is not modernity, it is a return to the oldest part of capitalism ... with new technologies" (*Izquierda castellana*, August 15, 2020).

Often, the difference between the old forms of "distant" or "home" work (see Marx, 1982, chapter XIII)—which have in common the subordination to capital—lies in the digital use of new technologies through applications in production and services.[3] We note that, however sophisticated it may appear, its *substance* continues to be the exploitation of labor by capital under the prevalence of relations of subordination and dependence of the former by the latter, with the reinforcement of the apparatuses of the capitalist State through institutions, regulations, laws and labour norms without which they could hardly be maintained.

Here, we see the commonality of interests between the State and capital: generally, the changes are undertaken by the latter and end up being legalized in

3 For example, regarding delivery applications, "Historically, delivery jobs relied on controllers—a person sitting in an office in front of monitors checking where the workers were and telling them: 'You need to go to X to make a delivery to Y.' Today, that process has been automated, and the type of assignment of workers to do those tasks is taken over by an application. The application that gives instructions to the worker is a kind of algorithmic manager" (Fachin, March 13, 2021, see note 57).

laws, statutes, and regulations by the former, as is happening today precisely with the home office and remote work under the protective mantle of the parliaments of several countries and international organizations such as the ILO.

A paradigmatic example of the above is offered by the Resolution Foundation (*The Telegraph*, March 04, 2017) in relation to the existence of the so-called "zero hours" contracts. Despite the fact that in Great Britain there are around 1 million workers under this modality—which consists of the fact that that worker must be willing to accept to perform a certain job, in addition to the fact that the employer is not obliged to give a minimum number of hours per week—there are no regulations in labor legislation and it is a practice very much favored by employers.

1.1.2 The Home Office in the Fashion of the House

In home office labor matters, things are not rosy. A UNAM research project entitled "Impact of Covid-19 in Mexican workers"—consisting in interviews with over 5000 employees who perform their work in the home office (*La Silla Rota*, November 06, 2020)—revealed that 81% of employees are afraid of losing their jobs. It adds that 61.9% have worked longer hours or performed work tasks in order not to lose their jobs, and 23.8% have stopped enjoying their work that they do from home because of the coronavirus contingency and its effects. 87% of those interviewed feel economically affected because 75% had a reduction in their income or have family members who received a cut of more than 50% of their salary. 90% are worried about household expenses. More, 63% of workers are affected by not seeing their friends or loved ones, and 44% of those surveyed reported having communication with bosses after working hours, according to psychologist Érica Villavicencio Ayub, UNAM academic.[4]

The home office or "virtual work office" lowers labor costs, while employers save constant capital (furniture, desks, chairs, cabinets, drawers, fixed or mobile telephones, Internet connection, PC, electricity, water, printers, *hardware* supplies such as printer cartridges; desks, pens, printing sheets, etc.). It also achieves savings for the capital in the use of the skills and knowledge of the workers that are applied to the tasks of the companies (variable capital), or educational activities in the case of teachers of all educational[5] levels that nurture their plans and programs at a distance in the profitable business cyberspace, as well as in the activities developed by call centers.

---

4 For an interesting study on the effects of Covid-19 on the working conditions, insecurity, and health of Spanish workers, see Salas, Llorens, Navarro, and Moncada, June 2020.

5 An analysis of the precarious work of subject and assistant professors at UNAM, in: CAM (March 24, 2021).

For example, in a call center of the Salinas group in Mexico, the average worker earns around 4,000 pesos a month, the work schedules are exhausting and cover 6 days a week, while the legal times established by the Federal Labor Law are rotated at the whim of the company and its profitability needs. Those who are lucky receive a bonus that fluctuates between 1,000 and 2,000, conditioned to the acceptance of the increase in the exploitation of their labor force (See: *La izquierda diario,* October 19, 2020).

Most of those who work in these centers are mothers, young women, and students, while, following patriarchal patterns, the heads of these centers are men. With salaries that on average do not exceed 4,000 pesos per month, they have to support a family with between one and three children. The workers denounce that under the pretext of the pandemic, the employers have reduced their salaries and increased the targeted goals to be met by up to twice as much in order to receive a bonus. This in a context in which mothers have to take care of their children and assist them in their classes from a distance, with the result being that in many cases these women have to abandon their own studies and careers. In addition, women workers report that they are constantly subjected to harassment and sexual harassment by their bosses and supervisors.

A worker expresses that:

> ... [W]e are the force that keeps the services running; they use our friendly voices and force us to answer in a friendly way to customers who, annoyed, communicate [with us] because of the lousy services that banks and telephone companies offer, while they fill their pockets selling poor quality products and paying us poverty wages.
>
> *La Izquierda Diario,* September 29, 2020

The result of the above quote is that work and home—confined into one—become a combined space through a process of "domicide" (expression popularized by Mould, 2019: 48; the original usage in: D. Porteous and S. Smith, *Domicide: The Global Destruction of Home* 2001) because "... 'working from home' is a process in which the former colonizes and in effect destroys the latter" at the same time that it "... further leaches the productivity of domestic labour toward its own proliferation. The home becomes a precarious *place* because it becomes an extended *space* of creative capitalist production" (Mould, 2019: 50, author's italics).

Evidently—when the home office is connected to and dependent on the business cycle of private companies—company decision makers, governments, NGOs, advertisers, administrators, and institutions do not take into account the labor, political, and social implications that this type of activity of the capitalist enterprise based on the home office entails for workers and the world of labor in general. That is why there are already proposals to generalize this form of work and exploitation that was being implemented before the coronavirus health crisis, among other measures that capital is adopting in the midst of the pandemic.

In this sense, Antunes (*La Haine*, June 15, 2020) warns: "The projects of big capital for the post-pandemic are already clear: to computerize everything, to abuse work at home, [and] to disarticulate the collective force of wage earners." In such a way that the paths of labor—which historically had bifurcated along various paths that ensured for the working masses certain social and labor rights in some cases without precaritization and with a certain welfare state—have converged on a path of no return, mercilessly sowing a "new" regime of socio-economic precariousness and super-exploitation of labor (Sotelo, 2020); it is sponsored by the "new normality"—a post-pandemic, proto-capitalist, and anti-human world, articulated with large migrations and immigrations, structural unemployment and poverty, and inequality and social injustice in all trajectories, without prospects for the majority of working humanity that is confined by the threats of the pandemic and death under the iron vigilance of capital and its infernal panopticon (see Zuboff, 2019). We are in an epoch that Sadin (2017: 81 et seq.) characterizes as the "era of the geolocalized/assisted individual"—as the Iron Lady Margaret Thatcher believed—or, as adjectivized by Hervé Aubron, where the "human figure" "… is not atomized, it is pixelated—split into multiple scintillations, enclaves, interfaces, like a game of cards. We did not disappear; we are dislocated. We are a field in ruins" (quoted by Sadin, 2017: 132).

In Riechmman's words (September 7, 2020): "Digitalization leads us to a 'capitalism of surveillance' whose possibilities of social control make pale all that the totalitarianisms of yesteryear could count on."—a type of surveillance that is capable of penetrating the spirit and the bones of human beings in order to control them and submit them to the empire of digital platforms and designs. For example, Kickidler is a "multi-purpose" tool for employee monitoring and attendance records that contains features such as live video streaming, screen recording, time tracking, productivity tracking, keystroke recording, and remote desktop control. It is a new generation of workforce monitoring. Kickidler's main purpose is to automate staff monitoring functions, protect information, and record work time. In addition, it can be used to optimize communications within the company, record workers' actions for further analysis and correction of errors, as well as to train new specialists. It monitors employees and tracks user activity, enables automation of personnel control and information security, and increases business efficiency.

The main features of this software are: online monitoring of computers, recording and playback of employee activity history, efficiency analysis, time tracking, and detection of violations by user-workers that allows the company to optimize communications internally and management to monitor the activity of workers remotely (See: Kickidler, n.d.). It is also worth mentioning the category of "Bossware" software; already denounced on many occasions for violation of workers privacy, these are surveillance tools in remote work that when installed on PCs or cell phones are capable of recording the keyboards inputs of workers to collect information in a hidden way. This information can be used by companies legally to substantiate labor lawsuits in court against them. In capitalism, as Han (2021: 13) says: "It is information, not things, that determines the world we live in. We no longer inhabit the earth and the sky, but Google Earth and the cloud. The world becomes increasingly intangible, cloudy, and spectral. *Nothing is just and tangible*, and this is what *cybersecurity* is all about!" (author's italics).

In capitalism in order to use the resources and technologies of remote work and the home office, it necessarily requires internet and a suitable computer that is capable of loading and supporting programs and applications that are owned and controlled by transnational companies, which are mainly American such as Windows, Microsoft, Apple, as well as private platforms such as Zoom, Microsoft Teams, Meet, Moodle, Google Classroom, Blackboard Collaborate, among others, which require permits, licenses and payments for their use. Violation of the latter is cause for penalties and can be very expensive for violators, including jail sentences or sanctions.

The problem is that at present, worldwide, only a limited proportion of humanity has this access and possesses the "master key" of Internet technology, while the social majorities (workers, students, peasants, indigenous people) are excluded from its use and benefits. Therefore, we are light years away from what one author pompously called the "era of access" (Rifkin, 2001), which is, indeed, but for the restricted and privileged social classes and elites of bourgeois society.

According to a study by Brussevich, Dabla-Norris, and Khalid (July 9, 2020), as millions of human beings have lost their jobs and swelled the ranks of the unemployed and underemployed, there are thousands of more workers who are not considered "essential" to business and government and, therefore, cannot work remotely through cyberspace. Rather, they are exposed to reductions in their income and working hours, temporary suspension, or, finally, dismissal. The researchers argue in this study that about 100 million people in 35 "advanced and emerging" countries cannot telecommute, or remote work, representing 15% of the workforce in relation to those countries. By

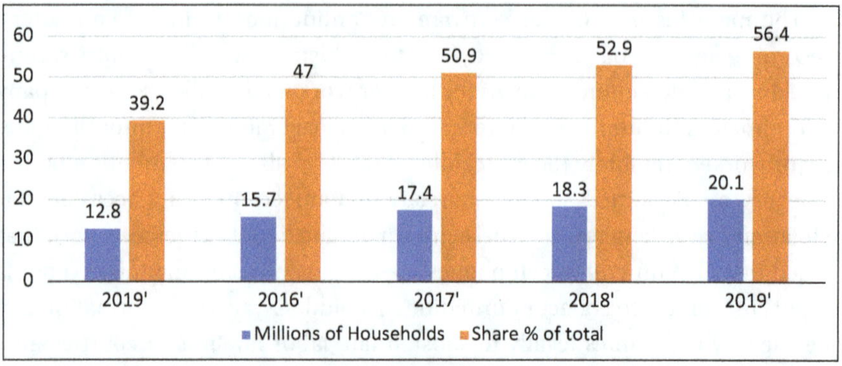

GRAPH 5 Mexico: Households with internet, 2015–2019
SOURCE: INEGI-IFC, GRAPH 8, FEBRUARY 17, 2020

constructing a "work feasibility index" in relation to GDP per capita, these authors conclude that remote work is more plausible in Norway and Singapore than in Turkey, Chile, Mexico, Ecuador and/or Peru, "... simply because more than half of the households in emerging and developing countries do not even have a computer at home."

Concretizing the above case studies, the effects on labor of no longer needing physical employees by many companies are exacerbated in dependent and underdeveloped countries such as Mexico where huge contingents of the population remain submerged in misery, unemployment, and precarious labor without access to the bare minimum necessities for the reproduction of human and social life (Sotelo, 2014, and CAM, July 15, 2020). Therefore, both precarious-informal workers as well as non-precarious-formal workers find it difficult to obtain the applications and tools to access this form of remote work.

In Mexico, for example, the National Survey on Availability and Use of Information Technologies in Households (ENDUTIH) of INEGI-IFC (February 17, 2020) estimates that there are 20,100,000 households that *have* Internet (15.96%), which represent 24.93% of the total number of national users, which is a figure of 80,600,000 people or about 64% of the total population in 2019 out of a total of 125,930,000 residents.

If we consider the proportion of households with Internet in Mexico (20.1 million) in 2019 (Graph 5)—regardless of the questions of the physical capacity in terms of hardware and gygabytes to install, store, and operate certain programs, applications, and tools[6]—in relation to the total number of

6 Consider that in order to install programs that support new applications (Office, Power Point, Excel, Digital Platforms such as Zoom, 3D design programs, etc.), computer equipment

users (80.6 million), we can begin to see the enormous difficulties and shortages faced by the majority of the population, especially with the pandemic and confinement which implies for many people the necessity to work online or develop educational activities for their children in virtual classrooms or mandatory remote classrooms. Finally, in a sample of 16 countries, this same source places Mexico in the last place in terms of Internet users, only above South Africa and Colombia. The other countries are in decreasing order: South Korea, United Kingdom, Sweden, Japan, Spain, Germany, United States, Chile, France, Italy, Turkey, and Brazil.

Among the most vulnerable sectors for the performance of remote work are food workers, hospitality, and trade (retail and wholesale), in addition to the delivery of services and goods at home that in recent months have made major mobilizations and struggles against labor precariousness and the superexploitation of labor in various parts of the world significantly in Mexico and Brazil—in the former by food and service delivery workers and in the latter by the well-known Motoboys who fight against private and monopolistic firms such as Uber or Walmart (*La Silla Rota*, July 6, 2020). This possibility of remote work is reduced for young workers and those without a university education and, of course, for the informal workers who number in the millions around the planet. The most affected group is that of women workers because they are located precisely in the sectors most sensitive to the pandemic, to labor precariousness, and to the capitalist crisis in places such as construction, restaurants, hotels, food services, domestic work, and care of children and the elderly (Alves, 2020).

Part-time employment, temporary employment, and those types of employment corresponding to medium, small, and micro enterprises are more vulnerable to job loss according to researchers Brussevich, Dabla-Norris and Khalid (July 9, 2020):

> Part-time workers and employees of small and medium-sized businesses face a higher risk of job loss. Workers in part-time jobs are often the first to lose their jobs when economic conditions deteriorate and the last to be hired when they improve. They are also less likely to have access to healthcare and formal insurance channels that can help them weather

with sufficient ram memory capacity is required to store the necessary information capable of activating the drivers for the proper functioning of the programs. In addition to the high costs of these programs, which generally require expensive licenses and updates, users are faced with a monopolistic market that prevents the use of the programs without the consent of the companies that own the patents, mostly transnational.

> the crisis. In developing economies, in particular, part-time workers and those in informal jobs face a much higher risk of falling into poverty.

Regardless of the ravages of a crisis such as the pandemic in the world of work—which mainly affects activities that require social distancing or healthy distance such as entertainment, restaurants, or personal care—the most vulnerable jobs of thousands of workers that will be lost and/or difficult to recover are those belonging to activities such as sales, office and administrative jobs, education in general, tourism and the construction industry, according to a study published by CNN (*La Silla Rota*, September 4, 2020). Although these jobs could be recovered once the pandemic is over, it is warned that it will be very difficult to reach their pre-pandemic levels, among other reasons due to automation and the development of e-commerce, remote work and telecommuting, the home office, e-learning and online training, which will cause new displacements and job losses in other activities linked to the industries and companies subject to these technological and organizational innovations of the 4.0 revolution in progress (see Chapter 6).

The problem is that unemployment is a structural and not a conjunctural phenomenon of capitalism so that, although many jobs lost during a crisis can be recovered, the long-term balance is negative both in quantitative terms and for the workers. Thus, as Baker (September 3, 2020) comments on a Wall Street Journal report,

> Desperate to maintain their profits, many large corporations are planning massive layoffs and acknowledging that currently furloughed workers are not going to have jobs to come back to. The Wall Street Journal reports that a recent study found, "nearly half of U.S. employers that furloughed or laid off staff because of COVID-19 are considering additional workplace cuts in the next 12 months." The companies say low-paid workers will be the first to be cut.Twice as many workers had their pay cut by July 1 as during the Bush-Obama recession that began in 2009, according to the Washington Post. More than 10 million private sector workers have had their wages cut or been forced to work part-time.

But unemployment has worsened with the syndemic note 1, page 58 severely affecting young people between 16 and 25 years of age as noted by the researchers of the Economic Policy Institute Gould and Kassa (October 14, 2020) when they state that in the United States, along with the country's existing inordinate unemployment rates, for young workers the unemployment rate increased from 8.4% to 24.4% between the second quarter of 2019 and the same quarter of 2020, while unemployment for those aged 25 and older increased from 2.8% to 11.3%, respectively. And according to the U.S. Institute, the unemployment situation worsens for young black, Hispanic, and Asian workers whose unemployment rates stand during the second quarter at 29.6%, 27.5% and 29.7%, respectively. This corroborates that a similar situation is experienced in practically all countries of the world where young working populations (women and men) are the most affected by both the pandemic and the brutal global capitalist crisis, particularly the categories located in the informal and precarious jobs that exhibit high rates of labor turnover and low wages. Thus, according to the aforementioned Institute, about 25% of young workers in the United States work in trade and service activities such as sales, transportation, administration, hospitality, business management, finance, among others "... where employment decreased 41% between February and May 2020," besides being the social sectors most affected by the coronavirus as we have seen.

1.1.3 Regulating Remote Work and the Home Office

There are proposals to legislate remote work and home offices in several countries that have even adopted them in their labor and business management practices—measures that are already implemented in Mexico and in other countries of the world, developed and underdeveloped, supposedly to "adapt" to the "new normality" of labor that in the background is nothing more than a euphemism that hides the return to more *of the same, but worse*! if the world continues under the inhospitable destructive iron fist of bloodthirsty and voracious capitalism.

In Germany, for example, the possibility of legally regulating the home office is being studied, as stated by the Minister of Labor Hubertus Heil (*Excelsior*, April 26, 2020) in an interview for the German newspaper Bild last April. On that occasion, he said: "Everyone who wants to and whose workplace allows it should be able to work from home, even when the pandemic of the new coronavirus is over," and proposed to that effect to create a law protecting the right to work from home even in the post-pandemic period, reinforcing his argument in the fact that it is estimated that the percentage of the population working from a home office in that country increased from 12% to 25% due to the disease in about 8 million people (*Excelsior*, April 26, 2020).

It should be clarified that although this type of work has so far been adopted in some activities and companies due to the coronavirus, it does not cancel out the real possibility that in the future capitalism will increasingly adopt these digitized and networked work platforms on a compulsory basis and that they will have to adapt to the new regulations of the world of work and labor relations—the new form that capitalist restructuring and the social organization of labor will take with the extension (and supplanting) of the digitization of manual and automated processes to the large capitalist and service industries that have not yet adopted the 4.0 to move into the era of digital networks and cyberspace.

In Mexico, telecommuting or remote work is being legislated in order to serve the needs of companies both in pandemic and post-pandemic. In this regard, the Labor Commission of the Chamber of Deputies approved on July 21, 2020 a reform opinion to regulate this type of remote work that was ratified in its plenary session on December 8, 2020 and one day later by the Senate of the Republic to reform and adapt Article 311 of the Federal Labor Law (LFT) and the addition of Chapter XII Bis, which contains five articles[7] (*La Silla Rota*, July 21, 2020). Subsequently, a Decree was issued in the *Official Gazette of the Federation* (DOF, January 11, 2021) reforming article 311 and adding chapter XII Bis of the Federal Labor Law regarding remote work, which it defines as:

> … a form of subordinate labor organization that consists in the performance of paid activities in places other than the establishment or establishments of the employer, so it is not required the physical presence of the worker under the modality of remote work in the workplace, using primarily the information and communication technologies for contact and command between the worker under the modality of teleworking and the employer.
>
> The worker under the modality of remote work will be the one who renders their personal, remunerated, and subordinate services in a place

7 "330-A. Definition of telework and teleworker; 330-B. Teleworking agreement and conditions of service under which employer and teleworker must operate; 330-C. Balance in the labor relationship of workers under this scheme in order to enjoy decent work; 330-D. Obligations and responsibilities of the employer and the teleworker; Safety, health and prevention of occupational hazards subject to a Mexican Official Standard that guarantees the rights of the teleworker: their privacy and intimacy, among others. 330-E. National network of advice, promotion and encouragement of teleworking among social, private and public organizations by the labor authorities".

> different from the facilities of the company or source of work of the employer and uses the information and communication technologies.
>
> For the purposes of the remote work modality, information and communication technologies shall be understood as the set of services, infrastructure, networks, software, computer applications, and devices whose purpose is to facilitate the tasks and functions in the workplace as well as those required for the management and transformation of information, in particular the technological components that allow the creation, modification, storage, protection, and retrieval of such information.
>
> DOF, January 11, 2021: 380

This Decree highlights that remote working or telecommuting applies when the worker or employee performs at least 40% of its activity at home or in the place or domicile chosen by the employer in addition to the fact that the employer will have the obligation to cover the expenses for electricity, internet, and those directly related to the company. Obviously, a methodology and the appropriate parameters will have to be generated to *specifically* quantify the expenses for this type of work charged to the employer's costs in addition to the benefits and other benefits for the workers.

The capitalist labor logic induces businessmen to demand that the virtual work regime be legislated and established in Mexico for their benefit. Thus, for example, the consulting firm PwC-Mexico (May 8, 2020) stated that in the opinion of 64% of the financial directors of companies in the country (CEOs), the "home office" should remain after the coronavirus contingency (*El Universal*, September 5, 2020). For his part, Nicholas Bloom, professor of Economics at Stanford, believes that work models must be redesigned since currently 40% of the world's employees have been converted into "teleworkers." According to him, before the pandemic, 15% already used this form of work in the United States at least one day a week, and the figure was similar in England.

They ask:

> - Q- "Has it multiplied?"
> - A: "There are 40% of jobs that can be done remotely; the rest require at least some face-to-face time ... that 40% of telecommuting has become real."
> - Q: "And what does the company gain by closing offices?"
> - A: "It saves more than €2,000 per year per employee who switches to telecommuting on items such as space, water, electricity, Wi-Fi, cleaning, equipment, maintenance, dining area, and meal vouchers."
>
> Bloom, June 9, 2020

Other business proposals that have emerged in the heat of the pandemic are: that the home office can be managed with a work schedule of 4 days of work with 3 days of rest (in total 7); staggered schedules, use of mouth covers, anti-bacterial gel, frequent temperature taking and regulating the home office. Obviously, in a situation of "new normality" post-pandemic, these resources and tools are not necessary to develop productive and service activities by virtual means, even face-to-face, representing great financial savings for companies.

Antoine Zervudacki, CEO of Letsmake Innovation, a company dedicated to the disruptive and sustainable growth of organizations through the development and culture of innovation, states that "we are entering the home office era, and we have to design a work experience that manages to define well the time at home and the time at the office" (Olías, August 31, 2020). In this way, the entrepreneur designed his "Post-Covid-19" company prototype to "survive" the "new work normality" in Mexico. Relevant points of the "prototype" include:

> 1. For companies to survive, they must adopt a "corporate vision" that seeks the "welfare of the community."
> 2. There must be a "technology vision for humanity" taking advantage of the digital transformations accelerated by the coronavirus.
> 3. To forge leaders with "hard and soft" skills so that companies with people with "spiritual skills" are the ones that survive."
>
> *Bridge Project*, June 7, 2020

In general terms, according to Olías (August 31, 2020), for the regulation of the home office both in Spain and in Europe, the European Framework Agreement on Telework of 2002 (reformed in 2005) defines remote work and the countries and modalities it covers.

Regarding this regulation:

> If we look at how telework is regulated in other European countries, the common reference is the Framework Agreement drawn up by the European social partners and updated in 2005. Telework is defined as a form of organization and/or performance of work using information technologies within the framework of a contract or employment relationship in which work that could also have been carried out on the employer's premises is usually performed outside those physical spaces. The definition makes it possible to cover different forms of 'regular work' under these conditions at a distance.

In connection with the Framework Agreement:

> ... [It] has served as a basis for European countries to establish their remote work conditions, which in the case of Spain (Article 13 of the Workers' Statute), France, and Portugal, for example, are specifically regulated in labor legislation; while Italy, the United Kingdom, and the Netherlands opt for broader 'flexible work' regulations, which include remote work but are not so specific or exclusive to this modality. Other states such as Germany, Sweden, and Finland develop telecommuting conditions through sectoral agreements, company agreements, and lower-ranking regulations.

Dave Nevogt, CEO and co-founder of Hubstaff, an American company specializing in personnel monitoring services through virtual space-time tracking software, revealed to the American business magazine Fast Company that there is a *key change* that many companies could take advantage of to "re-energize" the economy: having *a permanent remote workforce*. In a survey of 400 business owners and managers, the results showed that remote work helped prevent layoffs for 66% of companies, while 44.25% of companies expect remote work to increase profits.

Among others, the following are the reasons why the home office helps the economy, according to the analyst:

A. Companies save money because remote equipment eliminates physical office expenses such as rent, utilities, and office supplies, allowing companies to save costs that can be reinvested in other activities or businesses.
   a. They can move their headquarters to locations with a lower cost of living if they do not rely entirely on local talent to enable the ability to hire more employees.
   b. The daily commute time from home to work is reduced, giving employees back several hours a week.
   c. Employees have more control of their time and can choose to block out interruptions and distractions from co-workers. In an office environment, it is very easy to run over and interrupt someone with a question, and it is the number one reason why offices are so unproductive.

B. The talent pool expands:
   a. It removes the restrictions of having to hire locally based on the location of an office, which means that workers can come from

anywhere and allow them to live wherever they want, for example, where rents and home ownership costs are lower.

b. Employees can reinvest this additional capital in these local economies or make savings or investments in small businesses derived from cost savings on transportation, gasoline, street food, take-out coffee.

c. Businesses can help reduce unemployment rates in local economies that would have a harder time recovering (*La silla Rota* August 27, 2020).

In terms of the formation of an "ideal employee," perhaps what capital and its companies are aiming for is to achieve without qualms the idea narrated by Pierre Lemaitre in his novel *Inhuman Resources*: To value their employees and to know their "cold blood," their "capacity to resist violent pressures" (such as kidnapping or murder), and above all "to remain faithful to the values of the company" to which they belong in the face of a hostage-taking simulation that is justified because a large contracting company will announce the dismissal of 823 salaried workers for which it needs the adhesion of its managers so that they unconditionally and silently endorse such action. In the corporate psyche, which is that of the average global capital, this panoptic ideal configures the "model" of the company and society that it intends to erect through the 4.0 revolution and that for Sadin (2017: 60):

> It is about the emergence of a humanity that is no longer only interconnected, hyper-mobile, that makes access a capital value but that from now on is hybridized with systems that guide and decide collective and individual behaviors under still discrete but already pregnant modalities and that are destined to spread towards numerous fields of society.

In a context of falling world employment, the above is congruent with the new demands and occupations that delineate current jobs and those of the post-pandemic future within the framework of companies considered "successful" in the midst of human and social misfortune but, in particular, for the benefit of disaster and decadent capitalism.

In this regard, the ILO identifies the jobs and sectors that grew in the midst of the economic recession exacerbated by the health crisis:

> In contrast to almost all other sectors, employment in the information and communication sector as well as in finance and insurance continued to increase in the second and third quarters [of 2020: AS]. In line with an increasing demand for a digital economy and the strong performance

> of financial markets in that period, employment in the second quarter increased by 5.0 percent in the information and communication sector and by 3.4 percent in the financial and insurance sector. There was also an increase in employment particularly in the third quarter in the mining and quarrying sectors as well as in public services.
>
> ILO, January 25, 2021:15

Although there was a positive impact on sectors linked to Information and Communication Technologies (ICTs)—such as mining activity in the extraction of strategic minerals such as lithium, which is essential in the automotive industry and in the production of batteries, for example—the coronavirus had a negative impact on the world economy, causing the loss of thousands of jobs in most productive and service activities. However, the confinement and the subsequent change in consumer habits uncovered the need for companies and retailers to migrate to the digital realm—as they did in the past in other capitalist crises in sectors such as energy or real estate—creating jobs connected in cyberspace through the use of Apps and digital networks controlled by computerized business management.

This source indicates that what recruiters are looking for in the face of the changes brought about by the pandemic and the crisis are people who show "skills," "virtues," and "talents" capable of increasing the productivity of companies: creativity, persuasion, collaboration, adaptability, and the ability to manage time. For example, the Peruvian company *Quantum Talent. People analytics* (see: https://www.quantum-talent.com/), specialized in "talent selection" and downsizing through the application of artificial intelligence in order to increase productivity and capital profitability, highlights in its advertisement that: "After answering a 20-minute online test, an applicant can access a job vacancy through *Quantum Talent*, a technological platform that uses artificial intelligence (AI) and machine learning to connect companies and workers in a 100% digital process, very ad hoc for times of COVID-19 and social distancing."

Obviously, alongside the increase in labor productivity, there is the *essential objective* of capital: *to* maximize its rate of *profit* and in general its profitability.

1.2 *The Factory of the Future as a Builder of Skills and Talents*

An interesting document outlines what capitalism prefigures as the digitalized factory of the future and its functions in practically all its facets. It was prepared by the U.S. multinational corporation *ManpowerGroup* (December 6, 2016), which has several branches around the world.

In that document, Rebekah Kowalski, Vice President of Manpower North America, states that:

TABLE 6 Most in-demand jobs in-and post-pandemic in the digital age

DIGITAL AREA
- Software Engineer
- Graphic Designer
- Community Manager
- Data engineer (responsible for developing algorithms to help make raw data more useful to the business)
- Java Developer

SALES AREA
- Customer Service Manager
- Cashier
- Sales Executive
- Recruitment Specialist
- Marketing Specialist
- Key Account Manager (in charge of maintaining long-term relationships between clients and the company).

LOGISTICS
- Store Supervisor
- Driver for parcel delivery companies (such as iVoy and Amazon)
- Delivery person
- Project Manager (head of project management)
- Supply Chain Manager (in charge of the administration and management of all supply chain processes)

OTHER SECTORS
- Certified Public Accountant
- Psychologist
- Nurse
- Construction worker
- Translator

SOURCE: DATA ACCORDING TO *LINKEDIN*, CITED IN *REFORMA*, JULY 7, 2020

> Amid today's context of talent shortages and rapidly evolving skills needs, employers can no longer turn to the market, when they want to, to acquire new skills. They need to become talent builders to develop a workforce that has the skills they need to remain competitive. *Talent is our planet's most renewable resource* (2, our italics).

Chandra Brown, CEO of the MxD (Manufacturing x Digital) Institute associated with the U.S. Department of Defense—formerly called DMDII (Digital Manufacturing and Design Innovation Institute) and second of the 14 institutes known as Manufacturing USA—weighs in on the topic:

> The potential of the manufacturing sector has never been greater to transform other industries and drive economic growth, [and] this is due to the rapid advancement of new technologies. We can only achieve this potential through *new skills* and the evolution of the current and future workforce. This is a mission we are proud to support, along with our partners (p. 2, emphasis added).

The approach of both the corporation and this Institute, which jointly subscribed to this document, places as the axis and central objective of the coming "great transformation," paraphrasing Polanyi (2001), the "capture of talent" that is a "scarce commodity" (estimated at 2 million missing jobs in the United States) and that has to be articulated with the technical skills of the workforce and with the professions of the future (see Table 7)—65% of which have not yet been created for the new generations born after 1996, which the publication we are commenting on calls "Generation Z," referring to those born after that date and who are currently, on average, 25 years old.

According to this study, the first catalyzing force of this articulation was the automation of machinery Computerized Numerically Controlled Machine Tools. Today, the transformation of the digitized manufacturing industry involves the following processes: a) the Internet of Things, b) digitally connected enterprises, c) Big Data and algorithms[8] and, d) artificial intelligence (see Figure 3).

8 Big Data can be understood as a computational device for performing multiple combinations of data and information to answer or solve a specific problem. Other tools it uses include Hadoop, Spark, BBD, and NoSQl. As for algorithms, "… in order to work, algorithms must exist as part of assemblages that include hardware, data, data structures (such as lists, databases, memory, etc.), and the behaviours and actions of bodies. For the algorithm to become social software, in fact, 'it must gain its power as a social or cultural artifact and process by means of a better and better accommodation to behaviors and bodies which happen on its outside'" (Terranova, 2014: 382). Other algorithms include Google's PageRank; Facebook's EdgeRank, Klout, Appinions; Adobe Premier's Cinematch; and so on. To overcome the impression of those who believe that mathematics and algorithms are "merely technical things," we quote Negri's (2014: 05) statement: The use of mathematical models and algorithms by capital does not make them a feature of capital. It is not a problem of mathematics—it is a problem of power." And I would add for my part: of force between labor and capital fundamentally! From

TABLE 7 Technical generations of the manufacturing process: tools, types of work, and technologies

Generation 1 (1900–1970)	Generation 2 (1970–2005)	Generation 3 (2005–2020)	Generation 4 (2020 …)
Conventional manufacturing.	Software and hardware-automation systems.	Software and data enhancements (integration of digital networks).	Artificial Intelligence based systems, Big-Data. Internet of Things, 3D.

SOURCE: *MANPOWERGROUP*, (DECEMBER 6, 2016)

It is important to note that when we refer to "digital" in this study, we are analyzing:

> […] an integrated approach that combines software, data, interfaces, and controls in order to design, model, simulate, analyze, control, share, and manage the creation, delivery, and performance of products and services. Digital technology will touch every aspect of the organization and will ultimately end up being the way the organization will operate (p. 3. See Figure 3).

These new jobs and their respective professions and skills (see Table 7)—supported by the "virtuous combination" of digital technology, professional, talent, and skills production, which the study identifies as coming in the near *future*, but in our view, it is *accelerated* by the current global crisis of capitalism and exacerbated by the coronavirus pandemic—result from the technical and human evolution and transformation of tools and the workforce since the first industrial revolution in the 18th century.

As can be seen in Table 6 and in the Figures 2 and 3, the central device of the new configuration of the digital factory has as its center the cyberspace that articulates the devices of the fourth generation triggered—and accelerated as we said—by the industrial revolution in the making. To complete the picture

another perspective for Han (2021: 18), algorithms are "black boxes" where "… the world is lost in the deep layers of neural networks to which the human being has no access."

of this fourth generation of the workforce and technology, we must add the development of fifth generation (5G) digital telecommunications networks, which has triggered the biggest global trade dispute between the United States and China.

In congruence with our central hypothesis in this book: that in the face of the capitalist crisis and the exhaustion of the third industrial revolution (based on automation and microelectronics) the transformation of productive processes and of the labor force articulated to the new technical-labor paradigm advances with the digital transformation and the (in process) generalization of the fourth industrial-digital revolution in an attempt to restore the accumulation and valorization of capital according to the strategic objective of companies to increase their rate of profit and profitability in a context of profound civilizational crisis of the mode of production.

Much research (Merritt, 2016) has emphasized the effects of automation on employment or on the labor market as some call it. But not on its effects—direct or indirect—on production, work processes, or the valorization of capital and its relation in the creation of surplus value. One of the most visible changes in the new industrial revolution with respect to the previous one consists in the fact that now it is no longer only routine workers who are replaced by digitized automation but intellectual labor itself—the *general intellect* that continues to depend on the valorization (and is at the service) of capital under the influence of the development of artificial intelligence, Big Data, and algorithms, whose efficiency will require fewer and fewer computer or digital workers (for more, see Husson, January 9, 2021). In this sense, one should not lose sight of Lyotard's (1984: 46) forceful sentence: "Scientists, technicians, and instruments are purchased not to find truth, but to augment power." Of course, the power of capital!

In its pro-market and pro-business ideological language, the study referred to above (ManpowerGroup, December 6, 2016: 5) puts it in the following terms:

> Advances in mobile connectivity, the Internet of Things, AI, robotics, 3D printing, and advanced materials will radically transform manufacturing and production systems over the next five to ten years. This digital transformation is a key driver of radical change, which is going to result in a world that is more connected, in need of new skills, and open to new opportunities for companies to grow and create value.

In the paragraph above, the *key* is at the end: "create value." Of what value is this? Of course, the value that in the form of surplus value is appropriated by the capitalist as a result of the process of exploitation of labor power, without which there would be no point in promoting digitalization.

As we have said, the problem is that now the 4.0 revolution is replacing, in addition to the routinists, skilled digital workers. As Merritt (2016: 78) expresses: "Globally, the number of chip designers has stagnated because software programs now replace the work done by legions of logic designers and draftsmen."

And this author adds:

> ... the automation of higher-skilled and more complex jobs is accelerating due to advances in artificial intelligence and in the field of applied computational linguistics. Remarkable advances have recently been made in algorithms capable of deeper analysis of vast databases thanks to the fact that computers can now understand a little about the implicit meaning of human language as demonstrated by the victory of the Watson computer (Merritt, 2016: 79).[9]

In addition to Marx, a pioneer in this field since his *Grundrisse*, some authors had already warned of the advent of this demand for new jobs of highly qualified workers and technical personnel.

Thus, for example, Lyotard (1984: 48) points out that:

> If our general hypothesis is correct, there will be a growth in demand for experts and high and middle management executives in the leading sectors mentioned at the beginning of this study— [phonology, linguistics, communication and cybernetics, informatics, computers, data banks, telematics, among others: AS]—which is where the action will be in the years to come: any discipline with applicability to training in "telematics" (computer scientists, cyberneticists, linguists, mathematicians, logicians … .) will most likely receive priority in education. All the more so since an increase in the number of these experts should speed the research in other learning sectors, as has been the case with medicine and biology.

9 There is no doubt that China is the country leading technological change and driving new jobs in the new digital economy. This is confirmed by the McKinsey Global Institute (quoted in *Sputnik*, January 15, 2021), which projects that in 2030 around 220 million workers (30% of employees) will have to change their profession to adapt to the jobs demanded by digitalization, based on a revolution in professional training that starts with the radical transformation of its education system.

It is estimated that around half of the new jobs that will be created in the post-pandemic environment of the capitalist crisis will have to be adjusted to the needs and characteristics of the (new) digital industry, of which the ManpowerGroup study identifies 165 new functions distributed in 7 areas of technical specialization, also called "domains":

Each of the functions contained in these modules are performed by workers in various categories that the Manpower study (ManpowerGroup 2016: 5).) identifies in the following list:

- Service Technician.
- Predictive Maintenance Specialist.
- Robotic Engineer.
- Data Architect.
- Product Designer.
- Digital Manufacturing Manager.
- Supply Chain Strategist.
- Project Manager.
- Digital Twin Architect.
- Digital Thread Program Manager.
- Application Developer.
- Data Scientist.
- Community of Practice Manager.
- Technical Trainer, Level C Officer.
- Knowledge Curator and Ethicist.

TABLE 8 Percentage distribution of jobs and their functions by domain in the factory of the future

Domain	Function
Digital Manufacturing 28%	Production plant.
Digital Thread 21%	Data Archive Management.
Digital Company 16%	Organizational strategy and management.
Digital Product 18%	Feedback and after-sales support service.
Digital Design 10%	Tools, techniques, and mindset for design innovation.
Supply chain 11%	Supply and delivery technologies for products and services.
Omni Manufacturing 6%.	External Work Areas.

SOURCE: *MANPOWERGROUP*, (DECEMBER 6, 2016: 5)

In terms of skills, the following are indicated:
- Mechanics, electronics, and industrial logic
- Engineering principles and practices
- Mathematical and model-based engineering
- Commercial awareness or sensitization
- Focused design thinking and customer/worker experience
- Integrated Lean Systems
- Problem solving, innovation, and leadership for change
- Planning, control, improvement, and quality assurance.

Regarding the required technology:
- Design, manufacturing, materials, tooling, and assembly
- Modeling, simulation, and visualization
- Mechatronics, robotics, and automation control
- Internet of Things: technical and operational information
- AI/Machine learning and intelligent systems
- Systems integration and human interface design
- Visual analysis and reporting
- Data privacy/cybersecurity/risk mitigations
- Automated and user-managed testing
- Multi-platform design, implementation and operations.

Of the 7 domains that make up the digital factory, notes *ManPower* (p. 5, our italics), "the largest shift occurs between the *shop floor* and the *digital manufacturing* domain: 28% of the 165 new or evolved functions are in this domain": in the sphere of capital production requiring manual and psychic labor power located in the domain of the shop floor and digital manufacturing (see Table 8).

Perhaps the most important challenge of the digital industrial revolution contemplated in the elements of cyberspace (artificial intelligence, internet of things, Big Data, 3D, and self-learning) from the perspective of capital is to connect with and influence the material mutations and transformations of productive processes in all areas from industry and agriculture through commerce and services in an environment not only to raise the productivity and competitiveness of processes and companies but also to effectively contribute to the creation of value and surplus value with the essential support of the *collective workforce* in all its functions and categories involved.

While from this angle everything is promising and benign for the logic of the system, this is not the case for workers and in general the world of work, which will have to submit to the new norms, rules, and institutions established and demanded by the digital industrial revolution in the "new normality" that tends to be implemented in the post-pandemic world.

2 Conclusion

Salaried or not, the new digitalized jobs arising from the pandemic, the previous ones adjusted to it demanded by companies in the framework of the new digital factories and in jobs framed in the home office and remote work, as well as those related to the digital applications of companies such as Uber, Rappi, DiDi Food, fast food deliverers through digital platforms (which charge up to 30% commission for the delivery service, which makes products more expensive to the extent that the owners of the goods pass these increases on to consumers) in general are projected as flexible and precarious jobs, easily rotated, and adaptable to the demands and conditions imposed by companies in the framework of their class and organizational interests for which they advocate preventing any legislation or if it is adopted, that it be in a framework of diminished social and labor rights in a mimicry of what happens in outsourcing activities or informality.

This was possible thanks to the development of platforms and the control exercised by capital to prevent direct intervention by those involved in the defense of their rights.

Digital platforms—such as remote work and the home office as well as the components of the fourth industrial revolution—are projected as a whole to restructure and recycle capitalism in a new structural dimension that will allow it to overcome the crisis and contradictions of the pre-coronavirus stage, where the great industrial and technological revolutions took place and could not resolve them.

CHAPTER 6

The Vicissitudes of the Fourth Industrial Revolution

1 Introduction

This chapter deals with what has become popularly known as the fourth industrial revolution or simply revolution 4.0 and its repercussions on the world of work. It exposes the relationship between the components of that revolution (Big data, algorithms, artificial intelligence, 3D printing, etc.) with the law of value and the production of surplus value in the contour of what we call the digitized factory or simply digital factory in terms of commodity production and its relationship with the labor force.

1.1 *Marx's Theory of Value and the Fourth Industrial Revolution*

Capitalism is a historical system that evolves and spirals towards maturity and decadence on the basis of contradictions and mutations of rupture and continuity. It is these factors that drive its processes of production, reproduction, and crisis, and they are themselves the very forces that deepen and extend the crises of capitalism. But the essence of these contradictions lies in the clash between the *use-value* of labor power and its *exchange-value*, which makes possible the difference between the first value and the supplementary or surplus value it can produce. Its perpetual unfolding is the central axis of the mechanism of the production of surplus value—in any of its forms: absolute or relative—which remains the core sustenance of the capitalist system and without which it would inevitably collapse.

As Marx (2010a: 385, author's italics) points out:

> The *production of surplus value*—which implies the preservation of the value originally advanced—thus appears as the determining purpose, the driving concern, and the *final result* of the capitalist production process, as the means whereby the original value is converted into capital.

Has the fourth industrial revolution eradicated this fundamental objective of the capitalist system as is sometimes claimed generally without argument? Whether or not in conjunction with the State, any action undertaken by capital has as its logic and purpose the objective of maximizing its profit and

 | DOI:10.1163/9789004532717_008

resuming the processes of valorization and accumulation of capital that will ensure its continuity, even in times of crisis such as the pandemic. For this to happen, it is necessary to insist that, unlike the "factors" of production (as the neoclassical economists ideologically call them), namely: capital, land and labor (force), only the latter creates the (new) value and surplus labor (surplus value) that is appropriated in various ways by capital and its subject: the business owners of the capitalist class.

As Marx (1973: 618–621) indicates, this is due to the fact that *fixed capital*—machines, instruments of labor, technologies (even the most sophisticated)—only increases value in two cases: a) when it transfers value to the final product as past labor conferred by labor power and b) to the extent that it increases the proportion of surplus labor at the expense of necessary labor by increasing its productivity, which makes possible the creation of more goods (of use) in ever shorter times. In the latter case, it is a genuine method of production of relative surplus value achieved by reducing the labor time socially necessary for the production of labor power as such. The earth and its natural resources (*circulating constant capital*) produces value as long as they are filtered and removed by the physical-manual and cerebral-intellectual action of human labor[1] power—be it that of the peasant, the artisan, or the worker.

Due to the need of capital to valorize itself, we must clarify that the fact that the variable part of capital is reduced with the associated increase of the constant one does not imply drawing the conclusion made by the authors of the end of labor in the sense that:

> ... to *imagine that by eliminating living labor it* [capital] *could continue to reproduce itself.* It would not be possible to produce capital and neither would it be possible to complete the reproductive cycle through consumption, since it would be abstract to imagine consumption without wage earners.
>
> ANTUNES, 2005: 110

In this sense, any hope that this system can produce anything other than surplus value—for example, non-mercantile human satisfactions for the great mass of the population—constitutes, to say the least, a flagrant illusion. It is quite another thing to note that the crisis of capitalism derives from the incapacity of the mechanisms of the system to restore the production of value and

1 As Marx says (*Capital*, Vol. 1, 1982: 296–297) "... the raw material merely serves to absorb a definite quantity of labour. By being soaked in labour, the raw material is in fact changed into yarn, because labour-power is expended in the form of spinning and added to it; but the product, the yarn, is now nothing more than a measure of the labour absorbed by the cotton."

surplus value to their previous levels in order to guarantee the increase of the rate of profit, which is what governs the trajectory and the (ir)rational logic of the system.

This theoretical approach derives from Marx's thesis that labor (labor power) is the *only factor* that produces value and, therefore, surplus value; that, when capital does not remain in the sphere of production but in that of circulation (trade, services, finance), it is unproductive (Piqueras, 2018a) or, if you will, constitutes an *anti-value*, in such a way that "[t]his realization process is at the same time the de-realization process of labor. It posits itself objectively, but it posits this, its objectivity, as its own not-being or as the being of its not-being—of capital" (Marx, 1982a: 415).

It is necessary to understand and locate in the critical episteme this contradiction that sometimes goes unnoticed by analysts: to the extent that as surplus value falls along with the increase in the productivity of labor and the organic composition of capital, the quantity and volume of social wealth increases, which due to the first movement reduces its value and, therefore, the socially necessary labor time that is increasingly, in Marx's words, a miserable, meager portion (*geringen*) for the measurement and determination of value and wealth, which generates the phenomenon that we have called the *dismeasure of labour power* (Sotelo, 2010 and note 6, page 24).

In this way, Marx (1973: 624–625, author's italics) states that:

> *The theft of alien labor time, on which the present wealth is based,* appears a miserable foundation in face of this new one—[capital's appropriation of the global productive force, understanding, and mastery of nature]—created by large-scale industry itself. As soon as labor in the direct form has ceased to be the great well-spring of wealth, labor time ceases and must cease to be its measure, and hence exchange value (must cease to be the measure) of use value. *The surplus labor of the mass* has ceased to be the condition for the development of general wealth, just as the *non-labor of the few*, for the development of the general powers of the human head

Thus, Marx (628, author's italics) concludes:

> The measure of wealth is then not any longer, in any way, labor time, but rather disposable time— [available time]. *Labor time as the measure of value* posits wealth itself as founded on poverty, and disposable time as existing *in and because of the antithesis to surplus labor time*; or, the positing of an individual's entire time as labor time, and his degradation

> therefore to mere worker, subsumption under labor. *The most developed machinery thus forces the worker to work longer than the savage does, or than he himself did with the simplest, crudest tools.*

The *dismeasure of labour power* becomes more acute when capital shifts from industrial activities, agriculture, or services to the financial or speculative spheres—a characteristic of the capitalist present with its basis in the hegemony of fictitious capital—whose unproductive dynamics end up generating less and less value, severely punishing the rate of surplus value and, therefore, the *average* rate of profit (see Tables 2 and 3).

From these passages of Marx, hasty and erroneous conclusions have been drawn in at least two respects. For example, Gorz (1999: 85) states that: "When intelligence and imagination ('general intellect') become the main productive force, working time ceases to be the measure of labor; indeed, it ceases to be measurable." This *interpretation is* ambiguous and obscure. It makes it seems that Marx affirms that "labor time ceases to be the measure of labor," which is a tautology. What Marx is referring to, first of all, is that *immediate labor* (not labor in general as a social abstract) ceases to be the "source of wealth" (note: of wealth, not of value nor of surplus value, which is indeed affected by the reduction of socially necessary labor time—but this is not what is being discussed at the moment). Consequently, the same happens with *labor time*, which ceases to be its measure (of wealth). Therefore, Marx's conclusion quoted above: "... hence *exchange value* (*must cease to be the measure*) of *use value*" (our italics). And what is use value, labor? No!: Wealth is the product of the concrete labor of the worker determined, in turn, by the law of value. Secondly, as if capitalist technique were advancing in the sense of "liberating" the human being from the penalties and burdens of exploitation, alienation and wage labor *without* abolishing the capitalist mode of production, Gorz (1988: 93, our italics) asserts that:

> In a complex society, *heteronomy cannot be abolished completely* to be replaced by autonomy. It is possible, however, for tasks performed within the sphere of heteronomy itself to be reskilled, restructured and diversified—notably (though not exclusively) by a*llowing individuals to self-manage their working time*—in such a way as *to increase the degree of autonomy within heteronomy*. It would be wrong, therefore, to imagine there is a clear-cut separation between autonomous activities and heteronomous work, the realm of freedom and the realm of necessity. The former does indeed have repercussions on the latter but *can never subsume it entirely*.

In Gorz's model, "heteronomy" corresponds to the capitalist system, to the realm of necessity, to wage labor, and the division of labor, while the social sphere of "autonomy" corresponds to the world of life, to freedom, autonomous production, and work (such as small workshops or cooperatives, for example). It is, thus, a classic structural and social dualism (for a critique of dualism, see Frank 1969) that cannot be overcome. A similar thesis to that of Habermas (1984, particularly Chapter 6: et 161seq.) when he postulates that in contrast to the sphere of the "world of work"—integrated into the system, to the systemic structure of the technical, bureaucratized rationality of the institutions—there exists the "communicative action" that belongs to the sphere of the "world of life" and of the "subjects" with the capacity for transformation. Moreover, according to Gorz, this dualism is strengthened by the fact that the revolutionary subject embodied in the proletariat is no longer viable and is replaced by a new "subversive figure" that he calls: the "non-class of post-industrial proletarians" (Gorz, 1982: 75).

It should be emphasized that Marx differentiates the immediate labor time of the worker—which the development of machines, science, and, in general, of the productive forces of society turns into a miserable, meager basis for the production and determination of the value of social wealth— from labor time in general—the coagulation of labor—in which abstract labor consists and takes shape (producing the exchange value responsible for the production of surplus value) and whose result leads to the inevitability that the "... exchange value (must cease to be the measure) of use value." It stands out here the role that society's *available time*—as opposed to *labor time* as an *dismeasure of labour power* (Sotelo, 2010)—provokes to the detriment of the production of surplus labor and, therefore, of surplus value, as well as to the detriment of the production of antivalue or unproductive spaces. Both phenomena present difficulties in achieving the "self-valorization" of capital and, therefore, negatively affect to some extent the rate of profit, which capital finds it necessary to increase through an increase in the rate of exploitation. Let us note that this approach of Marx, which in his time was appreciated as a tendency, is today a faithful reflection of a structural behavior of the contradictory dynamics of contemporary capitalism, in which the hard core of the crisis lies in the mechanisms of production of value and surplus value practically all over the world.

As can be seen from the above—in spite of the *dismeasure* and the reduction of the *immediate work* involved in production and, therefore, of the necessary social labor time and of the share of surplus value—the rate of profit can continue to increase under different procedures such as the increase of the *mass of* surplus value with reduction of wages and labor costs; some of these procedures include the constant increases in the intensity of labor, the reduction of the workers' and popular consumption fund, the increase of the working day, labor precariousness, and "flexibility" of jobs and labor. All this is coupled together with a reduction of the value of constant capital under the influence of the increase of labor productivity, stimulated through the scientific-technological development that is now being transformed by the fourth industrial revolution as a device of the future capitalist restructuring and of the global world of labor.

Professor Husson (January 9, 2021) reflects on the effects of automation on employment before and after Covid-19, starting from a central question: why does automation through robotization, which replaces jobs, not result in an increase in productivity? After noting that this process did not generate the significant reductions in employment predicted by some theorists and analysts, he points out that this displacement did occur in the industries and sectors of routine, manual, or low-skilled workers. In the understanding that the objective of the increase in labor productivity and total factor productivity (including land and capital) is the rate of profit, the author notes that there was a fall in productivity and wonders whether the current crisis will be able to restore it:

> The exhaustion of productivity growth is a fundamental characteristic of contemporary capitalism: throughout the Glorious Thirties, labor productivity increased by around 5% per year. Today, it is no longer increasing by more than 1% or 2%, in the best of cases [...] both in Spain and in the Eurozone as a whole.

To address this problem, Husson compares two historical epochs of capitalism and introduces an "indicator" that he calls "deregulation."[2] In the first epoch, the increase in productivity slows down and the rate of profit falls, while the rate of deregulation remains constant, while b) in the second, when the neoliberal period begins in the 1980s, productivity continues to fall in conjunction with the increase in the rate of profit in parallel with the increase in the rate of deregulation. This is the key to the author's thesis: it will be the pair of the indicators (a) rate of profit and deregulation that will replace the pair of indicators (b) productivity and the rate of profit.

2 "Deregulation is defined here, in a broad sense, as the set of devices aimed at restoring profit despite the exhaustion of productivity growth. We compare the evolution of the rate of profit and productivity with a synthetic *deregulation index*, constructed from a set of indicators (wage share, trade deficits, household indebtedness, inequalities, financialization, globalization)."

From here the author investigates the causes of the decrease in productivity by virtue of considering that, according to logic and not dialectics, all technological and scientific development should lead, on the contrary, to an increase in the productivity of social work.

In spite of the substitution of routine work in the countries of advanced capitalism that has occurred in recent decades due to the effects of the third industrial revolution and in part due to the fourth in progress, it is noted that there has not been an increase in productivity—actually, there has been a "decreasing marginal productivity," the author points out—that has contributed to the increase in the rate of profit. According to the author, basing his work on another author (Artous), the cause of this phenomena is precisely because, in the end, there is insufficient investment to compensate for the fall in productivity. But he also indicates a second cause: the displacement of demand towards sectors of low productivity and profitability and concludes:

> This may be the underlying answer to Solow's paradox: the flow of technological innovations does not seem to be exhausted, but what is in the process of being exhausted is capitalism's capacity to incorporate them into its logic.[3]

Both elements have an impact, then, on a fall in labor productivity, and it is here that the increase in the rate of deregulation mentioned by Husson is highlighted as a counteracting factor, particularly on the side of the fall in wages. We consider that Marx since the *Grundrisse* solved this enigma—that apparent paradox or, rather, contradiction regarding the fact that despite the continuing development of technological innovations capitalism and its mechanics (and not only the enterprises) is unable to incorporate them into its reproduction processes in quantity and speed. Why?

In the *Grundrisse* (1973: 266–267), we find the answer:

> The larger the surplus value of capital before the increase of productive force, the larger the amount of presupposed surplus labor or surplus value of capital; or, the smaller the fractional part of the working day which

3 According to Merritt (2016: 56)—although the concept "productivity paradox" has its origin in a work of the prominent American economist Robert Solow (July 12, 1987), hence the term "Solow paradox"—the first to address the concept in an analytical and systemic way was the American from Stanford University Erik Brynjolfsson who detected the (apparent) contradiction between the advances in computer-derived automation and the slow pace of productivity growth, which is why he called this phenomenon the "productivity paradox."

> forms the equivalent of the worker, which expresses necessary labor, the smaller is the increase in surplus value which capital obtains from the increase of productive force. Its surplus value rises, but in an ever smaller relation to the development of the productive force. Thus, the more developed capital already is, the more surplus labor it has created, the more terribly must it develop the productive force in order to realize itself in only smaller proportion, i.e., to add surplus value—because its barrier always remains the relation between the fractional part of the day which expresses necessary labor, and the entire working day. It can move only within these boundaries. The smaller already the fractional part falling to necessary labor, the greater the surplus labor, the less can any increase in productive force perceptibly diminish necessary labor; since the denominator has grown enormously. The self-realization of capital becomes more difficult to the extent that it has already been realized. The increase of productive force would become irrelevant to capital; realization itself would become irrelevant, because its proportions have become minimal, and it would have ceased to be capital [...] But this happens not because wages have increased or the share of labor in the product, but because it has already fallen so low, regarded in its relation to the product of labor or to the living work day.

From the above quotation results the explanation of why capital investment is reduced to compensate for the effects of displacement of labor by automation as a function of the following articulated factors: a) reduction of necessary labor (which constitutes the value of labor power), b) the concomitant *marginal* increase of surplus labor not remunerated to the worker (surplus value), c) the increasing difficulties created for the self-valorization of capital due to the fact that valorization reaches its limits. All this, Marx concludes, leads to the increase of the productive forces—of productivity—and of the valorization of capital itself, becoming "indifferent to capital." Although, he clarifies, this does not happen because wages or their share in national income increase as postulated by neoclassical economics and the entrepreneurs themselves but just the opposite: because labor time has fallen so much due to the decrease in necessary working time, without the worker being compensated by an increase in his or her income. And here, of course, *the super-exploitation of labor plays an important role* in explaining this decline in wages and, in general, in the labor costs involving workers' social benefits in the daily life of the world of work.

From the above, we derive the following hypothesis: however much productivity increases—relatively or marginally—the technological revolution develops, and labor power is saved through the substitution of labor power and productive jobs for digital automation; this reduction of labor time, socially necessary for the production of goods and labor power, is increasingly difficult and in decreasing magnitude as a means to produce value and surplus value, even though social wealth is progressively increasing in terms of use values and global wealth.

Collaterally, the superfluity and discarding of junk goods (fast food, software, hardware, household appliances, computers, auto parts) is intensifying, which contradicts the employers' propaganda of the fetishistic, fallacious, and deceitful "total quality" that is expressed in the planned, programmed, and artificial reduction of the useful life of products and the time required for their manufacture. It is the society of perishability and disposable superfluity of things and of the human being (Antunes and Sotelo, 2003: 104 et seq.)—a completely irrational society that is constituted from what Mészáros (1995: 547–548) calls throughout his work the "decreasing rate of utilization" of capital, goods and labor force, which expresses the "triumph of generalized waste production." It is in this context that we frame Husson's thesis of the "rate of deregulation" that supplements the fall in generalized labor productivity.

1.2 *Three Industrial Revolutions*

Capitalism has experienced three industrial revolutions since the first one known as the Industrial Revolution in England, whose most active period occurred between 1795 and 1834 according to Polanyi (2001: 81); above all else, it was based on mechanization and the movement of hydraulic and steam power. The second introduced the assembly line and mass production that originated the well-known Fordism in the automobile industry. Finally, the third revolution—stimulated in part by the struggles of the workers but also by the technological development that capital gave as a response, both to those struggles and to the fierce inter-capitalist monopolistic competition (Antunes, 2000: 44)—was unleashed with automation, electronics, and computing (Internet) and had as its premise an intense concentration and centralization of capital. The latter can also be called the Toyota Production System (TPS) of intensified flexible production centered on the "just in time" system and on the principle of "autonomatization," which is a "[...] neologism forged from the contraction of the words autonomy and automation. The idea is to endow automated machines with a certain "autonomy" in order to introduce a self-stopping mechanism in case of malfunction" (Coriat, 1992: 39 et *seq.*).

As Marini (1996: 54–55) states:

> The problem could only be solved in the capitalist crisis of the 1970s that saw a wave of asset purchases and mergers as well as technological agreements that we are still witnessing and which are completed by the emergence of a new mechanism: outsourcing. In other words, as is the norm in situations of this nature, the crisis has given rise to unbridled centralization with which the masses of resources required to promote the development of new technologies and, thus, improve competitive conditions are being formed. This explains why, despite its irregular curve, the return of productive investments in these countries in the last third of the 1970s unleashed a formidable technological revolution, particularly in the fields of microelectronics and information technology, telecommunications, biotechnology, and new materials, as well as in energy production and the aerospace industry. This implied substantial changes in the levels of employment and remuneration, as well as in the modes of organization and management of capital and the labor force.

The Grupo Krisis (2018: 64) indicate the limits of the 3rd microelectronic revolution and the passage to the 4th:

> With the third industrial revolution of microelectronics, the labor society stumbles upon its absolute historical limit [...] It was foreseeable that this limit would be reached sooner or later. Because the commodity production system has suffered from its birth from an incurable contradiction: on the one hand, it lives by sucking human energy in massive quantities through the dilapidation of labor in its machinery, the more the better. On the other hand, the law of business competitiveness imposes a constant growth of productivity in which human labor power is replaced by capital in the form of scientific knowledge.

We have, thus, reached the fourth industrial revolution (Figure 1), a productive world stimulated by the worldwide pandemic of the coronavirus and sustained by artificial intelligence and intelligent robots integrated into production lines that develop activities similar to those of human intelligence; the development of Big Data (data and information stored on microchips in quantities fluctuating between a minimum of 30–50 Terabytes, where a Terabyte unit=1000 Gigabytes); and automatic learning through intelligent software, the Internet of Things and three-dimensional printing (3D).

In agreement with the economic analyst Pilotzi (July 15, 2020), the coronavirus pandemic drove a drastic change both in the world of work and in different sectors and industries, where Mexico is no exception. This change

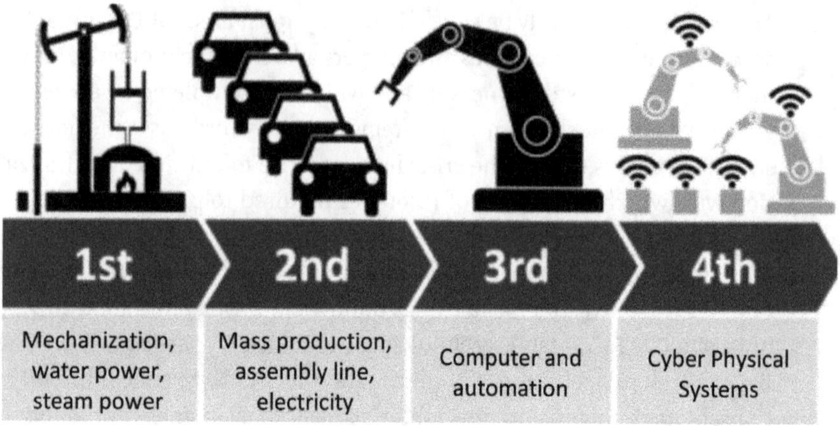

FIGURE 1 Industrial revolutions throughout history
SOURCE: CHRISTOPH ROSER. *AT ALLABOUTLEAN.COM*, AT: HTTPS://ES.WIKIPEDIA.ORG/WIKI/INDUSTRIA_4.0#/MEDIA/ARCHIVO:INDUSTRY_4.0.PNG

implies that from now on "... productive processes and methodologies will have to be adapted in strategies focused on digital inclusion, both in small and medium-sized companies and in multinationals," being the support and key of the digital revolution—which enables the transition from the physical to the virtual world but also its articulation—at the same time that these processes serve to store huge amounts of information and data that enable the remote management of processes, products, and user-customers. According to the aforementioned author, the most significant change of this digital revolution is that production and work processes "... will be able to restart their cycle in real time by combining physical and remote operation through digitization." But at the expense of the human being, since as Lassalle states (May 7, 2019): "The massive digitization of human experience, both on an individual and collective scale, is beginning to take on the aspect of a progressive, evolutionary catastrophe, reaching the entire Earth." A devaluation of humanity itself taken to infinity—of its existential, labor, and cultural condition in order to reify it even more and put it at the service of capital and its incessant and inexhaustible social metabolism and suction of labor and surplus value.

We postulate that according to the law of value/labor—ignored or denied by the thesis of the "end of labor" and by most engineers and designers of labor—it maintains the impossibility of dispensing with the labor force of the worker as the essential factor in the creation of value, of surplus value, and, therefore, of wealth and profits. The future productive and labor processes (and jobs) restructured by the industrial-digital revolution will necessarily be hybrids: they will have to combine, dialectically and necessarily, physical activities with increasingly intellectual ones as foreseen by the author of the *Grundrisse*:[4] the interaction through cyberspace between science and technique—considered as productive forces—with the psycho-manual-subjective activity of the worker producer—not only of physical goods but, in addition, of information and data stored in sophisticated software or programs through applications, computer platforms, and tools.

In this environment, in Mexico there are already companies using this type of digital technology, specifically in the state of Nuevo Leon, Mexico, that are "... focused on the digital transformation of energy and process automation" (Pilotzi July 15, 2020) for which the installation of software for remote diagnosis, configuration, and maintenance of equipment is of fundamental importance, in[5] addition to special security programs such as "24/7 cybersecurity" to preserve information and data.

In this context, Anuja Sonalker, CEO of Steer Tech—a Maryland-based company that sells self-parking technology—summarizes a new discourse that legitimizes the use of technology "... without human contact [because] ... Humans are biohazards, machines are not" (quoted by Naomi Klein, May 8, 2020). We arrive, thus, at the stage where the infernal panopticon unreservedly proclaims the "dangerousness of humanity," whereby "We are the object of a panoptic vision. The smart bed with various sensors carries out continuous monitoring even during sleep. Monitoring is increasingly being introduced into everyday life in the form of *convenience*. Infomata, which save us a lot of work, turn out to be efficient *informants*, which monitor and control us" (Han, 2021: 17–18, author's emphasis).

1.3 *The Fourth Industrial Revolution in the Making*

The technologies of the third industrial revolution—based on the automation of production and work processes and the development of computers and

4 "[It is,] hence, the tendency of capital to give production a scientific character; direct labour [is] reduced to a mere moment of this process" (Marx, 2010:618). But, contradictorily, in spite of that reduction, capital in general in its average must necessarily resort to exploitation and the super-exploitation of labor not only to survive but not to perish.

5 24/7 cybersecurity, which means 24/7 protection, is a global security system provided by transnational companies specialized in this segment to ensure business operations in an environment of protection of their private interests. It is particularly useful in circumstances of deployment of activities through remote work and home office and during situations of confinement as in the case of the coronavirus pandemic whose use becomes essential to monitor employees.

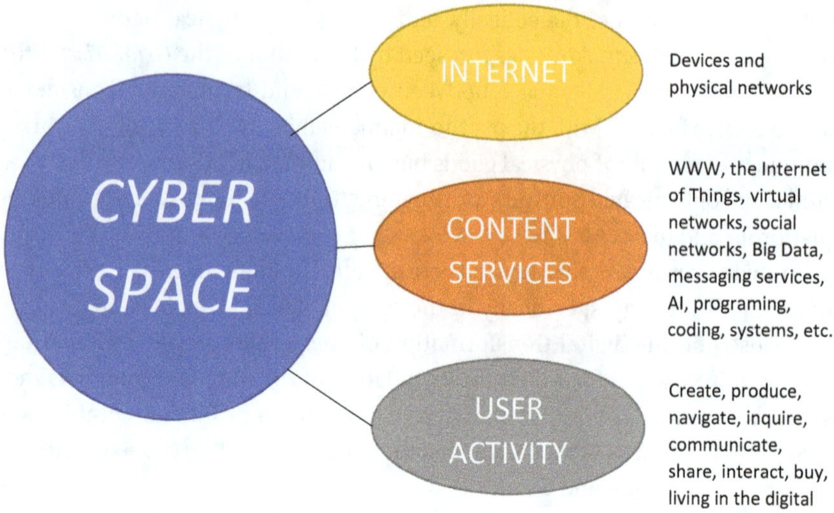

FIGURE 2 A material representation of cyberspace
SOURCE: *INFORMATION* AND *ICT*, MARCH 7, 2019

electronics—did not succeed in eliminating the physical limitations of working time through the formation of *cyberspace* (Figure 2).[6]

These technologies also failed to completely reduce production idle times and the porosity of working days with the intermediation of the computerized numerical control machine system. The much-desired "structural stability of the economy" touted by international organizations and the dominant thinking was not achieved, nor was it possible to generate economic and political conditions that would prevent the emergence of new crises such as those of 2008–2009 and the current one of 2019–2022.

The appropriation of human subjectivity and the intensification of the rhythms of production propitiated by this industrial revolution have a historical-structural limit that not even the technological revolution has been able to overcome. Therefore—and this is our hypothesis in this book—in the interstices of this capitalist crisis aggravated by the pandemic, capital has to unleash a new technical-scientific revolution (4.0) or fourth industrial revolution and deploy a series of articulated policies and strategies that aim to help

6 *Cyberspace* is a virtual reality inside a computer or PC, on tablets, smartphones connected to social networks and to the software of large companies that operate on the Internet to provide communication through platforms such as Google. The concept of "cyberspace" dates back to 1984 in the novel Neuromancer, where William Gibson defines cyberspace as "… an electronic matrix of global interconnectedness underpinned by the combination of the digital paradigm and networks with large volumes of digital information in circulation" (Information and ICT, March 7, 2019). For a broader view see: Lévy (2004).

to overcome it in such a way that a new cycle of capitalist development can be generated—which is extremely difficult to achieve, considering that together with this revolution interacts the class struggle and the possibility that in the future it will be hindered by the emergence of a new revolutionary subject commanded in its hard core by the working class and the political projects of overcoming the capitalist order. In this way, once again, the struggle between labor and capital presents itself as the midwife of history despite the slogans against the false auguries of the ideologists of the end of labor. As Mészáros (1995: 891) says with respect to both the mode of production and the antagonistic labor/capital relation:

> It is almost impossible to understand the development and self-reproduction of the capitalist mode of production without the notion of total social capital, which alone can explain many mysteries of mercantile society—from the 'average rate of profit' to the laws governing the expansion and concentration of capital. Similarly, it is almost impossible to understand the many thorny problems of labor, both in its national variation and in its social stratification, without keeping in mind all the time the necessary framework of a proper appraisal: namely, the irreconcilable antagonism between total social capital and the totality of labor.

From another perspective, it can be seen that:

> Robert Gordon has pointed out that the current phase of economic development the world is experiencing indicates an exhaustion of the great inventions that helped trigger the enormous productivity gains of the past decades. Gordon says that, despite the growing influence of ICTs in most productive activities, their net effect on productivity is still relatively low because they do not represent a drastic paradigm shift, as did at the time electric power or the internal combustion engine. It is, therefore, likely that the lingering effects of the 2008 economic crisis will continue to manifest themselves on a regular basis for several more years.
>
> MERRITT, 2016: 76

In addition, there are those who think—and in this we agree—that it is almost impossible for this revolution to be completed and generalized above all due to the problem of the scarcity of natural resources, particularly minerals "... as Emilio Santiago Muriño has pointed out: '... it is an insurmountable bottleneck for the 4th Industrial Revolution to be universalized. Its advances will be partial and directly proportional to the geopolitical privilege that imperial actors of the world-system can impose at the expense of the rest" (quoted by Riechmman, September 7, 2020).

We start from the fact that technology (at whatever stage of its development) is applied specifically to historically constituted material and social conditions. This makes it possible to distinguish different historical epochs (see Figure 1), even though its application and its fruits vary according to the specific way in which it is used in different economic regimes such as capitalism, feudalism, or socialism. This is what Marx alludes to (2010: 95–106) in a letter to Pavel Vasilievich Annenkov of December 28, 1846 when he warns of the difference between technology in general and its application that many authors erase:

> The present *use* of machinery is one of the relations of our present economic system, but the way in which machinery is exploited is quite distinct from the machinery itself. Powder is still powder, whether you use it to wound a man or to dress his wounds.
>
> ibid: 99, author's italics

Technology can be used to produce important social goods like vaccines, but in capitalism it must first be converted and priced into commodities and then distributed to segments of the population with purchasing power, excluding the poorer majority sectors of society as occurs in major health crises such as the one experienced by all humanity during COVID-19.

In capitalism, technology and its innovations are generally applied to the most advanced productive and work processes in line with the production of value and surplus value, mainly for the purpose of profit and profitability. In this sense, capitalist mutations are created and developed in the vicinity of crises and major social upheavals that mark points of rupture and continuity that trigger technical-scientific revolutions, responsible for the creation of new paradigms (Pérez, 2002), generally after the unleashing of major crises and wars, as were the second and third industrial revolutions, or major social and health catastrophes such as the current pandemic that shakes humanity in conjunction with the global capitalist crisis.

Underlying these prerogatives—incubated in the midst of a capitalist and pandemic crisis—capital is intensifying the productive and organizational restructuring of its work processes and its enterprises at the cost of the dismissal of thousands of workers, the intensification of work, and the strengthening of the super-exploitation of labor. This social and material base was already given both by the high volumes of unemployment, underemployment, and informality pre-existing in the world, as well as by the precariousness of work that includes job creation with jobs that do not entirely satisfy social needs.[7] For example, the ILO estimates that between January-September 2020, 1 billion 48-hour full-time jobs were lost worldwide, while in Latin America this loss reached almost 150 million as shown in Table 9 below.

It should be added that the system has the tools and applications based on automation and digitalization of production processes and IT platforms for these changes to take place (see ECLAC, August 26, 2020). Some call this common business practice "reengineering" (Hammer and Champy, 1994) or "starting over" or "from scratch," and it is very likely that the industrial-digital revolution will reintegrate it into its devices.

For Antunes (2018: 38), industry 4.0 constitutes a new phase of industrial automation that differs from the Industrial Revolution of the eighteenth century, the automotive industry of the twentieth century, and the productive restructuring that developed in the course of the 1970s. From here arises the fourth digital-informational phase characterized by the use and application of cell phones, tablets, smartphones, and social networks that control, supervise, and command this new stage of cybernetic industry in the 21st century.

The fourth Industrial Revolution consists of the prevalence of production based on *cyber physical systems*. It is preceded by the first, corresponding to mechanization based on river power; the second, on the steam engine; and the third, on the power of computers and automation, which began in the 1940s (for more on the subject, see Mandel, 1995; Naville, 1985; and/or Alves, 2013).

To understand this role of 4.0 in the capitalist restructuring or cybernetic recycling of the same, we refer to a famous passage of Marx's (1904: 9–15): "Preface" to *A Contribution to the Critique of Political Economy* originally published in 1859 where he writes that:

> No social order ever disappears before all the productive forces, for which there is room in it, have been developed; and new higher relations of production never appear before the material conditions of their existence have matured in the womb of the old society. Therefore, mankind always takes up only such problems as it can solve; since, looking at the matter more closely, we will always find that the problem itself arises only when the material conditions necessary for its solution already exist or are at least in the process of formation.
>
> ibid.: 12–13

7 For an interesting article on labor precariousness in Peru, see Lust (January 7, 2021).

TABLE 9 Loss of working hours at the global, regional, and subregional scales for the first three quarters of 2020 (% values and full-time equivalent jobs)

	Lost work hours (in %)			Full-time jobs equivalents (48 hours per week in millions)		
	2020			2020		
	Q1	Q2	Q3	Q1	Q2	Q3
World	5.6	17.3	12.1	*160*	*495*	*345*
Africa	1.9	15.6	11.5	7	60	43
North Africa	2.1	21.2	12.9	1	13	8
Sub-Saharan Africa	1.9	14.5	11.3	6	45	35
Central Africa	1.8	14.7	11.9	1	7	6
East Africa	2.0	14.0	11.8	3	19	16
Southern Africa	0.5	20.3	14.2	0	4	2
West Africa	2.1	13.9	9.9	2	15	11
Americas	3.0	28.0	19.8	11	105	75
Latin America and the Caribbean	3.7	33.5	25.6	*9*	*80*	*60*
Central America	0.8	35.8	29.9	1	24	20
South America	5.0	33.5	24.9	8	50	39
North America	1.8	18.4	9.6	2	25	13
Arab States	2.3	16.9	12.4	1	10	8
Asia and the Pacific	7.3	15.2	10.7	125	265	185
East Asia	12.0	5.5	4.9	100	45	40
Southeast Asia and the Pacific	3.3	16.7	10.7	10	49	31
Southeast Asia	3.4	17.1	10.9	9	48	30
South Asia	3.1	27.3	18.2	19	170	115
Europe and Central Asia	4.1	17.5	11.6	13	55	38
Northern, Southern, Western, and Eastern Europe	4.5	18.1	11.4	7	28	18
Northern Europe	1.1	16.6	10.8	0	6	4
Southern Europe	6.1	23.9	17.1	3	12	8
Western Europe	5.4	14.8	7.7	4	10	5
Eastern Europe	3.1	13.6	7.8	3	15	8

TABLE 9 Loss of working hours at the global, regional, and subregional scales (*cont.*)

	Lost work hours (in %)			**Full-time jobs equivalents (48 hours per week in millions)**		
Central and Western Asia	4.8	23.3	18.5	3	14	11

Note: Values equivalent to full-time jobs lost greater than 50 million are rounded to the nearest 5 million; values below that threshold are rounded to the nearest million. The number of full-time equivalent jobs provided is intended to reflect the extent of the estimates of hours lost. The values of full-time equivalent jobs are calculated based on the assumption that the decrease in working hours affected only a subset of full-time workers and that the number of working hours of other workers was not reduced. The figures in this table do not reflect the actual loss of jobs nor the actual increase in the level of unemployment.

SOURCE: ILO, SEPTEMBER 23, 2020. BOLDED FIGURES BY AUTHOR

In other words, we can infer from the above quote that:

1) Material productive forces must be developed so that a new social formation can appear. Here, Marx works on a historical-abstract level that operates on the level of the concept of *social formation*—from the primitive community, through slavery and feudalism, to the current capitalist world society—understood as "material social relations" whose sociological analysis made it possible to scientifically observe regularity and repetition and to synthesize the social systems of the various countries in the concept of "*social formation*" (see Lenin, 1977: 140–141) until apprehending and concretizing the concept of country, region, or locality.
2) The material conditions for the emergence of new relations of production and consumption within the old society must have matured, and the material and institutional conditions such as the state, law, and education must exist to some degree for a material revolution to take place that will drive the development of new relations of production and consumption in accordance with existing social relations.
3) The objectives that humanity sets for itself are only those that it can really achieve once the material conditions for their realization have been created. Within the capitalist mode of production, the objectives set by capital and its enterprises are plausible to achieve only in function of the existence of the material conditions for their realization such as the advances in science and technology or the quantities and masses of labor force necessary to manipulate the instruments and means of

> production to create value and surplus value in sufficient quantity to obtain profits and/or surplus profits for the capitalists, in addition to the political conditions and the correlation of forces being favorable to them in order to promote their plans and impose their class interests. In this sense, neoliberalism as a repressive political regime and management of the capitalist crisis has been fundamental to preserve and recreate the conditions conducive to the reproduction of capital, especially for the speculative financial capital that is dominant in the world.

Every crisis triggers mutations and changes in the economy and society tending to restore the conditions of valorization and profitability of capital. As noted above, for this to occur the material and institutional processes must have been incubated in advance, or at least be in the process of gestation, so that the productive forces and the corresponding type of social relations can be developed. In this sense, the third industrial revolution constitutes the support for the deployment and development of the fourth revolution and for this at the same time to redefine or destroy the industries and devices of the previous third revolution in the sense of Schumpeter's "creative destruction" (1994).

As far as the world of work is concerned, the new means of production and business organization need to adjust the labor force to its requirements, needs, and demands. In this sense, the central hypothesis of this book, which opens up a new line of research in the sociology of labor, holds that the new industrial revolution in the making requires a vast global army of unemployed to serve as leverage for a) the significant reduction in wages, b) the intensification of exploitation and the super-exploitation of labor, c) the disciplining of the workforce to counteract and weaken its collective action, and, d) making work more precarious with the support of the devices of that revolution such as artificial intelligence, Big Data, and algorithms, with the boost from remote work and the home office connected to productive and work processes through cyberspace. A new industrial revolution 4.0 whose course and results will depend on the class struggle between labor and capital as well as on the ability of workers to reverse the capitalist crisis for the benefit of a new mode of production, life, and work, framed in non-capitalist productive, social, and cooperative relations.

For the realization and testing of the hypothesis put forward, an exhaustive academic and empirical investigation is required, which is not part of this book but only the general theoretical-methodological framework to encourage it in the future. It is necessary to investigate the impact and power of the 4.0 revolution in the reduction of human labor in production and consequently of the time socially necessary for the production of goods—for example, automobiles, which has accelerated as a result of the development of science and technology applied to production and work processes in their automated and digital versions. In 1913, the assembly time of a Ford-T model vehicle lasted around 90 minutes; today, a fully assembled Honda Civic leaves the Japanese company's production line every 69 seconds. It is worth noting that in 2003 capital investment in the conception and design of a car, on average, absorbed around 75% of its total cost (Antunes and Sotelo, 2003: 106). 'Hot', of course, that proportion of cost is higher.

1.3.1 Revolution 4.0: Variable or Constant Capital?

As for the relationship between the theory of value and the 4.0 revolution, we only point out some indicative issues. As a starting point for the discussion, we highlight Terranova's (2014) thesis that locates algorithms—as components of information and communication technologies—as a "form of fixed capital" in the same way as Negri (2014): "informatization [i.e., information] remains the most valuable form of fixed capital" and, rather, as means of production (ibid: 08–10). Strictly speaking, constant capital, which allows converting social knowledge (of skilled workers, technicians and engineers, programmers) into exchange value for the capital accumulation of firms. This is of course a point of controversy.

Let us recall that, according to Marx, *constant capital* contains two modalities: fixed capital, referring fundamentally to machines and means of production, and *circulating capital,* which includes raw materials such as oil or lithium. It is *constant* because independently of its volume and physical size its global value is not modified. But—unlike *variable capital* which *does* modify[8] its value based upon its volume and size—constant capital only transfers value to the final product, to the merchandise. It is, therefore, preterit labor, dead labor.[9] And it is *fixed,* because it refers to the material aspect as productive

8 "That part of capital, therefore, which is turned into means of production, i.e. the raw material, the auxiliary material and the instruments of labour, does not undergo any quantitative alteration of value in the process of production. For this reason, I call it the constant part of capital, or more briefly, constant capital. On the other hand, that part of capital which is turned into labour-power does undergo an alteration of value in the process of production. It both reproduces the equivalent of its own value and produces an excess, a surplus-value, which may itself vary, and be more or less according to circumstances. This part of capital is continually being transformed from a constant into a variable magnitude. I therefore call it the variable part of capital, or more briefly, variable capital" (Marx, 1982, *Capital,* Vol. 1. Chapter 6: 317).

9 As Marx (1982, Vol. 1: 146) says: "By turning his money into commodities which serve as the building materials for a new product, and as factors in the labour process, by incorporating living labour into their lifeless objectivity, the capitalist simultaneously transforms value, i.e., past labour in its objectified and lifeless form, into capital, value which can

capital that appears as machinery, installations, buildings, infrastructure *without generating or creating new value*, only transferring it.

Marx's other key concept is *variable capital*, or the proportion of capital that capital invests in the wages that workers receive in exchange for the *sale of* the (use) *value* of their *labor power*. And precisely this *use* that capital buys in the labor market has *two* indissoluble *dimensions*: the physical-muscular value and the brain-intellectual, or cognitive, that the worker deploys in production—both property of the capitalist when they buy and exploit the labor force in order to create surplus value to appropriate and allocate, one part to accumulation and the other to their pockets for enrichment and private consumption.

If we understand by algorithm (see note 63) a set of data and information that serve to instruct solutions to certain problems or to follow the sequential steps marked, for example, by a commercial instruction manual or a user's manual for industrial equipment or a digital screen, it is evident that it must be placed on the side of variable capital and not fixed or constant capital, regardless of whether it is embodied in a material configuration (smartphone, PC, tablets, chips), since it is a genuine product of the human intellect. The fact that the algorithm transfers its cognitive value to the final product, to the commodity, means that it is incorporated into the collective worker, helping to fulfill this function. And the same can be said in relation to artificial intelligence, understood as an "emulation" of human intelligence[10] through machines that supposedly replace it to perform certain functions from the design to the manufacture of goods,[11] in addition to turning human beings and things into "infomatas," a portmanteau coming from the blending of the words "information" and "automatons" (Han, 2021: 15).

As Sadin (2018: 113) puts it:

> ... what characterizes the nature of today's expanding artificial intelligence is not the ability to duplicate our imaginative, creative, or playful resources and ultimately seek to surpass them but the ability to surpass without known measure human brain and cognitive power in certain

perform its own valorization process, an animated monster which begins to 'work', 'as if its body were by love possessed.'"

10 Han (2021:59) rightly observes that artificial intelligence is incapable of reaching the "conceptual level of knowledge," nor of understanding "the results of its calculations".

11 Table 8 corroborates our hypothesis that digitization does not eliminate the material production phase and the work process as some claim but rather maintains manufacturing (such as production manufacturing or the digital plant), which will constitute 28% of the space in the factory of the future.

> specific tasks in order to ensure the management of existing or new activities in an infinitely faster, optimized, and reliable way.

Capital invests in the *use* value of the labor force of engineers, programmers, skilled workers, trainees, and specialized technicians in variable capital to build artificial intelligence that is finally embodied in chips (these are also the product of human labor and, therefore, belong to constant capital) that contain the information and instructions of the operations to achieve these ends.

In fact, after showing the intimate relationship between work and science and between design and execution in relation to Japanese capitalism, this is what Antunes (2005: 114) rightly alludes to when he states that:

> The main mutation within the process of capital production in the 'Toyotized' and flexible factory is not to be found, therefore, in the *conversion of science into the main productive force that substitutes and eliminates labor in the process of value creation but in the growing interaction between labor and science, material and immaterial labor, fundamental elements in the contemporary productive (industrial and service) world.* (Author's italics.)

This interaction between science and labor, between living and dead labor (which is what is expressed in the organic composition of capital) increases productivity (Antunes and Sotelo, 2003: 104–105),

> … provoking the fall of the rate of profit and intensifying the mechanisms of extraction of surplus labor in an ever-shorter time by means of the extension of embodied labor in the technical-scientific machinery –constitutive characteristics of the process of organizational freeze-drying of the 'lean company', as the Spanish sociologist Juan J. Castillo suggestively called it.

Therefore, we insist it is a mistake to unidimensionalize, separate, and/or segment manual labor from intellectual labor—the objective activity of the worker from the subjective one—undermining their intimate dialectical articulation, both with respect to the individual worker as well as the collective. This error is the basis, as we have seen, of the erroneous thesis of the end of labor, which confuses manual labor with intellectual labor. They separate science from the productive process and autonomize it, erasing labor power as the principal and only factor of social wealth, of the production of value and surplus value, that at the same time is the responsibility of the collective worker, involving the labor of various categories of workers who carry out their activities in the sphere of the circulation of capital: transport, commerce, or financial services.

In synthesis, the value of merchandise is the result of the investment in constant capital (means of production used in the production of chips that constitute a sort of 'envelopes' or 'packages' of data and information), variable capital (the total remuneration received by the workers engaged in the construction of Big Data, in the design of algorithms and artificial intelligence), and, finally, in the surplus value produced in the direct production process (of software, hardware) and indirect, through its articulation with the collective worker (in the factories or mines from which raw materials such as lithium are extracted, for example). These value chains that articulate the work and labor processes start from the exploitation of nature, pass through the automated and semi-automated factories in interaction with the collective worker, and conclude in the production of the components of the 4.0 revolution.

1.3.2 Productive and Unproductive Work in the Fourth Industrial Revolution

It remains, finally, to find out whether Big Data and Artificial Intelligence are productive or unproductive activities; whether and how they create surplus value; and whether they do so directly or indirectly.

For Marini (1993a), the collective worker

> ... comprises different types of workers and is organized in differentiated strata, on some levels of which its members move 'on the margins' of the direct producers of value. However, involved like the others in the productive sphere, they are an integral part of the collective worker. Of course, the way in which this collective worker was presented in the middle of the last century has changed: today, laborers are not primarily children nor are higher-level personnel numerically unimportant, and they have diversified considerably. Thus, based on interviews with IBM employees and managers, Reich estimates that less than 20,000 of its 400,000 employees are classified as production workers employed in traditional manufacturing; the vast majority of its personnel are engaged in other activities such as research, design, engineering, sales, and the provision of services.

In his unpublished "Chapter 6: Results of the Direct Production Process," Marx reaffirms the conversion of the individual worker into a collective worker within the capitalist mode of production, expanding in this way its functionality and definition in the production of surplus value. The author of the *Grundrisse*

(1973: 619) affirms that in relation to the *conversion* of the labor process into a *scientific labor process*, "… individual labour as such has ceased altogether to appear as productive, is productive, rather, only in these common labours which subordinate the forces of nature to themselves, and while this elevation of direct labour into social labour appears as a reduction of individual labour to the level of helplessness in face of the communality [*Gemeinsamkeit*] represented by and concentrated in capital …" (in this regard, see Sotelo 2016a, Chapter 2).

According to Marini (1993a), Marx discusses this point in "Chapter XIV" of *Capital*:

> The question of productive labor, although clearly established since Book I as we emphasize, will only be completely rounded off in Chapter XVII of Book III, when studying the mercantile salaried workers.[12] The touchstone here is the distinction between social capital and individual capital.

Based on the above, the research must therefore determine whether the devices (Big Data, algorithms, 3D, Artificial Intelligence) have a direct impact on the accumulation of productive activities and processes for the benefit of the production of surplus value, either by reducing the socially necessary work time (relative surplus value), increasing the working day (absolute surplus value) and the intensity of work or, finally, their combination. In any case, the result is positive insofar as it results in the production of surplus value, so that the various jobs would be productive jobs, in Marx's sense, derived from the social division of labor in accordance with the collective worker of society.

1.3.3 The Digital Factory and the Law of Value

It is not possible to understand the global dimension of the changes that the so-called 4.0 revolution promises to unleash in the terms presented here both in the mode of production and in the world of work if its analysis is not carried out in function and with the tools of the law of value and the restructuring of capital to counteract the fall in the rate of profit, the reduction of economic growth, and the average productivity of social labor in the global system.

12 Indeed, in this chapter Marx (*Capital*, 1991, Vol. III, Chapter XVII: 407–408) resolves the difference regarding the production of surplus value between industrial wage laborers and commercial workers by concluding that: "Just as the labourer's unpaid labour directly creates surplus-value for productive capital, so the unpaid labour of the commercial wage-worker secures a share of this surplus-value" even though it is not responsible for the creation of the latter.

In order to approach the understanding of how the devices of the 4.0 revolution affect (or not) the material production of goods and services (one of the central objectives of capitalism) and, therefore, of value and surplus value (the essential objective), it is necessary to separate in this process 4.0 two dimensions for analytical reasons that, in reality, are articulated and constitute a singular unit.

On the one hand, the software part: Big Data, AI, Algorithms, 3D and Machine Learning (technology that creates systems that learn tasks automatically under human understanding). Here, the information that is directly connected to the sensors or devices that capture the properties of matter (light intensity, temperature, vibration, sound, quantity) is incorporated into the machines or the digital machine system and is elaborated, processed, ordered, and managed. These constitute the *second dimension*: the machinery itself, the digital factory, with levels of automation or "autonomatization" (Coriat; 1992) that can fluctuate between 90% and 100%, depending on the type and characteristics of their manufacture and the proportion they keep with respect to the labor force used.

This means that its organic composition is very high since the relationship with the labor force is superior both in technical terms and in investment of variable capital in relation to constant capital. The few employed workers—subjected to high rates of labor intensity and productivity—have higher than *average* levels of qualification and training to understand and manipulate the operation of machinery and computer systems incorporated into the production of goods.

Figure 3 shows that what constitutes the "cloud"—made up of the elements identified as constituting the fourth industrial revolution (Big Data, Algorithms, AI, Internet of Things, Machine Learning, etc.)—is the product of *general intellect*. In Marx's terminology: the knowledge that creates, processes, and distributes the information that is materially embodied in the products-goods that are made by consumer demand in accordance with the law of value and the production of surplus value. It should be emphasized that through such devices, companies collect millions of data that benefit them by being able to perfect their designs and production lines in "accordance" with the "preferences" of consumers, i.e., of the market.

Many analysts derive their conclusions from this dimension without considering that regardless of whether they are the product of human knowledge and intelligence they only acquire meaning when they are materially embodied in corporeal commodities-products that, therefore, are subject to the law of value, the exploitation of labor, and the accumulation of capital. By not considering this dialectical totality (where the material and the immaterial,

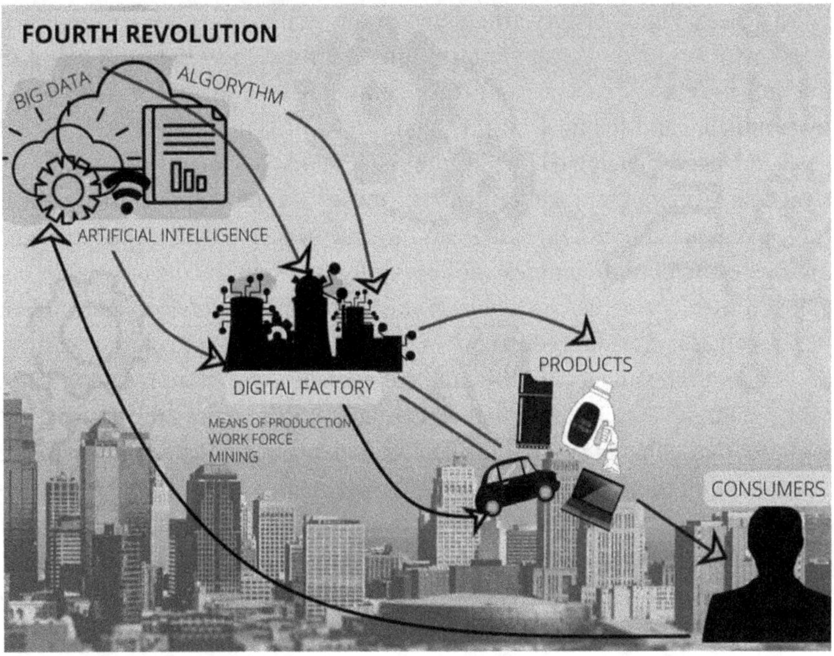

FIGURE 3 The digital factory
SOURCE: DESIGN BY MARIETTA V. SOLANES

use value and exchange value, and concrete and abstract labor are united), conclusions are drawn that are not only hasty but false regarding the fact that capitalism has reached a stage in which it can function *without* the participation of labor power in its double character of being concrete labor and abstract labor, which is the double character that encloses all merchandise and unfolds in the process of labor and capital valorization.

On the contrary, when we glimpse the relationship between such components of the fourth industrial revolution with the devices of the digital machine, the perspective changes.

It is necessary to introduce a *third dimension* made up of raw materials and work tools, starting with the production and mining of, for example, lithium, an essential mineral for the manufacture of batteries, without which 4.0 would simply be useless or difficult to impose.

Here, the cognitive-informatic aspect is intrinsic to the material-brain-intel lectual aspect of the labor force. In this way, information and material production configure the new physiognomy of the digital factory in the context of capitalism's need to restructure itself in order to reestablish its processes of valorization, accumulation, and increased rates of profitability.

The (new) digital factory articulated in the system of computers and platforms with computer sensors transmitting information to the work and production processes replaces both the Fordist-Taylorist factory, based on the assembly line and the mass worker, and the Toyota Production System (TPS) modeled factory, energized by the automated modular system, by *just-in-time*, stress management and work intensity, whose "... central and distinctive feature, in comparison with the American Taylorian way, is that instead of proceeding by destruction of complex workers' knowledge and by decomposition in elementary movements, the Japanese way will proceed by *de-specialization* of professionals to transform them not in parcel workers but into pluri-operators, polyvalent professionals, 'multifunctional workers' ..." (Coriat, 1992: 41). Thus, both paradigms are surpassed in their contents and programmatic designs. But we must clarify that in the new productive and organizational paradigm of the 4.0 revolution the previous forms of production and organization are refunctionalized in the new system, under its hegemony and prerogatives and under the leadership of the companies and the policies implemented by the State.

The *unity* of the three *dimensions*: a) that which incorporates information and platforms, b) the digital factory controlled by computers and information, and, finally, c) the dimension of the extraction and processing of raw materials makes it possible to obtain a vision of totality (Figure 3) of the meaning of the fourth industrial revolution *overdetermined* by the structural contradictions of capitalism, the law of value, and the accumulation of capital.

A merely technological view, which is reductionist, can account for the implications of the aforementioned industrial revolution but in a biased and fetishistic way because it hides the true substance: That this phenomenon takes place in the vicinity of the capitalist mode of production, not outside of it as it is frequently publicized by the business and communication media in conferences, videos, or in commercial advertising. These views present a fetishized world without human participation—a world that is diminished or frankly liquidated—in which the dynamic occurrence of life and the system operates exclusively by the functioning of intelligent machines, simulating and reifying the famous novel by the British writer Aldous Huxley: *Brave New World* (1932) which presents a one-dimensional automated, dystopian society administered by drugs (*soma*) and technology that guarantee that permanent state of "happiness" for the supposed "humans"—rather humanoids who inhabit it (with stylized characters such as Mustafa Mond, Linda, Lenina Crowne, Bernard Marx, Tomakin).

To the extent that capitalism minimizes humanity and turns it into mere merchandise, "[w]e witnesses the disruptive humanization of machines, no longer in the form of a naive anthropomorphism but through the acquisition of qualities that were hitherto considered privative of the human race and that today appear under more reliable and expanded modalities" (Sadin, 2017: 122). Thus, "[t]he original interrelationship of man with nature is transformed into the relationship between wage labour and capital" (Mészáros, 1970: 83); The "... 'real man'—the 'real, human person'—does not actually exist in a capitalist society except in the alienated and reified form in which we encounter him as 'Labour' and 'Capital' (Private Property) antagonistically opposing each other" (Mészáros, 1970: 111).

In this sense, Mészáros (1970: 35) points out that:

> "Alienation is therefore characterised by the universal extension of'saleability' (i.e. the transformation of everything into commodity); by the-conversion of human beings into "things" so that they could appear as commodities on the market (in other words: the "reification" of human relations), and by the fragmentation of the social body into "isolated individuals"

Continuing his point quoting Geothe,, "... all isolated particularity is to be rejected" (apud, 35–36). Additionally, Mészáros notes (36):

> [T]he social order of "civil society" sustains itself only on the basis of the conversion of the various areas of human experience into 'saleable commodities' and it could follow relatively undisturbed its course of development only so long as this universal marketing of all facets of human life, including the most private ones, did not reach its points of saturation.

Against the fetishistic and alienated visions criticized by Mészáros, the three-dimensional perspective raised above breaks the fragmented vision of an alleged post-industrial capitalism of digital platforms that would have replaced the human labor force and no longer have anything to do with the categories and concepts associated with capitalism and its mode of production. This ignores that these concepts and categories have a historical content that the dominant ideology tries to make invisible because "[a] great deal of modern 'functionalism' is, *mutatis mutandis*, an attempt at liquidating historicity" (Mészáros, 1970: 40), which configures a "digital order" that, as Han (2021: 17) emphasizes, is "... numerical, devoid of history and memory [that] consequently, fragments life."

In deference to that ideological and digital order that ends the "*era of truth*" and inaugurates that of the "*post-factual information society*" (Han, 2021: 19) in relation to social analysis, Mészáros comments that "... Marxian ontology is dynamically historical and objectively dynamic. Marx does not 'deduce' human society from the "categories" but, on the contrary, sees the latter as specific modes of existence of the social being" (Mészáros, 1970: 251). And if this social being called capitalism has not substantially changed except in its morphological mutations, the *developed* categories that gave it sustenance and explanation, therefore, remain in their spatio-temporal-historical dimension. As British-Canadian writer Nick Srnicek (2016: 64) states:

> For all the rhetoric of having overcome capitalism and of transitioning to a new mode of production—a rhetoric inherent in the postindustrial thesis of the 1960s, in the ideas of 'new economy' disciples in the 1990s, and in the radical and conservative paeans to the sharing economy of today—we still remain bound to a system of competition and profitability. Platforms offer new forms of competition and control, but in the end profitability is the great arbiter of success.

This conclusion is central to understanding the core of the 4.0 revolution: It precisely reveals not only the fragility of merely descriptive and technical explanations of capitalism's structure and characteristics but also its purpose in the environment of the capitalist mode of production—and by no means in a presumed post-capitalist or post-industrial society—which consists essentially in the attempt to reconstruct and format a metamorphosis of production, the management of the machinery, and the collective labor force in a new articulation and dimension that will make it possible for the system and capital to recover the diminished rates of productivity and profits that have seriously fallen in recent years as a result of the profound historical-structural crisis of capitalism, as we saw in Chapter 3 of this book.

From the point of view of the system—of the State and capital as components of the capitalist social formation—the purpose of promoting the technical-scientific and human devices of the 4.0 revolution is no other than to reinforce these systems, although in the surface propaganda it appears as if it were really able to solve the problems and needs of the working classes and society. In reality, the workers of the world remain subordinated to public and private policies and submit their interests and demands to coercive and ideological-persuasive actions such that people end up accepting them on pain of losing their jobs and income, which are the only means they have to subsist or survive in a world plagued by social inequality.

Moreover, because of the coronavirus, the mandated confinement generated the "demonstration effect" by inducing people to use digital platforms (which they may not have been aware of) to advance the mass use of new technologies in material production in factories and services, where workers become accustomed to accepting new forms and norms of work, exploitation, organization, and labor contracts in accordance with the statutes imposed by the companies supported by the States through labor and institutional reforms that have been carried out in the last two years taking advantage of the "calamities" of the syndemic, supposedly in order to protect the health, employment, and security of the population. But this was done basically to adopt the new mode of exploitation and regulation demanded by the 4.0 revolution, as we said, in order to raise productivity and profitability rates. In this context, remote work and the home office are inserted into the working class with the aim of achieving these systemic objectives of both companies and the State itself as an interacting entity (direct or indirect) in the processes of exploitation, control, and domination of the world of work.

2 Conclusion

The crisis of global capitalism exacerbated by the health pandemic of the coronavirus paved the way for the development and expansion of the industrial revolution in its digital and virtual phase in cyberspace, with all the consequences that we point out for the world of work. With the current perspective of the law of value, we articulate the three dimensions that constitute it: 1) its devices (Big Data, Artificial Intelligence, Internet of Things, etc.), 2) the digital factory connected through sensors that control business engineering, and 3) the process of material production involving raw materials, mining (lithium), and the labor force as a producer of value and surplus value. We conclude that only this integral vision of the totality makes it possible to understand in its right dimension the macro- and micro-changes that capitalist restructuring brings about—and will bring about—with its implementation in the economy and human societies of the 21st century.

Conclusion

Never before has the world capitalist economy been so dependent in terms of its growth possibilities on the epidemic factor derived from the coronavirus pandemic.

To the extent that this disease was not controlled in most countries, the growth balance of the world economy was negative by -3.3% on average in 2020 according to the International Monetary Fund (April 2021). According to the same source, the only country that obtained a positive growth was the Asian giant China with a positive rate of 2.3% in the same year, compared to falls in the United States (-3.5%), Euro Zone (-6.6%), Germany (-4.9%), France (-8.2%), Italy (-8.9%), Spain (-11%), Japan (-4.8%), United Kingdom (-9.9%), and Canada (-5.4%).

Latin America, a dependent and underdeveloped region, was hard hit with a negative balance of -7% with Mexico (-8.2%) and Brazil (-4.1%) standing out, according to the same source.

The IMF (April 2021) suggested a certain recovery by 2021, but this will depend, we must warn, on the immediate and long-term evolution of the regions and countries with respect to the control and cure of the coronavirus. It is, therefore, very difficult to predict what may happen in the future without considering the consequences of the crisis and its contradictions. More convincing is Roberts' argument (May 14, 2021) when he states that:

> If the IMF now says that we will have strong growth, it is mainly due to economies opening up. If a substantial part of an economy has been closed and can now reopen, there will obviously be a strong bounce back. But this pace will not be sustainable. It is really like a sugar rush and as you know, once the sugar is consumed, you feel a little sleepy and down afterwards.

Meanwhile, the capitalist crisis is deepening and seriously affecting jobs, wages, and the labor, living, and working conditions of a large part of humanity.

We have argued that the world economy had been experiencing since the recovery from the 2008–2009 crisis a series of difficulties such as the slowdown in growth, the fall in the rate of profit, and productivity (Roberts, 2016)—phenomena that led to the strengthening of fictitious capital (mainly due to the fall in profitability and the slowdown in the average rate of economic growth); the contraction of the industrial apparatus to the benefit of services and of the speculation of raw material prices; the precarization of labor; and

 | DOI:10.1163/9789004532717_009

the extension of the super-exploitation of labor to advanced countries without breaking with the hegemony of the regime of exploitation and production historically founded on the relative surplus value that integrates the scientific-technological development.

In this regard and from another angle in relation to the "Westernization of systemic Toyotism" in the world, we can affirm with Antunes (2000: 57, author's italics) that such "paradigm"—typical of the third industrial revolution that started in the seventies of the last century although with antecedents from the period after the SGG—is actually a process of mixing that is constituted by " [...] elements present in Japan with existing practices in the new receiving countries, resulting in *a differentiated, particularized, and even singularized process of adaptation of this residuary.*"

This thesis has a positive impact on the theses and problems contemplated by the theory of dependency particularly in Marini's *locus* when we note the differences in the implications of the extension of the super-exploitation of labor under the influence of the impact of export substitution industrialization, which many believed would install at least in the larger countries of the region such as Brazil, Mexico and Argentina the method of production of relative surplus value dynamized by technological development that by increasing the social average productivity of labor would supposedly result in the improvement of the working condition, in the reduction of social work time, and in the increase of wage-remunerations (almost) following the trajectories of the "Western model" of advanced capitalism in the best tradition of Rostow-style development theories. On the contrary, as we have insisted, it so happened that as the regimes prevailed hegemonically in the dependent capitalist countries that rely on the super-exploitation of labor, the impact of both the first industrial revolution in England in the 18th and 19th centuries, and those of the other two that followed (throughout the 20th century until the dawn of the fourth industrial revolution in the late 1970s and 1980s) did nothing more than adjust—mixing and adapting—like Toyotism, with the specific pre-existing historical-structures (economic, social, political, cultural and territorial) of each of the dependent and underdeveloped capitalist social formations adapting it to their needs of accumulation and reproduction of capital for the benefit of the centers of advanced capitalism.

On the other hand, the current industrial revolution 4.0 (digital) is the product of the crisis and exhaustion of the structural and technological devices of the previous revolution (scientific-technical), which began in the 1970s based on the development of automation, computing, and the Internet (Figure 1).

Thus, the digital revolution arises from that crisis and poses a new global restructuring of the capitalist system based on devices that we identify as Big

Data, Internet of Things, artificial intelligence, algorithms, 3D technology, among others.

We recover Marx's approach regarding the conditions required for these changes to take place: a) to have matured the material conditions, the social relations of production and the productive forces in society; b) the awareness on the part of the subjects involved (capitalists, rulers, technical personnel) of the fact that only such objectives are attainable if the material, economic and political conditions for their realization have been previously created.

Without points a and b, it is impossible to make a paradigm shift to another one that is embodied, for example, in the industrial revolution, which, without them, assumes the form of utopia. In the absence of the outbreak of a nuclear war or an environmental catastrophe of planetary scale, the combination of the capitalist crisis with the coronavirus pandemic—or with any other disease that might arise in the future—stimulated the development and expansion of the fourth industrial revolution with the aim of restructuring the ailing world economy, recovering profit rates, and renewing the social relations of exploitation in line with these objectives.

The theoretical-methodological approach of our study—"the impact of the industrial revolution on the world of work"—implies linking said revolution with the law of value and the accumulation of capital to demonstrate that the articulation of the dimensions that constitute it—the cloud of its computer applications, the complex of digitized factories, and mining—is what makes the production of surplus value possible.

Finally, the digital-computerized-automated model—a substitute for the Toyota Production System (TPS) model—has a multidimensional impact on the world of work: in its organization, in increasingly precarious jobs, fluctuating salaries with strong tendencies towards deterioration, as well as labor costs; an increase in the intensity and appropriation of worker subjectivity and its appropriation by capital.

To the extent that this new paradigm is universal and controlled by virtual-informatic means, it contributes to the greater operation of the super-exploitation of labor in advanced capitalist countries, as we said, under the hegemony of relative surplus value, mainly through wage deterioration, flexibility, and the monumental precarization of labor that only in an environment of struggle and resistance of the workers is it possible to counteract and, probably, overcome.

In short, the hypothesis supported in this book assumes that not only workers and the world of work in general are affected but also humanity itself that is being reduced and diminished in terms of its importance and influence, to the extent that the industrial revolution 4.0 extends its tentacles and applications to the domain of the economy, society, nature, and the human spirit.

Bibliography

Aglietta, Michele (2015). *A Theory of Capitalist Regulation: The US Experience.* Verso, New York and London.

Alves, Giovanni (2013). *Dimensões da precarização do trabalho. Ensaios de Sociologia do Trabalho*, Projeto Editorial Praxis, São Paulo.

Alves, Giovanni (2018). *O duplo negativo do capital. Ensaio sobre a crise do capitalismo global.* Praxis. Bauru, São Paulo.

Alves, Giovanni (January-March 2019). "Capitalismo global y superexplotación del trabajo. Breves notas teóricas," in Adrián Sotelo Valencia (editor). *El trabajo en el capitalismo global. Problemáticas y tendencias, Anthropos* no. 250, January-March 2019, Madrid.

Alves, Giovanni (2020). *As contradições metabólicas do capital. Crise ecológica, envelhecimento e extinção humana.* Canal 6-Editora Bauru/SP.

Alves, Giovanni (2021). "A nova precariedade salarial: A ofensiva do capital no limiar da Quarta Revoluo Industrial," in Giovanni Alves (editor), *Trabalho e valor O novo (e precario) mundo do trabalho no século XXI,* Editorial Praxis, 2021, pp. 213–262. https://drive.google.com/file/d/1GsAHmn6Fek-TYbicDuCzhoS33mC8qvtB/view.

Amin, Samir (1999). *Los desafíos de la mundialización*, Siglo XXI, México.

Antunes, Ricardo (2000). *Os sentidos do trabalho: Ensaio sobre a afirmação e a negação do trabalho.* (2ª edição revista e ampliada). São Paulo: Boitempo.

Antunes, Ricardo (2001). *¿Adiós al trabajo?, ensayo sobre las metamorfosis y la centralidad del mundo del trabajo.* Cortez, São Paulo.

Antunes, Ricardo y Sotelo, Adrián (2003). "A crise da sociedade do trabalho. Entre a perenidade e a superfluidade," *Questões do Século XXI*, Edição Especial #100, T. II, Cortez Editora, São Paulo.

Antunes, Ricardo (2005). *Los sentidos del trabajo*, Ediciones Herramienta Buenos Aires.

Antunes, Ricardo (2018). *O privilégio da Servidão. O novo proletariado de serviços na era digital.* BOITEMPO. São Paulo.

Antunes, Ricardo (June 15, 2020). "Cómo se desarrolla la 'uberización' total del trabajo," en *La Haine*, available: https://www.lahaine.org/mundo.php/como-se-desarrolla-la-uberizacion. Consulted June 16, 2020.

Baker, Nick (September 3, 2020) "In the Worst of Times, the Billionaire Elite Plunder Working Class America," CounterPunch, available: https://www.counterpunch.org/2020/09/03/in-the-worst-of-times-the-billionaire-elite-plunder-working-class-america/ Consulted September 13, 2020.

Bambirra, Vania (1978). *Teoría de la dependencia: una anticrítica*, ERA, México.

Baran, Paul and Sweezy, Paul (1966) *Monopoly Capital: An Essay on the American Economic and Social Order.* Modern Reader Paperbacks, New York and London.

Barranco, Carlos Omar (May 21, 2020). "Ciudad Juárez: 600 por ciento de incremento de casos y defunciones en treinta días",In *Norte Digital*, https://nortedigital.mx/ciudad-juarez-600-por-ciento-de-incremento-de-casos-y-defunciones-en-treinta-dias/. Consulted May 25, 2020.

Beck, Ulrich (1992) *Risk Society: Towards a New Modernity*. Sage Publications Ltd, Newbury Park.

Beinstein, Jorge (2001). *Capitalismo senil, a grande crise da economia global*. Rio de Janeiro. Record.

Beinstein, Jorge (Februrary 2009: 63–69). "Las crisis em la era senil del capitalismo. Esperando inútilmente el quinto Kondratieff." *El Viejo Topo* n. 253, Barcelona.

Bellamy, Foster, John (March 11, 2019). "El capitalismo ha fracasado, ¿qué viene a continuación?" *La Haine*, available: https://www.lahaine.org/mundo.php/el-capitalismo-ha-fracasado-ique Consulted June 18, 2020.

Bell, Daniel, (1960). *The End of Ideology*. Free Press, Glencoe.

Bell, Daniel, (1973). *The Coming of Post-industrial Society: A Venture in Social Forecasting*. New York. Basic Books.

Biondi, Guanais, Juliana (2018). *Pagamento por produção, intensificação do trabalho e superexploração na agronindústria canavieira brasileira*. FAPESP-Outras Expressões. São Paulo.

Biondi, Guanais, Juliana y GIL Felix (2018). *Superexploração do trabalho no século XX, debates contemporâneos*. Praxis. Bauru, SP.

Bloom, Nicholas (June 9, 2020) Interview, *La Vanguardia*, available: https://www.lavanguardia.com/lacontra/20200609/481688750649/iremos-a-trabajar-a-la-oficina-pero-solo-dos-o-tres-veces-por-semana.html. Consulted June 12, 2020.

Bolton, John (2020). *The Room Where It Happened*. A *White House Memoir*. Simon&Shuter. New York.

Boyer, Robert (2002) *Regulation Theory: The State of the Art*. Taylor & Francis, New York.

Brenner, Robert (2006) *The Economics of Global Turbulence: The Advanced Capitalist Economies from Long Boom to Long Downturn, 1945–2005*. Verso, New York and London.

brussevich, Mariya, Dabla-Norris, Era, and khalid, Salma (July 9, 2020). "El trabajo a distancia no es una opción para los pobres, los jóvenes y las mujeres." Inter Press Service, Agencia de Noticias. Available: http://www.ipsnoticias.net/2020/07/trabajo-distancia-no-una-opcion-los-pobres-los-jovenes-las-mujeres/. Consulted July 20, 2020.

Carcanholo, Reinaldo (2013). *Capital, essência e aparência*, Vol. 1 and Vol. 2, Expressão Popular, São Paulo.

Carcanholo, Reinaldo, and Nakatani, Paulo (2015). "Capitalismo especulativo e alternativas para América Latina," in Gomes, Helder (editor), *Especulação e lucros fictícios. Formas parasitárias de acumulação contemporânea, Outras Expressões*, SP, 2015, pp. 89–124.

Castel, Robert (1998). *As metamorfoses da questão social. Uma crónica do salário.* Editora Vozes, Petrópolis.

Chesnais, Françoise (November 1993) "A fisionomia das crises no regime de acumulação sob dominância financeira," In: *Novos Estudos*, CEBRAP, no. 52. pp. 21–53.

Collins, Chuck, Ocampo, Omar, and Paslaski, Siphia (April 23, 2020). *Billionaire Bonanza 2020: Wealth Windfalls, Tumbling, Taxes, and Pandemic Profiteers.* Institute for Policy Studies. Available: https://ips-dc.org/wp-content/uploads/2020/04/Billionaire-Bonanza-2020.pdf. Consulted April 28, 2020.

Colmenarez, Silva Simón (March 25, 2015) Interview by *Telesur.* Available: https://www.youtube.com/watch?v=_lJlh2NZnio. Consulted June 31, 2020.

Colmenárez, Silva, Simón (2014). *Huellas neoliberales, hegemonía y neocolonialismo del Estado burgués capitalista.* Fondo Editorial de la Asamblea Nacional. William Lara, Caracas. Consulted June 31, 2020.

Coriat, Benjamín (1985). El taller y el cronómetro. México, Siglo XXI.

Coriat, Benjamín (1992). Pensar al revés. Siglo XXI. México.

Cueva, Agustín (1993, 14ª. Edición). *El desarrollo del capitalismo en América Latina.* Siglo XXI. México.

Dardot, Pierre and Laval, Christian (July 24, 2019). "El desorden global: anatomía del nuevo neoliberalismo," *La Haine*, available: https://www.lahaine.org/mundo.php/el-desorden-global-anatomia-del. Consulted July 29, 2020.

De Bernis, Gerard (1988). *El capitalismo contemporáneo,* Editorial Nuestro Tiempo, México.

De Oliveira, Eurenice (2004). *Toyotismo no Brasil, desencantamento da fábrica, envolvimento e resistência.* Expressão Popular. São Paulo.

Dos Santos, Theotonio (1971). *La crisis norteamericana y América Latina.* Ediciones Prensa Latinoamericana. Santiago.

Dos Santos, Theotonio (1987). *Revolução técnico-científica e acumulação de capital.* Vozes. Petrópolis.

Dos Santos, Theotonio (2002). *La teoría de la dependencia. Balance y perspectivas,* Plaza&Janés, México.

Dos Santos, Theotonio (2004). *Economía mundial. La integración latinoamericana.* Plaza&Janés, México.

Duffin, Erin, "U.S.—Real GDP growth by year 1990–2019," in: *Statista*, February 3, 2020. Available: https://www.statista.com/statistics/188165/annual-gdp-growth-of-the-united-states-since-1990/. Consulted June 23, 2020.

Engels, Frederick (2010) "Outlines of the Critique of Political Economy," in *Marx & Engles Collected Works: Volume 29, Marx 1857–61.* Lawrence & Wishart, London. Available: https://www.marxists.org/archive/marx/works/1844/df-jahrbucher/outlines.htm

Fachin, Patricia (March 13, 2021). "El capitalismo de plataforma y su impacto en la reorganización del trabajo," Interview of Callum Cant *Viento Sur.* Available:

https://vientosur.info/el-capitalismo-de-plataforma-y-su-impacto-en-la-reorganizacion-del-trabajo/. Consulted March 15, 2021.

Fazio, Carlos (April 5 2020). *La jornada*, "Lawfare y guerra asimétrica vs. Venezuela," Available: https://www.jornada.com.mx/2020/04/05/opinion/023a1mun Consulted April 5 2020.

Felix, Gil (2019). *Mobilidade e superexploração do trabalho. O enigma da circulação*, FAPESP-Lamparina Editora, RJ.

Frank, Andre Gunder (1969). *Latin America: Underdevelopment or Revolution*. First Modern Reader, New York and London.

Fukuyama, Francis, *The End of History and the Last Man*, The Free Press, New York, 1992.

Furtado, Celso (1966.). *Subdesenvolvimento e Estagnação na América Latina*, Editôra Civilização Brasileira, Rio de Janeiro.

Gallegos, Rocío y Gabriela Minjárez (October 26 2020). "En emergencia por covid-19, las maquilas trabajan con mayor actividad," Pie de Página. Available: https://piedepagina.mx/en-emergencia-por-covid-19-las-maquilas-trabajan-con-mayor-actividad/. Consulted October 28 2020.

Germani, Gino (1968). *Política y sociedad en una época de transición*. Paidós Buenos Aires.

Gorz, André (1980). *Farwell to the Working Class: An Essay on Post-Industrial Socialism*. Pluto Press, London.

Gorz, André (1982). *Adiós al proletariado. Más allá del socialismo*. El Viejo Topo, Barcelona.

Gorz, Andre (1988). *Critique of Economic Reason*. Verso, London New York.

Gorz, André (1997). *Metamorfosis del trabajo*, Editorial Sistema, Madrid.

Gorz, Andre (1999). *Reclaiming Work: Beyond the Wage-Based Society*. Polity Press, Malden.

Gorz, André (2003, 2ª reimp). *Miserias del presente, riqueza posible*, Paidós, Buenos Aires.

Gorz, André (January 7 2008). «Le travail dans la sortie du capitalisme, » in *Ecoren, Revue Critique d'Ecologie Politique*. Available: http://ecorev.org/spip.php?article641.

Gould, Elise (May 8, 2020). "A waking nightmare. Today's Jobs report shows 20.5 million jobs lost in April," *Economic Policy Institute*. Available: https://www.epi.org/press/a-waking-nightmare-todays-jobs-report-shows-20-5-million-jobs-lost-in-april/?utm_source=Economic+Policy+Institute&utm_campaign=9f1d451bfd-EMAIL_CAMPAIGN_2019_02_22_11_12_COPY_01&utm_medium=email&utm_term=0_e7c5826c50-9f1d451bfd-59324437&mc_cid=9f1d451bfd&mc_eid=abecff23e5. Consulted May 17, 2020.

Gould, Elise and Kassa, Melat (14 de octubre de 2020). "Young workers hit hard by the COVID-19 economy," Economic Policy Institute. Available : https://www.epi.org/publication/young-workers-covid-recession/?utm_source=Economic+Policy+Institute&utm_campaign=3b154ae817-EMAIL_CAMPAIGN_2019_02_21_07_37_COPY_01&utm_medium=email&utm_term=0_e7c5826c50-3b154ae817-60019701&mc_cid=3b154ae817&mc_eid=9d8953a98c. Consulted October 17, 2020.

Gounet, Thomas, *Fordismo e toyotismo na civilização do automóvel*, Boitempo, São Paulo, 1999.

Grupo Krisis (2018). Manifiesto contra el trabajo, VIRUS editorial, Barcelona. Disponible en: https://www.viruseditorial.net/paginas/pdf.php?pdf=manifiesto-.

Guillén, Romo, Héctor (2005). *México frente a la mundialización neoliberal.* ERA, México.

Habermas, Jurgen (1984) *The Theory of Communicative Action, Vol 1., Reason and the Rationalization of Society*. Beacon Press, Boston.

Hammer, J. and Champy, James (1994). *Reingeniería*, Norma, 5ª reimpresión, Bogotá.

Han, Byung-Chul (2021). *No-cosas. Quiebras del mundo de hoy*. Taurus: México.

Harvey, David (2010) *The Enigma of Capital: And the Crises of Capitalism.* Oxford University Press, USA.

Husson, Michel (January 9, 2021). "Robotización, productividad y Covid-1." *La Haine*, Available: https://www.lahaine.org/mundo.php/robotizacion-productividad-y-covid-19. Consulted January 10, 2021.

Kelly, Kevin (1997). "New Rules for the New Economy: Twelve Dependable Principles for Thriving in a Turbulent World," *Wired Magazine*, No. 11, 1997, pp. 140–197. Available: https://www.wired.com/1997/09/newrules/.

Kennedy, Paul (1987) *The Rise and Fall of the Great Powers*. Random House, New York.

Klein, Naomi (2007). *The Shock Doctrine.* New York: Metropolitan Books.

Klein, Naomi (May 8, 2020) "Screen New Deal: Under Cover of Mass Death, Andrew Cuomo Calls in the Billionaires to Build a High-Tech Dystopia," in *The Intercept*. Available: https://theintercept.com/2020/05/08/andrew-cuomo-eric-schmidt-coronavirus-tech-shock-doctrine/. Consulted January 3, 2021.

Kohan, Néstor (2013). *mercancía y poder en el pensamiento de Karl Marx*, Editorial Biblos, Buenos Aires.

Lenin, V.I. (1963) "Imperialism, the Highest Stage of Capitalism," In *Lenin's Selected Works*, Vol. 1, Progress Publishers, Moscow.

Lenin, V.I. (1977) "What the 'Friends of the People' Are and How They Fight the Social-Democrats," In *Lenin's Selected Works*, Vol. 1, Progress Publishers, Moscow.

Levitt, Theodore (May 1983). "The Globalization of Markets," *Harvard Business Review*, Available: https://hbr.org/1983/05/the-globalization-of-markets.

Lévy, Pierre (2004). *Inteligencia colectiva*. Washington, DC, Available: https://ciudadanosconstituyentes.files.wordpress.com/2016/05/lc3a9vy-pierre-inteligencia-colectiva-por-una-antropologc3ada-del-ciberespacio-2004.pdf. Consulted August 4 2020.

Lukács, György (1978). *The Ontology of Social Being*. Merlin Press, London.

Lust, Jan (January 7, 2021). "El carácter estructural de la precariedad laboral en el Perú." *La Haine*. Available: https://www.lahaine.org/mundo.php/el-caracter-estructural-de-la. Consulted January 8, 2021.

Lyotard, Jean-François (1984). *The Postmodern Condition: A Report on Knowledge*. Manchester University Press, Manchester.

Mandel, Ernest (1976). *Late Capitalism*. NLB, London.

Mandel, Ernest (1995). *Long Waves of Capitalist Development: A Marxist Interpretation*. Verso, London.

Mandel, Michael (December 26, 1996). "The Triumph of the New Economy: A Powerful Payoff from Globalization and the Info Revolution," *Bloomberg*. Available: https://www.bloomberg.com/news/articles/1996-12-29/the-triumph-of-the-new-economy. Consulted October 23, 2019.

Marini, Ruy Mauro (1973). *Dialéctica de la dependencia*. ERA, México.

Marini, Ruy Mauro (1978). "Las razones del neodesarrollismo" (respuesta a Fernando Enrique Cardoso y José Serra), Revista Mexicana de Sociología, Año XL/vol. XL, núm. extraordinario, México, IIS-UNAM, pp.57–106.

Marini, Ruy Mauro (1979, pp. 37–55). "El ciclo del capital en la economía dependiente," in Úrsula Oswald (coord.), *Mercado y dependencia*, Nueva Imagen México.

Marini, Ruy Mauro (1985). *Subdesarrollo y revolución*. Siglo XXI. México. 12ª Ed.

Marini, Ruy Mauro (1993). "Preface" to the book by Adrián Sotelo *México: dependencia y modernización*, Ediciones El Caballito, México. Available: http://www.marini-escritos.unam.mx/082_mexico_modernizacion.html.

Marini, Ruy Mauro (1993a). "El concepto de trabajo productivo," available: http://www.marini-escritos.unam.mx/078_trabajo_productivo.html#_ednref1. Consulted October 17, 2020.

Marini, Ruy Mauro (1995: pp. 17–41). "La década de 1970 revisitada," in Marini y Millán (coord.). *La teoría social latinoamericana*, Vol. III. Ediciones el Caballito, México.

Marini, Ruy Mauro (April-June 1979). "Plusvalía extraordinaria y acumulación de capital," *Cuadernos Políticos*, n. 20, México, April-June 1979, pp. 19–39. Available: http://www.marini-escritos.unam.mx/057_plusvalia_extraordinaria.html.

Marini, Ruy Mauro (July-September 1977, pp. 76–84). "Estado y crisis en Brasil," in *Cuadernos Políticos*, núm. 13, México.

Marini, Ruy Mauro (1996, pp. 49–68). "Proceso y tendencias de la globalización capitalista," in Marini y Millán (coord.), *La teoría social latinoamericana: Cuestiones contemporáneas*, Vol. IV. México, Ediciones El Caballito.

Marini, Ruy Mauro (2022) *Dialectics of dependency*, Monthly Review Press, NY.

Martins, Carlos Eduardo (2011). *Globalização, dependência e neoliberalismo na América Latina*, Boitempo Editorial, São Paulo.

Martins, Carlos Eduardo (September-December 2017). "Algumas reflexões sobre o conceito de superexploração do trabalho," in *Revista da Sociedade Brasileira de Economía Política*, Vol. 48, RJ, pp. 28–43.

Martins, Carlos Eduardo (2020). *Dependency, Neoliberalism, and Globalization in Latin America*. Brill, Leiden-BOSTON.

Marx, Karl (1904). "Preface" in *A Contribution to the Critique of Political Economy*. Charles H. Kerr & Company, Chicago.

Marx, Karl (1973). Grundrisse: *Foundations of the Critique of Political Economy (Rough Draft)*. Penguin Books in association with New Left Review, London.

Marx, Karl (1982) *Capital: A Critique of Political Economy*. Vol. 1, Penguin Books in association with New Left Review, London.

Marx, Karl (1982a, T.I). *Elementos fundamentales para la crítica de la economía política (Grundrisse)* 1857–1858, T.I., Siglo XXI, 12ª Ed, México.

Marx, Karl (1991) *Capital: A Critique of Political Economy*. Vol. III, Penguin Books in association with New Left Review, London.

Marx, Karl (2010). "Letter from Marx to Pavel Vasilyevich Annenkov, December 28, 1846" in *Marx & Engels Collected Works, Volume 38: Letters 1844–51*. Lawrence & Wishart, London.

Marx, Karl (2010a). "Chapter 6. Results of the Direct Production Process (draft)" in *Marx & Engels Collected Works, Volume 34: Marx 1861–64*. Lawrence & Wishart, London.

Mattis, James N. and Hoffman, Frank G. (2005). "Future Warfare: The Rise of Hybrid Wars." *U.S. Naval Institute* (USNI). Available: http://milnewstbay.pbworks.com/f/MattisFourBlockWarUSNINov2005.pdf. Consulted July 14, 2020.

Méda, Dominique (1995). *Le Travail. Une Valeur en vie de Disparition*, Aubier, Paris.

Merritt, Tapia (2016). *Cambio tecnológico y empleo: el futuro del trabajo a la luz de su automatización*, Colofón, México.

Mészáros, István (1970) *Marx's Theory of Alienation*. The Merlin Press Ltd, London.

Mészáros, István (1995). *Beyond Capital: Towards a Theory of Transition*. The Merlin Press Ltd, London.

Meza, Naycli (February 6, 2019). "Maquila dividida," *Reporte índigo*. Available: https://www.reporteindigo.com/indigonomics/maquila-industria-dividida-criticas-condiciones-laborales-desigualdad-economia/.

Miller, Riel (1999). "The Future of the Global Economy: Towards a Long Boom?," *OECD Observer* No. 217/218, Summer 1999. Available: https://www.researchgate.net/publication/285206517_The_future_of_the_global_economy_Towards_a_long_boom. Consulted July 9, 2020.

Mischel, Lawrence and Bivens, Josh (May 13, 2021). "Identifying the Policy Levers Generating Wage Suppression and Wage Inequality," Economic Policy Institute. Available: https://www.epi.org/unequalpower/publications/wage-suppression-inequality/. Consulted May 21, 2021.

Mittelman, James (2000) *The Globalization Syndrome*. Princeton University Press, Princeton.

Morley, Morris (1999) "Neoliberal Political Cycles" in Petras, James (editor) *The Left Strikes Back: Class Conflict in the Age of Neoliberalism*. Latin American Perspectives. Westview Press, Boulder.

Mould, Oli (2019). *Contra la creatividad. Capitalismo y domesticación del talento*. Alfabeto, Madrid.

Naville, Pierre (1985). *¿Hacia el automatismo social? Problemas del trabajo y de la automación*. FCE, México.

Negri, Antonio (2014). "Some Reflections on the #Accelerate Manifesto," in: Avanessian, Armen and Reis, Mauro (editors), *#Accelerate: The Accelerationist Reader*. Urbanomic, Falmouth.

Novoa, Girón, Sergio. (2019) "Trabajo y subjetividad," in Sotelo, Adrián (editor). *El trabajo en el capitalismo global. Problemáticas y tendencias*. Revista *Anthropos*, Madrid, no. 250, January-March 2019: 179–191.

Offe, Claus (1985). "Work: The Key Sociological Category?," in Claus Offe (editor) *Disorganized Capitalism*. Cambridge, The MIT Press, pp. 129–150.

Olías, Laura (August 31, 2020). "Derechos y obligaciones del teletrabajo," in *Rebelión*. Available: https://rebelion.org/derechos-y-obligaciones-del-teletrabajo/. Consulted September 4, 2020.

Oprinari, Pablo (May 31, 2020). "Maquiladoras y COVID: explotación capitalista y resistencia obrera en la frontera norte de México," *La izquierda diario*. Available: http://www.laizquierdadiario.mx/Maquiladoras-explotacion-capitalista-y-resistencia-obrera-en-la-frontera-norte-de-Mexico. Consulted June 3, 2020.

Porteous, D. and Smith, S. (2001) *Domicide: The Global Destruction of Home*. McGill-Queen's University Press, Montreal.

Pérez, Carlota (2002) *Technological Revolutions and Financial Capital: The Dynamics of Bubbles and Golden Ages*. Edward Elgar Publishing, Cheltenham.

Perondi, Eduardo (2020). *El proceso de precarización del trabajo en México y Brasil (1994–2018): un análisis desde la economía política*, Doctorate thesis in Latin American Studies [Estudios Latinoamericanos], Programa de Posgrado en Estudios Latinoamericanos, FCPyS, UNAM, México.

Pilotzi, Julio (July 15, 2020). "Regreso a la normalidad en procesos industriales," *Forbes*. Available: https://www.forbes.com.mx/regreso-a-la-normalidad-en-procesos-industriales/. Consulted September 15, 2020.

Piqueras, Andrés (2014). *La opción reformista: entre el despotismo y la revolución. Una explicación del capitalismo histórico a través de las luchas de clase*, Anthropos, Madrid.

Piqueras, Andrés (2018). *Las sociedades de las personas sin valor. Cuarta revolución industrial, des-substanciación del capital, desvalorización generalizada*. El Viejo Topo, Madrid.

Piqueras, Andrés and Dierckxsens, Win (2018a). *O capital frente ao seu declínio*, Expressão Popular, São Paulo.

Polanyi, Karl (2001) *The Great Transformation: The Political and Economic Origins of Our Time*. Beacon Press, Boston.

Postone, Moishe (2003) *Time, Labor, and Social Domination*. Cambridge University Press, Cambridge.

Ramonet, Ignacio (25 de abril de 2020). *La jornada*. Consultado el 27 de abril de 2020.

Reich, Robert (1992) *The Work of Nations*. Penguin Random House, New York.

Reilly, Katie (September 13, 2018). "'I Work 3 Jobs and Donate Blood Plasma To Pay the Bills.': This is What It's Like To Be a Teacher in America." *Time*. Available: https://time.com/longform/teaching-in-america/). Consulted May 22, 2020.

Ribeiro, Silvia (May 19, 2021) "Enfrentar al capitalismo digital," *Desinformémonos*. Available:https://desinformemonos.org/enfrentar-al-capitalismo-digital/.Consulted May 22, 2021.

Riechmman, Jorge (September 7, 2020). "Decrecer, desdigitalizar —quince tesis," *15/15/15 Revista Para Una Nueva Civilización*. Available: https://www.15-15-15.org/webzine/2020/09/07/decrecer-desdigitalizar-quince-tesis/#vueltanota24. Consulted January 1, 2021.

Rifkin, Jeremy (1995). *The End of Work: The Decline of the Global Labor Force and the Dawn of the Post-Market Era*. Putnam Publishing Group. New York.

Rifkin, Jeremy (2001) *The Age of Access: The New Culture of Hypercapitalism*. Penguin Random House, New York.

Roberts, Michael (2016) *The Long Depression: Marxism and the Global Crisis of Capitalism*. Haymarket Books, Chicago.

Roberts, Michael (November 4, 2019). "US rate of profit measures for 2018." *The Next Recession*. Available: https://thenextrecession.wordpress.com/2019/11/04/us-rate-of-profit-measures-for-2018/ Consulted November 19, 2020.

Roberts, Michael (September 13, 2020). "The US rate of profit before the COVID" *The Next Recession*. Available: https://thenextrecession.wordpress.com/2020/09/13/the-us-rate-of-profit-before-the-covid/ Consulted September 19, 2020.

Roberts, Michael (September 20, 2020). "More on a world rate of profit." *The Next Recession*. Available: https://thenextrecession.wordpress.com/2020/09/20/more-on-a-world-rate-of-profit/ Consulted October 2, 2020.

Roberts, Michael (December 2, 2020). "A credit crash ahead?" *The Next Recession*. Available:https://thenextrecession.wordpress.com/2020/12/02/a-credit-crash-ahead/ Consulted December 14, 2020.

Roberts, Michael (January 20, 2021). "Biden's four years." *The Next Recession*. Available: https://thenextrecession.wordpress.com/2021/01/20/bidens-four-years/ Consulted January 29, 2021.

Roberts, Michael (January 25, 2021). "Covid and fictitious capital" *The Next Recession*. Available: https://thenextrecession.wordpress.com/2021/01/25/covid-and-fictitious-capital/ Consulted January 31, 2021.

Roberts, Michael (May 14, 2021). "Some notes on the world economy now." *The Next Recession*. Available: https://thenextrecession.wordpress.com/2021/05/14/some-notes-on-the-world-economy-now/ Consulted May 15, 2021.

Robinson, William I. (2008). *Latin America and Global Capitalism: A Critical Globalization Perspective (Johns Hopkins Studies in Globalization)*. The Johns Hopkins University Press, Baltimore.

Robinson, William I. (2014). *Global Capitalism and the Crisis of Humanity.* Cambridge University Press, Cambridge.

Rostow, W.W. (1971). *The Stages of Economic Growth. A Non-Communist Manifesto.* Cambridge University Press, Cambridge.

Rubin, I.I. (1972). *Essays on Marx's Theory of Value*. Black and Red, Detroit.

Sadin, Éric (2017). *La humanidad aumentada. La administración digital del mundo.* Caja Negra, Buenos Aires.

Sadin, Éric (2018). *La silicolonización del mundo. La irresistible expansión del liberalismo*, Caja Negra, Buenos Aires.

Salas, Nicás, Sergio, Llorens, Serrano, Clara, Navarro, Alberto and Moncada, Lluís Salvador (June 2020). "Condiciones de trabajo, inseguridad y salud en el contexto del COViD-19: estudio de la población asalariada de la encuesta COTS. Barcelona: UAB, ISTAS-CCOO." Available: https://www.ccoo.es/5a2456b71be76180daaf0ffd563d62eb000001.pdf. Consulted July 19, 2020.

Santos, B. de Sousa (2018) *The End of the Cognitive Empire: The Coming of Age of Epistemologies of the South.* Duke University Press, Durham.

Sassen, Saskia (2014) *Expulsions: Brutality and Complexity in the Global Economy.* Harvard University Press, Boston.

Schumpeter, Joseph (1994) *Capitalism, Socialism, and Democracy.* Routledge, London and New York.

Shaikh, Anwar (2006). *Valor, acumulación y crisis. Ensayos de economía política.* Ediciones RYR, Buenos Aires.

Smith, Ashley (November 6, 2019). "Rebellion, Reformism, and Reaction in Latin America: An Interview with Jeffery R. Webber" *Verso Books*. Available: https://www.versobooks.com/blogs/4477-rebellion-reformism-and-reaction-in-latin-america-an-interview-with-jeffery-r-webber. Consulted November 25, 2019.

Solow, Robert (July 12, 1987). "We'd better watch out," New York Times Book Review. Available: http://www.standupeconomist.com/pdf/misc/solow-computer-productivity.pdf. Consulted January 14, 2021.

Sotelo Valencia, Adrián (2005). *América Latina, de crisis y paradigmas: la teoría de la dependencia en el siglo XXI*. Coedición Plaza y Valdés-FCPyS-UOM, México.

Sotelo Valencia, Adrián (2010). *Crisis capitalista y desmedida del valor: un enfoque desde los Grundrisse*. Editorial ITACA-UNAM-FCPyS, México.

Sotelo Valencia, Adrián (2014) *México (re)cargado. Dependencia, neoliberalismo y crisis.* Coedición Editorial Itaca-FCPyS-UNAM, México, 2014.

Sotelo, Valencia Adrián (October 4, 2015). "Encrucijadas, límites y perspectivas del ciclo progresista en América latina," *La Haine*. Available: https://www.lahaine.org/mundo.php/encrucijadas-limites-y-perspectivas-del.

Sotelo, Valencia, Adrián (2016). *Precariado ou proletariado?.* Editora Praxis, Bauru, São Paulo.

Sotelo, Valencia, Adrián (2016a). *The Future of Work: Super-exploitation and Social Precariousness in the 21st Century.* Brill, Leiden-Boston.

Sotelo, Valencia, Adrián (November 30, 2019). "Bolivia: del progresismo al golpe de Estado y la réplica de Guaidó." *La Haine.* Available: https://www.lahaine.org/mm_ss_mundo.php/bolivia-del-progresismo-al-golpe.

Sotelo, Valencia, Adrián (December 17, 2019). "T-MEC, 'agregados laborales' o injerencia colonialista de EEUU en México." *La Haine.* Available: https://www.lahaine.org/mm_ss_mundo.php/t-mec-agregados-laborales-o.

Sotelo, Valencia, Adrián (March 20, 2020). "México: el T-MEC y la dependencia estructural," *La Haine.* Available : https://www.lahaine.org/mm_ss_mundo.php/mexico-el-t-mec-y.

Sotelo, Valencia Adrián (April 6, 2020). "El Covid-19 y el mundo del trabajo," *La Haine.* Available: http://lhblog.nuevaradio.org/b2-img/Covid19.pdf.

Sotelo, Valencia, Adrián (April 23, 2020). "El Covid-19 en un mundo multipolar," *Rebelión,* https://rebelion.org/el-covid-19-en-un-mundo-multipolar/.

Sotelo, Valencia, Adrián (2020). U*nited States in a World in Crisis: The Geopolitics of Precarious Work and Super-Exploitation.* Brill, Leiden-Boston.

Srnicek, Nick (2016) *Platform Capitalism.* Wiley, New York.

Steindl, Josef (1976). *Maturity and Stagnation in American Capitalism.* Monthly Review Press, New York. 185.

Stiglitz, Joseph (2002) *Globalization and Its Discontents.* W.W. Norton & Company Inc., New York.

Sweezy, Paul and Magdoff, Harry (2009) *Stagnation and the Financial Explosion,* Vol. IV. NYU Press, New York.

Teruggi, Marco (May 26, 2020). "Las implicaciones de la llegada de los barcos petroleros iraníes a Venezuela," *La Haine.* Available: https://www.lahaine.org/mundo.php/las-implicancias-de-la-llegada. Consulted May 29, 2020.

Terranova, Tiziana (2014) "Red Stack Attack! Algorithms, Capital, and the Automation of the Common," in: Avanessian, Armen and Reis, Mauro (editors), *#Accelerate: The Accelerationist Reader.* Urbanomic, Falmouth.

Valenzuela, Feijóo, José (2017). *¿De la crisis neoliberal al nacionalismo fascistoide? México y Estados Unidos.* Universidad Autónoma Metropolitana-Iztapalapa. México.

Varela, Raquel. (December 11, 2020). "El teletrabajo convierte en tortura nuestras casas," Interview of Mónica Salas for *El Faro de Vigo* of Galicia. Available: https://finlandiaestacion.com/2020/12/11/raquel-varela-el-teletrabajo-convierte-en-tortura-nuestras-casas/. Consulted December 31, 2020.

Weil, Simone (2014). *La condición obrera,* Editorial Trotta, Madrid.

Zuboff, Shoshana (2019). *The Age of Surveillance Capitalism: The Fight for a Human Future at the New Frontier of Power.* Profile Books, London.

Other Sources Consulted

ANIMAL POLÍTICO (January 11, 2021). "Empleos recuperados en México durante la pandemia son eventuales y mal pagados," available at: https://www.animalpolitico.com/2021/01/empleos-recuperados-pandemia-eventuales-mal-pagados/.

BANCO DE MEXICO (May 26, 2020: 94). Informe Trimestral enero-marzo 2020, at: https://www.banxico.org.mx/publicaciones-y-prensa/informes-trimestrales/%7B23C2DCA8-4AD3-FBE0-B0BF-4D30C8066B84%7D.pdf. Accessed June 27, 2020.

BBC News (October 4, 2020). "Coronavirus and telecommuting: 5 'office of the future' models emerging thanks to the pandemic," at: https://www.bbc.com/mundo/noticias-54356853. Accessed October 5, 2020.

BBC News (October 9, 2020). "Covid-19 is not a pandemic: the scientists who believe coronavirus is a syndemic (and what this means for its treatment)," at: https://www.bbc.com/mundo/noticias-54386816. Accessed October 12, 2020.

CAM (July 15, 2020). Research Report 132: "The social costs of the Covid-19 pandemic." Faculty of Economics, UNAM, Mexico. Available online: https://cam.economia.unam.mx/reporte-de-investigacion-132-los-costos-sociales-por-la-pandemia-del-covid-19/?fbclid=IwAR1eRLQTxwJrH-cfzh05cgNe0k9_qjkSCcZr8MNYprIxLGnxSUOXc-UfM08. Accessed July 15, 2020.

CAM (March 24, 2021). Special Research Report 135: "El poder adquisitivo del salario de las profesoras y los profesores de la UNAM: 2001–2021". Faculty of Economics, UNAM, Mexico. Available online: https://cam.economia.unam.mx/category/reportes-especiales/. Accessed June 18, 2021.

Castilian Left (August 15, 2020). "El trabajo en domicilio. De las tricotosas al teletrabajo." La Haine, at: https://www.lahaine.org/est_espanol.php/el-trabajo-en-domicilio-de. Accessed August 22, 2020.

CEFP, Centro de Estudios de las Finanzas Públicas-Cámara de Diputados (May 29, 2020). Reporte Económico: "Indicadores de Establecimientos IMMEX."

Coneval (July 27, 2020). Communiqué: "Ante la crisis sanitaria por la Covid-19, el CONEVAL presenta información referente a la pobreza laboral con la Encuesta Telefónica de Ocupación y Empleo (ETOE)." Available at: https://www.coneval.org.mx/SalaPrensa/Comunicadosprensa/Documents/2020/COMUNICADO_017_POBREZA_LABORAL_CON_LA_ETOE.pdf. Accessed July 27, 2020.

Congress of the United States (July 23, 2020). Washington, DC 20515, at: https://waysandmeans.house.gov/sites/democrats.waysandmeans.house.gov/files/documents/20200723%20House%20Ltr%20to%20DOL%20and%20USTR%20re%20USMCA%20Funding%20for%20Worker%20Centered%20Programs.pdf. Accessed August 3, 2020.

DEPARTMENT OF LABOR, U.S. BUREAU OF LABOR STATISTICS (July 2, 2020). "The Employment Situation." At: https://www.bls.gov/news.release/pdf/empsit.pdf. Accessed July 12, 2020.

ECLAC (September 2010), Economic Survey of Latin America and the Caribbean, 2009–2010, "Impacto distributivo de las políticas públicas," Santiago, 2010. Available at: https://repositorio.cepal.org/bitstream/handle/11362/1070/1/2009-2010_es.pdf.

ECLAC (2019). Preliminary Overview of the Economies of Latin America and the Caribbean, 2019 (LC/PUB.2019/25-P). Santiago, 2019. Available at: https://repositorio.cepal.org/bitstream/handle/11362/45000/125/S1901097_es.pdf. Accessed January 18, 2020.

ECLAC (April 21, 2020). Informe Especial#2, Covid-19, Dimensionar los efectos del COVOD-19 para pensar en la reactivación¸ United Nations, Santiago. Available at: https://repositorio.cepal.org/bitstream/handle/11362/45445/4/S2000286_es.pdf. Accessed May 28, 2020.

ECLAC (August 26, 2020). Special Report no. 7, Covid-19: "Universalizing access to digital technologies to address the effects of COVID-19," United Nations, available at: https://repositorio.cepal.org/bitstream/handle/11362/45938/4/S2000550_es.pdf. Accessed August 28, 2020.

ECLAC (April 3, 2020). Informe Especial#1, Covid-19, América Latina y el Caribe ante la pandemia del COVID-19. Efectos económicos y sociales, United Nations, Santiago, Available at: https://repositorio.cepal.org/bitstream/handle/11362/45337/6/S2000264_es.pdf. Accessed April 17, 2020.

ECLAC (August 2020). COVID-19 reports, "Impact of COVID-19 on the U.S. economy and policy responses." United Nations, Santiago. Available at: https://repositorio.cepal.org/bitstream/handle/11362/45981/1/S2000541_es.pdf. Accessed September 30, 2020.

ECLAC/ILO (May 2020). "El trabajo en tiempos de pandemia: desafíos frente a la enfermedad por coronavirus (COVID-19)." Coyuntura Laboral en América Latina y el Caribe, No. 22 (LC/TS.2020/46), Santiago, 2020. https://repositorio.cepal.org/bitstream/handle/11362/45557/1/S2000307_es.pdf. Accessed June 8, 2020.

Economic Policy Institute (July 24, 2020). "Why we still need the $600 unemployment benefit," en https://www.epi.org/blog/why-we-still-need-the-600-unemployment-benefit/?utm_source=Economic+Policy+Institute&utm_campaign=0646dd4526-EMAIL_CAMPAIGN_2019_02_22_11_12_COPY_01&utm_medium=email&utm_term=0_e7c5826c50-0646dd4526-60019701&mc_cid=0646dd4526&mc_eid=9d8953a98c. Accessed July 29, 2020.

Economic Policy Institute (January 14, 2021). "A more comprehensive look at unemployment rates," in Chart: A more comprehensive look at unemployment rates: Unemployment rates for select workers by race/ethnicity and gender, December 2019 and December 2020 | Economic Policy Institute (epi.org). Accessed January 15, 2021.

El Economista (April 8, 2020). "Se han perdido 346,878 empleos formales por la contingencia de Covid-19: STPS." Available at: https://www.eleconomista.com.mx/empresas/Se-han-perdido-346878-empleos-formales-por-la-contingencia-de-Covid-19-STPS-20200408-0046.html. Accessed April 11, 2020.

El Ladrillo (1992). Bases de la política económica del gobierno militar chileno, Centro de Estudios Públicos, Santiago, available at: http://www.memoriachilena.gob.cl/archivos2/pdfs/MC0032306.pdf.

El Universal (September 5, 2020). "Telework ¿llegó para quedarse?," available at: https://www.eluniversal.com.mx/mundo/teletrabajo-llego-para-quedarse. Accessed September 6, 2020.

EUROSTAT (n/d). "Economic indicators" GDP-Volume (%), available at: https://ec.europa.eu/eurostat/cache/infographs/economy/desktop/index.html. Accessed June 18, 2020.

Excélsior (April 26, 2020). "Planea Alemania Ley sobre Home office," available at: https://www.excelsior.com.mx/global/planea-alemania-ley-sobre-home-office/1378327. Accessed April 28, 2020.

FRAGUA (June 12, 2020). "En las conciliaciones el pueblo pone los muertos." Rebelión. Available at: https://rebelion.org/en-las-conciliaciones-el-pueblo-pone-los-muertos/. Accessed June 13, 2020.

HISPANTV (March 18, 2020). "US released its biological weapon, COVID-19, to dominate the world," at: https://www.hispantv.com/noticias/opinion/451885/arma-biologica-china-coronavirus-guerra). Accessed March 20, 2020.

HISPANTV (March 28, 2020). "One in four Americans loses job to coronavirus," at: https://www.hispantv.com/noticias/ee-uu-/462570/desempleo-coronavirus-sondeo. Accessed March 31, 2020.

HISPANTV (April 4, 2020). "Trump's anti-Venezuela plan seeks to cover up US health crisis." At https://www.hispantv.com/noticias/ee-uu-/463028/trump-venezuela-maduro-coronavirus. Accessed April 12, 2020.

However (October 8, 2020). "Autoridades registran 2 nuevos brotes de COVID-19 en maquilas de Chihuahua"; hay al menos 8 contagios, at: https://www.sinembargo.mx/08-10-2020/3873874. Accessed October 8, 2020.

ILO (2016). "The Challenges and Opportunities of Telework for Workers and Employers in the Information and Communication Technology (ICT) and Financial Services Sectors," Geneva. Available at: https://www.ilo.org/wcmsp5/groups/public/---ed_dialogue/---sector/documents/publication/wcms_531116.pdf. Accessed September 22, 2020.

ILO (2020). "Global Wage Report 2020–2021. Wages and minimum wages in times of COVID-19," Genoa, available in English at: https://www.ilo.org/wcmsp5/groups/public/@dgreports/@dcomm/@publ/documents/publication/wcms_762534.pdf. Accessed December 11, 2020.

ILO (April 29, 2020). ILO Observatory: COVID-19 and the world of work. Third edition Updated estimates and analysis, Available at: https://www.ilo.org/wcmsp5/groups/public/---dgreports/---dcomm/documents/briefingnote/wcms_743154.pdf. Accessed June 26, 2020.

ILO (September 23, 2020). ILO Observatory. COVID-19 and the world of work. Sixth Edition. Updated estimates and analysis, available at: https://www.ilo.org/wcmsp5/groups/public/---dgreports/---dcomm/documents/briefingnote/wcms_755917.pdf. Accessed September 27, 2020.

ILO (January 25, 2021) "ILO Observatory: COVID-19 and the world of work. Seventh edition. Updated estimates and analysis," at: https://www.ilo.org/wcmsp5/groups/public/---dgreports/---dcomm/documents/briefingnote/wcms_767045.pdf. Accessed March 9, 2021).

IMF (12 January 2020). Statistics Times "List of Countries by GDP (Nominal)". Available at: http://statisticstimes.com/economy/countries-by-gdp.php. Accessed June 22, 2020.

IMF (2020). Real GDP growth. At: https://www.imf.org/external/datamapper/NGDP_RPCH@WEO/OEMDC/ADVEC/WEOWORLD. Accessed June 29, 2020.

IMF (April 2021). "World Economic Outlook Reports," "Managing Diverging Recoveries." Available at: https://www.imf.org/es/Publications/WEO/Issues/2021/03/23/world-economic-outlook-april-2021. Accessed May 14, 2021.

IMSS (July 12, 2020). Communiqué: "Puestos de trabajo afiliados al Instituto Mexicano del Seguro Social," Mexico, available at: http://www.imss.gob.mx/prensa/archivo/202007/471. Accessed July 19, 2020.

INEGI (July 30, 2020). Press Release no. 381/20: "Estimación oportuna del Producto Interno Bruto en México durante el Segundo Trimestre de 2020 (cifras desestacionalizadas)," available at: https://www.inegi.org.mx/contenidos/saladeprensa/boletines/2020/pib_eo/pib_eo2020_07.pdf. Accessed July 30, 2020.

INEGI-IFC (February 17, 2020). Press Release n. 103/20. "En México hay 80.6 millones de usuarios de internet y 86.5 millones de usuarios de teléfonos celulares: ENDUTIH 2019," available at: https://www.inegi.org.mx/contenidos/saladeprensa/boletines/2020/OtrTemEcon/ENDUTIH_2019.pdf. Accessed February 23, 2020).

INEGI (January 29, 2021). Press Release n. 97/21, "Timely estimate of gross domestic product in Mexico during the fourth quarter of 2020," available at: https://www.inegi.org.mx/contenidos/saladeprensa/boletines/2021/pib_eo/pib_eo2021_01.pdf. Accessed January 31, 2021.

Information and ICT (March 7, 2019). "Emerging Literacies in Cyberspace 1," available at: https://informacionytic.com/2019/03/07/alfabetizaciones-emergentes-en-el-ciberespacio-1/. No author reference. Accessed August 4, 2020.

Kickidler (n/d). "Monitoramento online de computadores," at: https://www.kickidler.com/br/?fbclid=IwAR19EewgypZM22dF80CSeUAQY9vy6BAxxc6Vb6gn26ovOy8kGlZ6RoZxoeI. Accessed October 20, 2020.

La Izquierda Diario (March 28, 2020). "First general strike under pandemic breaks 'national unity' in Italy," at: https://rebelion.org/la-primera-huelga-general-bajo-la-pandemia-rompe-la-unidad-nacional-en-italia/). Accessed March 30, 2020.

La Izquierda Diario (June 3, 2020). "Did something change? Working in a call center in the "new normal,"" at: http://www.laizquierdadiario.mx/Cambio-algo-Trabajar-en-un-call-center-en-la-nueva-normalidad. Accessed June 3, 2020.

La izquierda diario, June 24, 2020. "Movimiento Nacional Contra la Precarización Laboral y Los Despidos, Conferencia de Prensa," Available online: http://www.laizquierdadiario.mx/Presentacion-del-Movimiento-Nacional-contra-la-Precarizacion-Laboral-y-los-Despidos. Accessed June 26, 2020.

La Izquierda Diario (June 30, 2020). "What is labor precariousness and how does it affect us?." Available online: http://www.laizquierdadiario.mx/Que-es-la-precarizacion-laboral-y-como-nos-afecta. Accessed July 5, 2020.

La Izquierda Diario (October 1, 2020). "Tecnoestrés: padecimiento de los trabajadores por precarización y home office," at: https://www.laizquierdadiario.mx/Tecnoestres-padecimiento-de-los-trabajadores-por-precarizacion-y-home-office. Accessed October 4, 2020.

La Izquierda Diario (October 19, 2020). "En call center de Grupo Salinas se violan los derechos laborales," at: http://www.laizquierdadiario.mx/En-call-center-de-Grupo-Salinas-se-violan-derechos-laborales. Retrieved October 20, 202.

La Izquierda Diario (May 25, 2020). "Industrial homicide: more than 30 killed by Covid-19 at Lear plant in Mexico," available at: http://www.laizquierdadiario.com/Homicidio-industrial-mas-de-30-muertos-por-Covid-19-en-la-planta-de-Lear-en-Mexico. Accessed June 1, 2020.

La Izquierda Diario (September 22, 2020). "Siguen en aumento las muertes por contagio en las maquilas,", available at: http://www.laizquierdadiario.mx/Siguen-en-aumento-las-muertes-por-contagio-en-las-maquilas. Accessed September 23, 2020.

La Izquierda Diario (September 29, 2020). "Esenciales, precarizadas y mujeres: Somos las trabajadoras de Call Center," at: http://www.laizquierdadiario.mx/Esenciales-precarizadas-y-mujeres-Somos-las-trabajadora-del-Call-Center. Accessed October 2, 2020.

La Jornada (November 18, 2020). "Comienza hoy en ocho estados la primera fase de la reforma laboral," at: https://www.jornada.com.mx/2020/11/18/politica/023n1pol. Accessed November 18, 2020.

La Jornada (July 31, 2020). "En la frontera México-EU, más de un millón de contagios," available at: https://www.jornada.com.mx/2020/07/31/politica/004n1pol. Accessed July 31, 2020.

La Jornada (May 8, 2020). "Al menos 104 obreros muertos por el virus en Juárez, asegura abogada," https://www.jornada.com.mx/2020/05/08/estados/025n1est. Accessed May 11, 2020.

La Silla Rota (July 6, 2020). "The end of a food delivery app; it gets taken over by a giant," At: https://lasillarota.com/dinero/el-fin-de-una-app-de-comida-a-domicilio-la-absorbe-un-gigante-pandemia-coronavirus-covid-19-postmates/409827. Accessed July 6, 2020.

La Silla Rota(July 21, 2020). "Así es como se busca regular el home office en México." Available at: https://lasillarota.com/nacion/asi-es-como-se-busca-regular-el-home-office-en-mexico-home-office-pandemia-covid-19-reforma/415240. Accessed July 21, 2020.

La Silla Rota (August 27, 2020). "Home office, the class to activate the economy's recovery," available at: https://lasillarota.com/dinero/el-home-office-la-clave-para-activar-la-recuperacion-de-la-economia-home-office-economia-economicos-trabajo-remoto/428694. Accessed August 27, 2020.

La Silla Rota (September 4, 2020). "The jobs that will be lost even after the pandemic ends," at: https://lasillarota.com/dinero/los-empleos-que-se-perderan-incluso-despues-de-que-termine-la-pandemia-empleo-cnn-pandemia-covid-19/431489. Accessed September 12, 2020).

La Silla Rota (November 06, 2020). "Con temor al desempleo 8 de cada 10 empleados que hacen home office," at: https://lasillarota.com/dinero/con-temor-al-desempleo-8-de-cada-10-empleados-que-hacen-home-office/452390. Accessed November 06, 2020.

Manpower, The Factory of the Future. Mapping the Skills That Will Drive Manufacturing, December 6, 2016, available at: https://www.manpowergroup.com.mx/wps/wcm/connect/manpowergroup/01bfe6bf-14d6-4ca9-8674-5fa6726d9d77/MPG_Future_Factory_Manufacturing_ESP_compressed.pdf?MOD=AJPERES&CONVERT_TO=url&CACHEID=01bfe6bf-14d6-4ca9-8674-5fa6726d9d77.

National Bureau of Statistics of China (January 18, 2021). "National Economy Recovered Steadily in 2020 with Main Goals Accomplished Better Than Expectation," available at: http://www.stats.gov.cn/english/PressRelease/202101/t20210118_1812432.html. Accessed January 18, 2021.

National Institute of Statistics (July 31, 2020), at: https://www.ine.es/dyngs/INEbase/es/operacion.htm?c=Estadistica_C&cid=1254736164439&menu=ultiDatos&idp=1254735576581. Accessed July 31, 2020.

OECD (June 2020). OECD Economic Outlook. "The global economy on a tightrope." Available: http://www.oecd.org/perspectivas-economicas/junio-2020/. Accessed July 2, 2020.

OECD (1999). The Future of the Global Economy: Towards a Long Boom? Paris. Accessed July 9, 2020.

OFFICIAL JOURNAL OF THE FEDERATION (DOF, June 29, 2020). Mexico. Available at: http://dof.gob.mx/2020/SRE/T_MEC_290620.pdf. Accessed June 30, 2020.

OFFICIAL JOURNAL OF THE FEDERATION (DOF, January 11, 2021). DECREE reforming Article 311 and adding Chapter XII Bis of the Federal Labor Law, regarding Telework, available at: https://www.dof.gob.mx/nota_detalle.php?codigo=5609683&fecha=11/01/2021. Consulted on January 12, 2021.

Oxfam (July 2020). "Who Pays the Bill? Taxing Wealth to Address the COVID-19 Crisis in Latin America and the Caribbean." https://oxfamilibrary.openrepository.com/bitstream/handle/10546/621033/bp-quien-paga-la-cuenta-covid-19-270720-es.pdf. Accessed July 27, 2020.

Oxfam (May 20, 2021). "COVID vaccines créate 9 new billionaires with combined wealth greater tan cost of vaccinatin world's poorest countries," at: https://www.oxfam.org/en/press-releases/covid-vaccines-create-9-new-billionaires-combined-wealth-greater-cost-vaccinating. Accessed May 24, 2021.

ProMéxico (November 8, 2017), at: https://www.google.com.mx/amp/s/manufactura.mx/industria/2017/11/08/27-del-pib-de-mexico-viene-de-la-manufactura-avanzada%3f_amp=true. Accessed June 27, 2020.

Puente Project (June 7, 2020). "4-hour days, home office," at: https://proyectopuente.com.mx/2020/06/07/jornadas-de-4-dias-home-office-horarios-escalonados-covid-19-transforma-el-trabajo-en-mexico/. Accessed June 9, 2020.

PwC (May 8, 2020). Report "Covid-19 CFO Pulse Survey by PwC," in The Economist, available at: https://factorcapitalhumano.com/mundo-del-trabajo/el-home-office-llego-para-quedarse-64-de-los-cfo-planea-hacerlo-permanente/2020/05/. Accessed May 12, 2020.

Reforma (June 12, 2020). "Vuelve maquila en BC pese a ascenso de contagios," available at: https://www.reforma.com/aplicacioneslibre/preacceso/articulo/default.aspx?__rval=1&urlredirect=https://www.reforma.com/vuelve-maquila-en-bc-pese-a-ascenso-de-contagios/ar1964529?referer=--7d616165662f3a3a6262623b727a7a7279703b767a783a--Consultado on June 14, 2020).

Reforma (July 7, 2020). "Empleos en auge pese a la pandemia," In: https://www.reforma.com/empleos-en-auge-pese-a-la-pandemia/gr/ar1981900?md5=b5f012d5fe70dc173341032a65ae6aa0&ta=0dfdbac11765226904c16cb9ad1b2efe&utm_source=elemento_web&utm_medium=email&utm_campaign=promocion_suscriptor. Accessed July 8, 2020.

RESOLUTION FOUNDATION (March 4, 2017). "Zero-hours contracts reach 910,000 in UK,".

Reuters (June 2, 2020). "Trabajadores regresan a las fábricas mexicanas ante reactivación del sector automotive." Available at: https://lta.reuters.com/articulo/salud-coronavirus-manufactura-reapertura-idLTAKBN2391RV-OUSLT. Accessed June 3, 2020).

Sputnik (June 8, 2020). "How the US Federal Reserve would make world markets collapse." Available at: https://mundo.sputniknews.com/economia/202006081091689124-como-la-reserva-federal-de-eeuu-haria-colapsar-los-mercados-mundiales/. Accessed June 9, 2020. Accessed June 10, 2020.

Sputnik (June 9, 2020). "U.S. officially falls into recession amid pandemic," at: https://mundo.sputniknews.com/america_del_norte/202006091091697882-eeuu-cae-oficialmente-en-recesion-en-medio-de-la-pandemia/.

Sputnik (July 7, 2020). "UN Confirms WHO's U.S. Health," available at https://mundo.sputniknews.com/america_del_norte/202007071092002801-la-onu-confirma-la-salida-de-eeuu-de-la-oms/. Accessed July 7, 2020.

Sputnik (July 25, 2020). "Why Is Faith in the American Economic Miracle Fading?," available at: https://mundo.sputniknews.com/economia/202007251092210653-por-que-se-esta-desvaneciendo-fe-milagro-americano/. Accessed July 25, 2020.

Sputnik (January 15, 2021). "Will China Lead the World into the Age of the Digital Economy?," available at: https://mundo.sputniknews.com/economia/202101151094128153-sera-china-la-que-llevara-mundo-era-economia-digital/. Accessed January 18, 2021.

Statistiches Bundesamt (Destatis), 2020 (July 30, 2020), at: https://www.destatis.de/DE/Themen/Wirtschaft/Volkswirtschaftliche-Gesamtrechnungen-Inlandsprodukt/Tabellen/bip-bubbles.html. Accessed July 30, 2020.

Stputnik (May 26, 2020). "Iran overcomes oil embargo right under US nose," at: https://mundo.sputniknews.com/politica/202005261091536510-iran-supera-el-embargo-petrolero-delante-de-las-narices-de-eeuu/. Accessed May 26, 2020.

STyPS (May 1, 2029). "Decreto por el que se reforman, adicionan y derogan diversas disposiciones de la Ley Federal del Trabajo, de la Ley Orgánica del Poder Judicial de la Federación, de la Ley Federal de la Defensoría Pública, de la Ley del Instituto del Fondo Nacional de la Vivienda para los Trabajadores y de la Ley del Seguro Social, en materia de Justicia Laboral, Libertad Sindical y Negociación Colectiva," available at: http://www.diputados.gob.mx/LeyesBiblio/ref/lft/LFT_ref30_01may19.pdf. Accessed May 18, May 7, 2020.

Telesur (March 24, 2015). Interview with Simón Colmenares (VIDEO), on YouTube: https://www.youtube.com/watch?v=_lJlh2NZnio.

The Captor (April 15, 2020). "Economic alarm; IMF projects labor crisis in Spain nine times higher than in Germany." Accessed April 18, 2020.

The Economist (June 24, 2019). "US achieves the longest economic expansion in its history, but the least intense ever," https://www.eleconomista.es/economia/noticias/9956877/06/19/EEUU-logra-la-expansion-economica-mas-larga-de-su-historia-poniendo-la-guinda-a-la-era-de-los-superciclos.html. Retrieved August 18, 2019.

The New York Times (May 29, 2020). "Blaming China for Pandemic, Trump Says U.S. Will Leave the W.H.O.," available at: https://www.nytimes.com/2020/05/29/health/virus-who.html. Accessed June 30, 2020.

The Telegraph (March 04, 2017). https://www.eltelegrafo.com.ec/noticias/mundo/8/los-contratos-de-cero-horas-llegan-a-910-000-en-reino-unido. Accessed March 15, 2021.

The Washington Post (August 8, 2020). "Trump attempts to wrest tax and spending powers from Congress with new executive actions," available at: https://www.washingtonpost.com/business/2020/08/08/trump-executive-order-coronavirus/. Accessed August 9, 2020.

U.S. Department of Commerce (July 30, 2020). Bureau Economic Analysis. "Gross Domestic Product, 2nd Quarter 2020 (Advance Estimate) and Annual Update," available at https://www.bea.gov/index.php/news/2020/gross-domestic-product-2nd-quarter-2020-advance-estimate-and-annual-update. Accessed July 30, 2020.

UCLA (August, 10, 2020. "Undocumented durin COVID-19 essential for the economy but exluded from relief," at: https://latino.ucla.edu/research/undocumented-during-covid-19-essential-for-the-economy-but-excluded-from-relief/. Accessed August 10, 2020.

World Bank (2020). Viral Effect: COVID-19 and the Accelerated Transformation of Employment in Latin America and the Caribbean. At: https://openknowledge.worldbank.org/bitstream/handle/10986/34413/211448SP.pdf. Accessed October 9, 2020.

WORLD BANK (February 2001). "Global economic outlook heralds soft landing." Available online: http://documentos.bancomundial.org/curated/es/512841468135917561/pdf/226790SPANISH0notes52es.pdf. Accessed June 23, 2020.

World Bank, (June 2020). Global Economic Prospect, Washington, DC.

World Bank (January 2021). Flagship Report. "Global Economic Prospects. Flagship Report. "Global Economic Prospects". Washington, D.C. at: https://openknowledge.worldbank.org/bitstream/handle/10986/34710/9781464816123.pdf?sequence=15&isAllowed=y. Accessed March, 2021.

WORLD BANK (n/d). GDP growth (annual %). Available online: https://datos.bancomundial.org/indicador/NY.GDP.MKTP.KD.ZG. Accessed June 29, 2020.

WTO, Press Release (April 8, 2020). "Trade Plummets as COVID-19 Pandemic Disrupts Global Economy," Available online: https://www.wto.org/spanish/news_s/pres20_s/pr855_s.htm. Accessed June 23, 2020.

Index

www.ingramcontent.com/pod-product-compliance
Lightning Source LLC
LaVergne TN
LVHW010626300926
849162LV00001B/83